Italo Svevo

Twayne's World Authors Series
Italian Literature

Anthony Oldcorn, Editor

Brown University

TWAS 795

ITALO SVEVO
(1861–1928)
Svevo seated in front of his library.

Italo Svevo

By Beno Weiss

Pennsylvania State University

Twayne Publishers
A Division of G.K. Hall & Co. • Boston

Italo Svevo
Beno Weiss

Copyright 1987 by G.K. Hall & Co.
All rights reserved.
Published by Twayne Publishers
A Division of G.K. Hall & Co.
70 Lincoln Street
Boston, Massachusetts 02111

Copyediting supervised by Lewis DeSimone
Book production by John Amburg
Book design by Barbara Anderson

Typeset in 11 pt. Garamond
by Compset, Inc., Beverly, Massachusetts

Printed on permanent/durable acid-free paper
and bound in the United States of America

Library of Congress Cataloging-in-Publication Data

Weiss, Beno, 1933–
 Italo Svevo.

 (Twayne's world authors series ; TWAS 795.
Italian literature)
 Bibliography: p.
 Includes index.
 1. Svevo, Italo, 1861–1928—Criticism and
interpretation. I. Title. II. Series: Twayne's
world authors series ; TWAS 795. III. Series: Twayne's
world authors series. Italian literature.
PQ4841.C482Z95   1987   853'.8   87-17714
ISBN 0-8057-6649-9

*In memory of my beloved father, Isaac,
the son of Abraham*

Contents

About the Author
Preface
Chronology

> *Chapter One*
> Svevo's Life   1
>
> *Chapter Two*
> A Life   16
>
> *Chapter Three*
> As a Man Grows Older   34
>
> *Chapter Four*
> Confessions of Zeno   52
>
> *Chapter Five*
> Svevo's Secret Passion: The Theater   93
>
> *Chapter Six*
> Short Stories   122
>
> *Chapter Seven*
> Conclusion   134

Notes and References   137
Selected Bibliography   155
Index   166

About the Author

Beno Weiss, a native of Abbazia (Fiume), grew up in Italy, where he completed his secondary education. He earned his B.A., M.A., and Ph.D. degrees at New York University. He taught for several years at N.Y.U. before joining the faculty at Pennsylvania State University, where he is presently associate professor of Italian, specializing in nineteenth- and twentieth-century Italian literature. He is the author of *An Annotated Bibliography on the Theatre of Italo Svevo* and the coauthor of *Juan de la Cueva's "Los Inventores de las Cosas."* He has also contributed to the *Journal of Modern Literature, Modern Fiction Studies, Anterem,* the *Forum, MLA International Bibliography, Modern Language Journal, Italica, Sin Nombre, García Lorca Review,* and *Modern International Drama.*

Preface

When we speak of the modern European novel, we think of Joyce, Pirandello, Kafka, Musil, Proust, Lawrence, Gide, and Mann, and a few others, as seminal forces. Among Italian writers, Italo Svevo, on account of his distinctive originality, his sensitivity to the new currents that dominated his time, his wealth of interests, and his intuitive capacity to probe into the inner motivations of man, has by now been fully assimilated into this canon and rightfully belongs among the ranks of these great writers. Svevo was the first Italian—if not European—author to make use of Freud's new and, at that time, revolutionary ideas. Yet, in spite of a prose brimming endlessly with insights, and despite the limited critical acclaim that followed the publication of *La coscienza di Zeno (Confessions of Zeno)*, he remained until after World War II something of an elusive figure for Italian readers, particularly those nurtured under the influence of Croce and D'Annunzio, who found it difficult to accept Svevo's anticlassical and antirhetorical experimentation in style, language, theme, and narrative technique. Today, at last, *La coscienza di Zeno* and Svevo's other works have finally become best-sellers, among the most popular novels in Italy.

I hope that the present study will serve not only as an introduction for English-speaking readers to the life and works of the Triestine writer, but that it may also prove of some interest to specialists in Italian and European literatures. My purpose is to provide a personal and critical account of Svevo's life, fiction, and drama, which, taking into consideration recent criticism and scholarship, will elucidate the substance of Svevo's thought and artistic production. For reasons of space, I have not been able to include all of his critical writings or his vast collection of letters.

I wish to thank the American Philosophical Society, The Institute for the Arts and Humanistic Studies, and the Office of Research and Graduate Studies (College of the Liberal Arts, Pennsylvania State University) for grants which made possible research for this study. I also wish to express my appreciation to my friend and colleague Professor Louis C. Pérez and to the editor Anthony Oldcorn for their encouragement and helpful criticism. Finally, I wish to thank Signora Letizia

Svevo Fonda Savio for her invaluable help, for graciously allowing me to examine the original manuscripts of Svevo's works, and for permission to reproduce a photograph of her father on the frontispiece to this volume.

Beno Weiss

Pennsylvania State University

Chronology

1861 19 December: Aron Hector (Ettore) Schmitz born in Trieste.
1863 21 October: younger brother Elio born.
1867 Ettore attends the Scuola Israelitica Elementare.
1868 6 June: the painter Umberto Veruda born in Trieste.
1872 Ettore begins to attend the Scuola Commerciale run by Emanuele Edeles.
1874 Ettore together with older brother Adolfo leaves Trieste for Germany to study at the Brussel'sche Handels-und Erziehungsinstitut in Segnitz-am-Mein, near Würzburg (Bavaria). 7 December: Ettore's future wife, Livia Fausta Veneziani, born in Trieste.
1876 Elio Schmitz joins his brothers in Segnitz.
1878 The Schmitz brothers return to Trieste. Ettore enrolls at the Istituto Superiore Commerciale Revoltella.
1880 His first literary effort, the unfinished play *Ariosto Governatore*. Starts work at the Unionbank. Publishes his first article, "Shylock," using the pseudonym Ettore Samigli, thereby beginning a long association with *L'Indipendente,* the newspaper in which he publishes most of his critical writings.
1881 Around this time he completes his first plays, *Le ire di Giuliano* (Giuliano's anger) and *Una commedia inedita* (An unpublished comedy). Writes a brief "History of My Works."
1883 Elio falls ill with a chronic kidney ailment.
1884 Meets Eleonora Duse. Writes the play *Le teorie del Conte Alberto* (Count Albert's theories).
1886 26 September: Elio dies. Ettore writes the memoir "Elio's Romance."
1887 Writes an essay on "Feeling in Art" and begins his first novel, *Una vita (A Life)*. Umberto Veruda becomes his close friend.
1888 Under the name of E. Samigli, he publishes his first short

story, "Una lotta" (A contest), while continuing to contribute review articles to the local press.

1890   Publishes another short story "L'assassinio di Via Belpoggio" (Murder on Belpoggio Street), and an article on "Smoking."

1891   Publishes his first theatrical work, *Prima del ballo* (Before the ball). Giuseppina Zergol becomes his lover. About this time he starts working part-time for the newspaper *Il Piccolo*.

1892   Probably writes the play *Il ladro in casa* (A thief in the house). 1 April: his father dies; December: his first novel *Una vita* published under the pen name of Italo Svevo.

1893   Begins his teaching career at the Revoltella Institute.

1895   4 October: his mother dies; 20 December: he becomes engaged to his cousin Livia Veneziani. He begins to write his *Diario per la fidanzata* (Diary for my fiancée).

1896   Starts writing his second novel, *Senilità* (*As a Man Grows Older*). 3 July: Ettore and Livia are married in a civil ceremony.

1897   Ettore is baptized, and on 25 August the couple are married in church. 20 September: birth of their daughter Letizia Fausta Pia. In November he publishes the story "La tribù" ("The Tribe").

1898   From 15 June to 16 September *Senilità* first appears in serialized form and is later published by Vram. He leaves his job at the Unionbank and starts working for the Veneziani paint firm.

1899   Begins but does not complete the play *Degenerazione* (Degeneration).

1901   Resigns his position at Revoltella and begins extensive travel throughout Europe: France, Ireland, Germany, Italy, and primarily England, where he opens a branch of the Veneziani paint factory in Charlton.

1902   Gives up his work at *Il Piccolo*.

1903   Completes the play *Un marito* (A Husband).

1904   4 May: death of Veruda.

1906   Starts taking English lessons from James Joyce.

1907   Writes an English composition for Joyce entitled "Mr. James Joyce described by his faithful pupil Ettore Schmitz."

Chronology

1911	Becomes acquainted with some of Freud's ideas, and meets Dr. Wilhelm Stekel, one of Freud's collaborators.
1915	War between Italy and Austria. The Veneziani factory is closed by the Austrian authorities and all the equipment is confiscated. During the war he resumes playing the violin and writes "Trattato sulla teoria della pace" (Treatise on the theory of peace).
1916	Starts reading Freud.
1918	Italian troops march into Trieste. Svevo translates Freud's *Ueber der Traum* (*The Interpretation of Dreams*).
1919	Starts writing *La coscienza di Zeno* (*Confessions of Zeno*). 23 April: wedding of daughter Letizia. Meeting with Joyce in Paris.
1920	The play *Terzetto spezzato* (*Broken Triangle*) is probably written during this year.
1922	Completion of *La coscienza di Zeno*.
1923	1 May: publication of *La coscienza di Zeno*.
1924	Sends *La coscienza* to Joyce in Paris.
1925	Svevo begins to be recognized as an important writer. Travels to Paris where Joyce introduces him to Crémieux and Larbaud. He begins to write the "Corto viaggio sentimentale" (Short sentimental journey). Montale brings Svevo's writings to the attention of the Italian public.
1926	Montale's second article on Svevo. Almost an entire issue of *Le Navire d'Argent* is devoted to Svevo. Publishes an article on Joyce. In Trieste he meets Pirandello and Marta Abba.
1927	Lectures on Joyce at the offices of *Il Convegno* in Milano. *Terzetto spezzato* is performed in Rome. Second edition of *Senilità*.
1928	Works on a number of continuations of *La coscienza di Zeno*. Honored at the Pen Club in Paris. Writes his "Profilo autobiografico" (Autobiographical sketch). Injured in an automobile accident on 10 September. Dies on 13 September in the hospital of Motta di Livenza at age sixty-seven. He is buried in the Catholic Cemetery of Trieste.

Chapter One
Svevo's Life

Aron Hector (or Ettore) Schmitz—known to posterity by his pen name Italo Svevo—was born into a patriarchal Jewish family in Trieste on 19 December 1861. The Schmitz family had migrated to Trieste from Hungary. Abraham Adolfo Schmitz, Ettore's grandfather, once a minor official of the Hapsburg Empire, had married an Italian Jewess from Treviso, thereby introducing the first element of Italian blood into the family. The father, Francesco, was a typical immigrant who felt and absorbed profoundly the cultural influences of Italy and the heritage of his maternal forebears. A self-made man and a successful businessman—he began his career peddling wares in cafés at thirteen—he brought up his children in the traditional no-nonsense, disciplined, nineteenth-century way. The mother, Allegra Moravia, tempered with love and tenderness her husband's extreme severity.

There had been sixteen children, of whom only eight survived into adulthood: Natalia, Paola, Noemi, Adolfo, Ettore, Elio, Ortensia, and Ottavio. From an early age Ettore displayed the manner and style of the future writer. He and his brothers issued a handwritten family newspaper describing various family occurrences. In his section Ettore revealed a certain precocity and wit.

Francesco Schmitz was a prominent member of the Jewish community and the Schmitz family respected and observed certain important Jewish customs and practices. The children attended the Scuola Israelitica Elementare (Jewish Elementary School), where the study of religion and Judaism was integrated with traditional Italian secular courses, while at home they were frequently in touch with their uncle, Abramo Ancona, an extremely orthodox Jew, and Aunt Peppina, who taught them how to pray in Hebrew. On Holy Days they all attended the Great Temple of Trieste, and most likely Ettore himself celebrated there his own bar mitzvah as well as those of his brothers and relatives. Nevertheless, the Schmitz family was by no means fanatical in its observance.

When Ettore was twelve, the family decided to send him and his brothers, Adolfo and Elio, to study in Germany. They attended a commercial school in Segnitz-am-Mein; their father felt that a good businessman ought to know German. Furthermore, he believed that the traditional German education, with its formality and discipline, would be highly advantageous for his sons. This paternal choice of place and quality of education was to have a great influence on Ettore's later life. The school was frequented predominantly by Jewish boys and Jewish religion was part of the curriculum.

In Segnitz a new life began for young Ettore Schmitz. Within a few months he perfected his German and surrounded himself with a small "intellectual" group with whom he carried on philosophical and literary debates. He had a great thirst for knowledge and read widely—from Shakespeare to the Russian novelist Ivan Sergeyevich Turgenev (1818–83). He was particularly fond of the German classics: the dramatist Friedrich Schiller (1759–1805), the poet Johann Wolfgang von Goethe (1749–1832), and the philosopher Arthur Schopenhauer (1788–1860); he found in the wry humor of Friedrich Richter (1763–1825) a special attraction.

His favorite brother Elio, physically ailing and of a delicate, sensitive nature, returned to Trieste after a brief stay in Germany. Ettore and Adolfo remained there until 1878 when they completed their studies and returned home. Ettore was almost eighteen and enrolled, without much enthusiasm, in the Istituto Superiore Commerciale Revoltella, a more advanced business school in Trieste. Although he loved to read and dreamed of becoming a writer, he accepted, however resentfully, the idea that his future lay in business; he was too weak, or perhaps too young, to oppose his father's will. Totally absorbed by his business ventures, the father failed to understand both Ettore's and Elio's sensitive natures.

Trieste was fortunate in having many theaters and concert halls where the most popular Italian and European plays and artists appeared, and Ettore went often to the theater. In 1882, when he first saw Ernesto Rossi's *Hamlet,* he was so stagestruck he decided to become an actor. He was given an audition by the famous actor-director Tommaso Salvini, who turned him down for a part because he was unable to pronounce the Italian *r* sound correctly. Although Ettore Schmitz is best known today for his novels, it is worth pointing out that his earliest writings were in fact plays.

At home Elio was the only one who really understood Ettore and encouraged his theatrical and literary aspirations. We get a very detailed picture of this formative period from Elio's diary (to which Ettore at times contributed):

> ... Ettore had already read all the French novels that we could get hold of. ... The poets Schiller and Goethe were his best friends when he was in boarding-school. ... As soon as I was able to understand German, he used to take me to his room and would not let me go without first reading to me one or two passages from a classic work. He gives the impression of indifference since he finds meaning for his life within himself. ... Bit by bit he got [the idea of becoming a writer] into his head, to the point that it controls him totally today. He studied all the German classics and tried to become as learned as possible through them. I remember that he put together a library with his savings. I can still see them on that shelf lined up in orderly fashion—the only orderly thing about our room—Schiller, Hauff, Koerner, Heine and others. Goethe, however, is missing. He had bought the book, which he read, commented, and then raffled off among the students; with the money he bought a German translation of *Hamlet*. Once the book was his he stayed up all night reading it, and subsequently spent many sleepless nights poring over it. He memorized it, became pale, and his appearance deteriorated.[1]

The critic Giacinto Spagnoletti, in a classic study of Ettore's formative years, points out that in this page of Elio's diary one can find the generic outlines of an enthusiastic youth: romantic love for Shakespearean characters such as Hamlet, the heroic cult of Schiller, and admiration for Goethe. But we also find something peculiar to Ettore: in his restless youth were the beginnings of a passion for inner drama—"To be or not to be"—in other words, a vocation for the theater.[2]

It is through Elio's diary that we learn of his brother's playwriting experiments. Elio grasped intuitively the value of Ettore's as yet unfocused excitement and ideas, and there can be no doubt that he was the first to stimulate his brother's aspirations and to guide him. He kept abreast of all his attempts at writing, his failures and partial successes. In referring to *Ariosto governatore,* an unfinished verse play written in 1880, Elio laments the fact that Ettore cannot complete it.

In 1880 the family suffered financial reverses. Franceso Schmitz had embarked upon a new business venture and it had failed. Ettore was compelled to leave school and seek employment in order to help support the family. After some searching, and one rejection on racial grounds,[3] Ettore found a job as a correspondence clerk at the Trieste branch of the Viennese Unionbank; he began to lead the typical life of a petit-bourgeois bank employee. A boring existence, it is well described in several of his stories, particularly in the novel *Una vita (A Life)* where he takes to task the Triestine middle class for its mediocrity and hypocrisy.

Many years later, after Ettore's death, his widow Livia Veneziani wrote a biography of her husband. Speaking of this period, she informs us that he began to acquire a dual personality: outwardly he was the diligent bank employee; secretly he was the aspiring writer searching for an identity and for success.[4] With Elio's prodding and counsel he realized that in order to succeed as an Italian writer he had to become familiar with Italian authors, and so he devoted much of his free time to this task. Using the great Romantic critic Francesco de Sanctis (1835–1907) as a guide, he set about reading the Italian classics, among them the works of the Renaissance prose writers Niccolò Machiavelli (1469–1527), Francesco Guicciardini (1483–1540), and Giovanni Boccaccio (1313–75), as well as the patriotic nineteenth-century poet and Nobel Prize winner Giosuè Carducci (1835–1907). But soon his taste changed and he began to be attracted to the novel, and eventually to the contemporary French naturalists. He read the novels of the French masters Gustave Flaubert (1821–80), Honoré de Balzac (1799–1850), Alphonse Daudet (1840–97), and lastly the founder of naturalism, Emile Zola (1840–1902), who immediately became his idol. Regarding his brother's conversion to naturalism, Elio notes as follows in his diary for 12 May 1881: "He has become a Naturalist. Reading Zola has convinced him that the purpose and interest of a play lie in the characters and not in the action. Everything must be true and simple."[5] This was an entirely new concept for Ettore, one that he was to follow in most of his future plays and novels. Indeed, all his works will downplay dramatic movement and will concentrate primarily upon characterization and inner psychological probing.

When he was eighteen years old, he started to take an active part in the intellectual life of Trieste. This international city, not yet a part of Italy, was, on account of its geographical and political position, a meeting place of heterogeneous peoples and cultures. It was also a clearing house of new moments and ideas, given its position as the Adriatic port of the Hapsburg Empire. The arts flourished, and Ettore frequented various intellectual circles, among these the Circolo Musicale, the Circolo Artistico, the Minerva, a literary society directed by the Triestine patriot and man of letters Attilio Hortis (1850–1926), as well as the salon of the poetess Elisa Tagliapietra-Cambon.[6]

In 1880 he began his lifelong association with the Triestine paper

L'Indipendente, well known for its "irredentist" leanings, that is, its support for the secession of Trieste and its region from Austria and their incorporation into the recently formed Kingdom of Italy. It was edited by Giuseppe Caprin and among its collaborators were Attilio Hortis and the journalist and author Silvio Benco (1874–1949). It was in this paper that most local writers acquired their first literary experience and exposure. And so it was with Ettore who, on 2 December 1880, after having seen a performance of *The Merchant of Venice,* published, under the pen name of E. Samigli, his first article: "Shylock." He continued to use this pseudonym until 1892 when he published *Una vita* under the name by which he is now universally known, Italo Svevo. Unlike Samigli, the name Italo Svevo was not chosen at random. Its two component adjectives of nationality were selected to underline the dual aspect of his culture, environment, education, and nationality: "Italo" Italian and "Svevo" Swabian or German.[7] After this modest exordium as a writer, Ettore continued his daily toil at the bank, but it became increasingly clear that his true interest lay in literature.

Throughout his life Svevo tried to evaluate periodically his literary production and progress; he was extremely severe (and wryly humorous) in his self-assessments. In his brother's diary, on 24 February 1881, he wrote:

A History of My Works

I. "Ariosto the Governor." I spent more time thinking about it than actually writing it. All the details seemed so promising that I was sure that this first attempt of mine was going to be successful. But how wrong I was! I never completed Scene I because at that point I recognized the abstruseness [of the idea] and the awkwardness of my verses.

II. "Discords of the Heart." One scene of this exists and it makes me blush. Conventional sentences, awkward movements, a prose that yearns to be poetic, but isn't even good prose. The ending (or rather the idea of an ending) I find logical but impossible. The play could have been dedicated to the Chinese because it resembles so much their favorite *Hoci-lai-ki.* The title is tragic, but the play itself hovered on the brink of comedy.

III. "Regeneration." Unfortunately I completed two acts and I wish I hadn't. Something that could have been included in one act, I tried to expand into four.[8]

The struggle that Ettore was undergoing in his writings and the objectivity of his self-criticism are clear. The faults he notes in language, style, composition, and technique are precisely those that, years later, the critics were to point out. Unfortunately, very little is left of Svevo's early attempts; in fact, he rarely mentions his plays in his writings. One has to wonder how many theatrical works Svevo undertook during this period. In the opinion of at least one critic, Spagnoletti, one a month.[9] Certainly, there must have been many attempts that were later abandoned.

Ettore's (and Elio's) disappointment with his inability to bring any of his writings to a satisfactory conclusion was soon to end, since during this period he actually completed several plays: *Le ire di Giuliano* (Giuliano's anger), *Le teorie del conte Alberto* (Count Albert's theories), and *Una commedia inedita* (An unpublished comedy). These were strongly influenced by the Italian naturalistic writers, such as Giuseppe Giacosa (1847–1906), Paolo Ferrari (1822–89), and Marco Praga (1862–1929), whose works he was currently reading and seeing performed on the stage.

Elio died in September 1886 after an extended illness punctuated by painful but vain attempts to find a cure for his nephritis. This was a tremendous blow to Svevo who as a consequence of his brother's death now felt utterly alone, discouraged, and bewildered. Other family deaths and misfortunes aggravated his depression, instilling a bitterness in the aspiring writer that never fully abandoned him. Life could no longer offer an acceptable solution to his difficulties; only literature could provide him solace and purpose.

In December 1887 Svevo began work on his first novel, *Una vita (A Life)*. The original title *Un inetto* (A failure) was changed at the publisher's insistence. It aptly characterized, however, the feelings, incapacities, and frustrations of the young Svevo. It took him several years to complete the book, years which he spent alternating between work at the bank and time spent at the *Indipendente* where, in addition to writing articles and short stories, he did editorial work, clipping the foreign press for items of interest. On 19 December 1889 he included in his own diary the following self-criticism:

Today I am 28 years old. My dissatisfaction with myself and with others could not be worse. I record these feelings so that if in a few years I should look back, I will be able to call myself a fool anew and perhaps even get some comfort from finding that my situation has not improved. My financial position is growing worse; I'm not happy with either my health, my work, or the people around me. It is only fitting that, since I myself am not satisfied

Svevo's Life

with my work, I can't expect others to be. Regardless of all the exaggerated ambitions I once had, it is terrible not to have found anyone, "no one at all," who would take an interest in what I was thinking or doing; I find myself instead forced always to take an interest in other people's doings, since that is the only way of getting their attention. Exactly two years ago I began that novel which was supposed to be God knows what. Instead it's mere rubbish that will nauseate me sooner or later. Hope has always been my strength, but alas even that is diminishing.[10]

The book mentioned is the novel *A Life*, in which one cannot help but notice the obvious similarities between the author and Alfonso Nitti, the main character of the novel.

Svevo's despair may have been caused in part by an unhappy romance with Giulia Gabersi, a tall, slender, and extremely beautiful girl. Around 1890 Svevo began courting her quite seriously, but this lasted only a short time. Her father, a strict and devout Catholic, quickly put a stop to it, as soon as he found out that the young suitor was a Jew. He forbade his daughter to even speak to Svevo. Their friendship continued, however, because Giulia's sister married Giuseppe Roncoldier whose brother Carlo was Svevo's good friend and colleague at the bank. Carlo loved literature and followed Svevo's career. Ettore, Giuseppe, Carlo, and the artist Veruda would often get together for drinks at the Birreria Dreher, which, at that time, was located near the bank.[11]

Despite his pessimism, Svevo persisted and slowly began to make a name for himself, at least in Trieste. He continued to write articles for *L'Indipendente* and in 1890 published a long short story or novella called *L'assassinio di Via Belpoggio* (Murder on Belpoggio Street). At the same time he went on writing plays. In the same year Svevo met Umberto Veruda, the painter who introduced the techniques of impressionism to Trieste: in *Senilità (As A Man Grows Older)*, Svevo's second novel, Veruda was to be portrayed as the sculptor Balli. This new friendship filled the void created by Elio's death and decreased, to a certain extent, Svevo's loneliness by bringing him out of his pessimistic withdrawal. Svevo's wife later indicated (presumably on the basis of information she received directly from her husband) that Veruda's understanding of Svevo was complete and that for many years they shared their thoughts and creations.[12]

Ettore's father died in 1892, dealing still another blow to the aspiring writer. That same year he published *A Life* (which he had in fact completed two years before). It was published at Svevo's own expense by the Triestine publisher Vram, who printed only one thousand copies. Unable to sell them, Svevo gave most of them away to his friends and acquaintances. The book, save for one or two reviews in the local press and a brief mention in the *Corriere della Sera,* was greeted with complete silence. Svevo wrote that had the book been well received he would have changed his way of life entirely: he would have given up his business career and become a full-time writer.[13] This silence on the part of the critics was merely the beginning of the now famous "Svevo case."[14] Six years later, in 1898, he published his second novel *Senilità* with the same publisher, again at his own expense. It was received with even greater indifference than his first, a fact which caused Svevo great bitterness and disappointment.

In 1895 Svevo lost his mother and the following year he married his cousin Livia Veneziani in a civil ceremony, and moved into her parents' home. One year later, after he had converted to Catholicism, they were married in church and shortly thereafter Livia gave birth to a girl whom they baptized Letizia.

Why did Svevo become a "religious renegade"? (We choose this term because it is the term he himself used with reference to the German poet Heine in his article on the Jew Shylock.)[15] The woman he married had been brought up in a very Catholic home and educated by nuns, even though her family was of Jewish origin. Livia Veneziani Svevo, in her biography *Vita di mio marito* (The life of my husband), describes her husband's conversion as she perhaps wished it had been. In discussing the religious problems that she and Ettore faced during their engagement, she writes:

Suddenly, one day, everything was resolved in the least expected way: Livia, unable to find any way out, had already resigned herself to Ettore's will, that is to say to a civil ceremony, when he said to her: "You, then, are willing to tie yourself to a Jew?" Yes, she replied firmly. And Ettore exclaimed happily: "Then, I'll get baptized!" The baptism took place in the church of S. Giacomo, in the working-class part of town, where the wedding was also celebrated.[16]

Actually, the facts are quite different. The only truth in this self-serving account is that they were married in the church of S. Giacomo. The civil ceremony took place on 30 July 1896, and the religious rite did not take place till 25 August 1897, more than a year later, and one month before the birth of their daughter. Ettore, apparently, had not been too willing or ready to renounce his Jewishness. He did so, only after being forced into it by circumstances and by his wife's relentless coercion. The civil marriage had been only a temporary compromise for Livia. In order to be married at city hall, which was permitted only for nonbelievers, Ettore and Livia had been compelled to abjure their religion and declare that they did not believe in God. This could not have been too difficult for Ettore, since he was an agnostic by now, but was extremely difficult for Livia, a very devout Catholic. We can assume, therefore, that both she and her family must have exerted tremendous pressure on Ettore. He finally offered to be baptized and married in church primarily because of Livia's illness during her pregnancy, and her fear of dying in mortal sin. Livia was overjoyed and promptly recovered. Many years later Svevo confided ironically to Marie-Anne Comnène Crémieux that he was uncertain whether Livia's miraculous cure had been brought about by the God of the Jews or that of the Christians.[17]

Another factor may have been the embarrassing experience of Livia's mother, Olga Veneziani, which must have gnawed away at the Venezianis' sense of bourgeois propriety, and which they did not want to happen a second time. The family secret was that Olga and her brothers and sisters were all born out of wedlock. Olga's father, Giuseppe Isacco Moravia, the brother of Svevo's mother Allegra Moravia, lived for many years with Anna Wolf (also known as Fanny) without being married. At the time, neither the church nor the Austrian authorities would permit marriages between people of different religions. Giuseppe, of course, was Jewish and Fanny was Catholic. They cohabitated for twenty-two years before they were finally able to legitimize their position, first by claiming Italian citizenship and then by getting married at the Italian Consulate in Trieste, where these restrictions did not prevail. When they were married, their daughter Olga was already in her twenties and engaged to Gioachino Veneziani, her future husband.

Svevo began to visit a priest who instructed him in the Catholic faith. Shortly after, however, unable or unwilling to memorize the catechism, he delivered an ultimatum: either the priest baptize him without further indoctrination, or not at all. Svevo was baptized and shortly after, when Livia felt better—she was already in her ninth month—they were married in a private ceremony, apparently embarrassed by the entire affair.[18]

The conversion would appear, then, to have been a necessary formality for Svevo, imposed by exceptional circumstances. Yet, this did not sit easy with Ettore who felt guilty for his apostasy even though he was not a believer. In his play *Con la penna d'oro* (With a golden pen), one of the characters states that in order to get a divorce "one has to change nationality and give up one's religion. Religion doesn't cost much. It is far more expensive to change one's nationality."[19] Svevo, on the contrary, seems to have paid dearly for his conversion and throughout the remainder of his life his position vis-à-vis the Catholic Church was totally negative. A few years after the marriage, while in Venice, he happened to be in Saint Mark's Cathedral and listened to a sermon. He subsequently wrote home to his wife:

. . . the effect of listening to that amazing rubbish in surroundings so splendid with wealth and meaning was incredible. What made it worse was that it was mouthed by a hoarse and raving actor. He spoke of the Supreme Pontiff, whom I suddenly found pleasant. I said to myself: "If I had to choose between you and him, I'd choose him, because I don't know him." It's no good any more: you and Titina [their daughter Letizia] are the only things to do with Christianity I can stand.[20]

In several other letters Svevo expressed his uneasiness, his incompatibility with Christianity. When his daughter's education was to be decided, he vehemently resisted Livia's determination to give the child a strict Catholic education. Livia wanted her daughter to be educated by the nuns of the Istituto Notre Dame de Sion, the same school she had attended. When Svevo finally gave in, he gave his consent with the greatest reluctance, and insisted that it be for only one year. He wrote home:

. . . we both know what each of us wants. Let's face it, this is a disagreement and not a misunderstanding. It's the same disagreement that almost prevented our union. We should be glad that it's our only one and that in so many years there haven't been others. However, we must keep it in mind. I believe that our family—given our condition (or better mine)—is Catholic enough and there's no need for it to become more so. Naturally, if you thought that it wasn't enough I would eventually yield, since a girl's education is more the responsibility of the mother than the father. But deep in my heart I would always be convinced that you had committed an injustice. So let us wait for this year, which I have freely conceded in order to make you happy, to pass, and then let us try to go back to the way things were, as we had decided.[21]

This "disagreement" continued to plague Ettore's and Livia's otherwise happy marriage for many years. His guilt feelings may be summed up in another letter written to his wife in which he states: "You have committed a foolish act that you now regret like a Jew who lets himself by baptized."[22]

After the wedding, he continued his work at the bank, wrote for *L'Indipendente* and also for *Il Piccolo,* another Triestine paper, and began to teach business courses at Revoltella, his former school. After his literary disappointments, as on previous occasions, Svevo once more took stock of his efforts as a writer, and concluded bitterly: "I can't fathom this incomprehension. It shows that people just do not understand. It's useless for me to write and publish."[23] He painfully withdrew into himself, giving up his literary ambitions. He no longer spoke to his friends about his writings; nevertheless, he continued to write and to read Ibsen, Dostoyevski, and Tolstoy incessantly during his free time.

In 1899, after being employed there for nineteen years, Svevo left the bank and went to work for his wife's family, thus greatly improving his financial prospects. The Veneziani family owned a very successful factory that specialized in protective underwater paints for ships' hulls. Thus, a new life began for him: he traveled extensively throughout Europe, but particularly to England, where there was a branch of the factory. Eventually, Svevo became a prosperous businessman and a proud family man. Although his new way of life provided him with a sense of satisfaction, it did not fulfill his inner needs. Only writing, it seems, could do that. He rationalized these conflicting ambitions by noting that "in this world one is compelled to write, but not necessarily to publish."[24] He thus began to make notes and collect scraps of paper on which he analyzed everything he saw or thought, hoping to achieve a better understanding of himself and of life in general. He felt that this practice would make him a better writer: "I believe, I sincerely believe, that there is no better way of becoming a serious writer than to scribble every day. One must try to bring out from the depths of one's innermost being a sound, an accent, a fossil, or a vegetable residue of something that may or may not be a feeling, or rather a whim, a regret, a sorrow, something sincere dissected, and that's all . . . In other words there is no salvation except in the pen. . . ."[25] Meeting this successful businessman, it must have been difficult to imagine that beneath the prosperous and jovial exterior there lay a restless, troubled spirit.

The business world now demanded more and more of him, leaving him little time or energy for his hidden passion. The industrialist appeared to overwhelm the creative writer. However, though he tried repeatedly to give up writing, he never succeeded. It was only through the pen that he could see things clearly and that he could understand himself. In 1902 he wrote in his diary: "At this time I have definitely eliminated from my life that pernicious and ridiculous thing called literature."[26] It is interesting to note that this perennial giving up of literature is similar, if not identical, to Svevo's lifelong resolutions to give up smoking. Like the hero of *La coscienza di Zeno (Confessions of Zeno)*, Svevo too throughout his life used to write himself resolutions vowing to give up this addiction, but he never succeeded in keeping his promise that the next would be his "last cigarette."

Fearing that he might succumb once more to his literary temptations, Svevo began to play the violin during his free time and continued to take an active interest in the theater. In his diary *Soggiorno londinese* (London sojourn) he analyzed and commented on English plays and actors, and on playwrights ranging from Shakespeare to Sheridan, Shaw, and Galsworthy.[27] He was particularly interested in the Theater of Ideas, in Ibsen and Strindberg whose plays he attended frequently.

Svevo's life took a decisive turn in 1905. He met James Joyce, who had come to the Berlitz School in Trieste as an English teacher. Because he needed English for his trips, Svevo became his pupil; soon the two of them, instead of concerning themselves with English grammar, were spending hours talking about literature and their writings. Joyce was impressed with Svevo's two books, so much so that he memorized parts of *Senilità*. The two authors discovered that they had things in common: they had both started out as disciples of naturalism and both had found a way to go beyond it. The most important aspect of this friendship for Svevo was that he again had someone to talk to about his writings, a confidant like his brother Elio and like his painter friend Veruda (who had died in 1904). Svevo found many similarities between Joyce's Bohemian style of life and Veruda's. This new relationship gave him the necessary encouragement to realize that his own works were not as bad as he had thought. It instilled in him a new sense of purpose as a writer.

When Italo Svevo wrote *La coscienza di Zeno* in 1919, he was a new man. He had read Freud and translated into Italian *The Interpretation of Dreams*, he had written a treatise on universal peace, and he no longer felt the uncertainties and inadequacies that had haunted him throughout his life. Italy had been involved in World War I and Svevo had even performed several heroic deeds in the struggle for the Italianization of Trieste, which had finally become part of Italy.[28] In 1918 he had been one of the first collaborators of *La Nazione,* a major new Italian newspaper published in Trieste. He no longer had doubts about literature, nor did he feel hesitant to write as he had during most of his life. His wife tells us that these were days full of excitement and that, although her husband had returned to his successful business affairs, which had been interrupted by the war, "Ettore fully embraced literature."[29]

La coscienza di Zeno, his last novel, was published in 1923 by Cappelli, once again, however, at Svevo's expense. And once again the Italian critics ignored his work. True, a few local writers praised it highly, although their doyen, Silvio Benco, gave it a mixed review. But this was no longer sufficient for Svevo—by now sixty-two years old—who felt embittered by this long and undeserved lack of recognition. He accused the critics of being blatantly hostile toward him. He went to see the critic Giulio Caprin of *Il Corriere della Sera* in 1924 but was dismissed by him and informed that the paper did not have enough space to bother with his book. As an act of rebellion he sent the novel to his friend Joyce, who was now living in Paris. Joyce showed *La coscienza* and Svevo's other novels to Benjamin Crémieux and Valéry Larbaud, key figures on the Parisian literary scene. They both were fascinated by Svevo's work and promised to make him known in *Le Navire d'Argent,* a new Parisian literary magazine. But success would only come at the end of 1925. Ironically, although everything pointed to a breakthrough in France, Svevo was vindicated, much to his satisfaction, by Italy's foremost twentieth-century poet, Eugenio Montale, who devoted a searching and substantial study to Svevo's works in the December 1925 issue of the periodical *Esame,* bringing him to the attention of Italian readers. After many delays, an entire issue of *Navire* was devoted to Svevo in 1926, thus finally making him known to the world.

His dramatic efforts—he had written altogether about fifteen complete plays—bore fruit in April 1927 with the performance of *Terzetto spezzato (The Broken Triangle),* written around 1920.[30] This play is the only one that reached the stage during Svevo's lifetime. It was performed in Rome at the Teatro degli Indipendenti, under the direction of the renowned Anton Giulio Bragaglia who, at the time, was presenting at his experimental theater widely known Italian and European playwrights. Unfortunately, Svevo never saw it performed because illness prevented him making the long journey to Rome. During this period, the mid 1920s, he read Marcel Proust and discovered the work of Franz Kafka, who became his "last literary love."[31]

Finally, Italo Svevo was enjoying his much deserved success—giving lectures, being interviewed, participating in various functions as a celebrity, preparing new editions of his books, editing and proofreading translations of his works—when on 13 September 1928 he suddenly passed away, a few days after a freak automobile accident had left him with no more than a broken thighbone. Since he had been suffering for years from a heart condition, however, it was probably the shock of the accident that caused his death. When it became evident that there was no hope for him, his wife records that she asked if he wanted to pray. He replied (according to Livia Veneziani) that it would be useless for someone who had not prayed all his life to do so now. In a conversation with their daughter, however, I learned that her father asked to be buried in the traditional Jewish shroud.[32] Thus, the Triestine author in a small but symbolic way returned to his "ancestral" custom, fulfilling Jewish law which holds that an apostate, despite his actions, may return—without any formal ceremony—to the Jewish nation. Ironically, however, Svevo was buried in the Catholic cemetery of Trieste, where he is listed in the register as Aron Hector Schmitz. The rest of his paternal and maternal family lie buried nearby in the Jewish cemetery.

It is difficult to establish a clear concept of Svevo's personality because he was a composite of many often contradictory traits; however, there are two pictures that do emerge clearly: on the one hand, the average bourgeois, the good husband and father, reliable if somewhat absentminded, a good provider and successful businessman; on the other, a man of letters who nurtured for a lifetime in the face of an uncomprehending public a literary production that is indeed destined to last. For his biography, we are obliged to rely primarily upon his wife's account *Vita di mio marito* which, although essential for the reconstruction of his marriage, does not clarify Svevo's inner life; nor does it sufficiently reveal the relationship between the man and his writings. It tells us little about the intimate nature, the spiritual agonies, and the pessimistic irony of the author of *Confessions of Zeno*. As Montale remarks, Livia Veneziani seems to have known only the exterior Svevo, the industrialist and the dilettante writer, without ever discovering the man who was very much the double of his literary character Zeno.[33] Furthermore, we lack a complete knowledge of all his writings, particularly of his plays, since he destroyed some and failed to date others. The same can be said about most of his private correspondence which—at least according to his daughter Letizia—is not related to Svevo the man of letters. Finally, the task of re-creating the man is made difficult by Svevo himself, who hardly ever discussed his theater or his first novels. Indeed, he seems to have tried, as Lavagetto points out,[34] to foster the Svevo myth, depicting himself as a writer who published nothing for twenty-five years but continued to write in secret.[35] He kept up this false image even when success was his. Even more puzzling, considering that he had been brought up as a Jew in a moderately observant Jewish family and in a city where the Jewish population had a central role in culture and commerce, is the fact that there are no references in his works to his Jewishness. Nor are any of the characters of his dramas and fiction overtly Jewish. With a few exceptions, we find only indirect and well-hidden references to his roots in his published writings. What becomes immediately clear is that he chose not to draw any attention to the *"condition juive,"* and that he intentionally tried to mislead us by expressly referring to his father as an "assimilated Jew." Perhaps he even tried to conceal his Jewishness. The use of various pseudonyms: *Erode, E. Muranese, E. Samigli,* and *Italo Svevo* could be construed as additional proof of this.[36] According to Brian Moloney, the use of these pseudonyms "certainly concealed one fact—that the author was a Jew."[37] His brother Elio on the other hand had no such inhibitions concerning his religion: his diary, in fact, is full of religious references. Ettore, notwithstanding the Jewish emancipation in Trieste, his professed agnosticism, and his later conversion to the Catholic faith (as we have seen, a practical formality), could not have escaped his roots, any more than his Irish-born friend Joyce could have escaped his. Indeed, Joyce saw Svevo as a typical Jew and used him as one of the models for Leopold Bloom in *Ulysses.* We have been able to re-create, to some extent, the true character of Svevo by relying upon indirect references and by scrutinizing what Lavagetto calls "a semi-clandestine literature"[38]—his published letters, Elio's diary, and of course Livia Veneziani's biography. Svevo's own "Profilo autobiografico" (Autobiographical sketch) is evasive and sheds little light on his "real" and private life.

Chapter Two
A Life

A Life (Una vita) is the tragic story of a young man, Alfonso Nitti, who comes to Trieste from a small town in the remote Carso to work as a clerk at the Maller Bank. He finds it difficult to adjust to city life and longs to return home to his old widowed mother Carolina. Alfonso, who holds a university degree in literature, finds the routine work at the bank demeaning and boring. He feels that his talents are being wasted. His job is to copy endlessly by hand impersonal business letters, a task that requires no imagination or ability. Alfonso's tendency to dream and fantasize prevents him from concentrating; he makes careless errors, with the result that he is constantly suffering humiliation at the hands of his colleagues and superiors.

Alfonso lives as a boarder with the Lanuccis, a lower middle-class family fallen on hard times, who admire Alfonso and hold him in high esteem. In contrast to his inferior status at the bank, with them he enjoys a degree of respect and importance. Mrs. Lanucci earns a meager salary as a schoolteacher, and could hope for nothing better than a marriage between her daughter Lucia and the young boarder whom she considers to be on the way to a brilliant career. The husband who has given up his job because he refuses to work for someone else, is trying unsuccessfully to make a living as a free-lance salesman. The son Gustavo, unsettled and listless, works only sporadically. Alfonso feels sorry for the family, yet he remains blind to their romantic schemes involving himself and the unattractive and unintelligent Lucia. He misguidedly tries to help the daughter by teaching her correct Italian grammar, but is soon exasperated by her stupidity.

Alfonso's first visit to the Maller residence turns out badly. He is received by Annetta, the bank director's spoiled but attractive daughter. Vain, pretentious, and arrogant, she devotes all her attention to her cousin Macario, a suave and self-confident young lawyer. She totally snubs the timid and tongue-tied Alfonso, who is unable to participate in the general conversation. He vows never to return to the banker's house.

A Life

Alfonso's apprenticeship at the Maller Bank soon becomes more complicated—and humiliating. Required not only to copy letters, but now to write them as well, Alfonso's incompetence results in harsh reprimands from his superior Sanneo. He tries to overcome his frustration by taking refuge each evening in the public library where he can return to his one true vocation: literature. He reads and gathers material for a projected treatise on moral philosophy. However, he never gets past the title page.

One day he happens to meet Annetta, who, much to his surprise, invites him back to her home. He starts to frequent her second-rate literary and artistic salon where he meets its other habitués: young men more interested in winning favor with their hostess than in literature or art. Alfonso is overwhelmed by the girl's beguiling beauty and by his privileged new social position, which affords him a special status at the bank. Annetta, on the other hand, wants him to collaborate with her in writing a novel. He agrees because it allows him to be near her. While he outlines the plot, she develops the novel's individual scenes, which consist of banal, sentimental, romantic drivel. Alfonso is humiliated by this work, nevertheless—hopelessly smitten—he persists. At first he is intimidated by his new surroundings and by Annetta's arrogant superiority. Later on, however, when his clumsy advances are not rejected, he becomes more assertive and intimate with her. Finally, aided by the complicity of Francesca (who, as Maller's mistress, wants Annetta married off, so that she can marry the girl's father), he overcomes his uncertainties and succeeds in seducing her—though it might be more accurate to say that she seduces him.

Alfonso, who could easily improve his lot by marrying the banker's wealthy daughter, is incapable of profiting from this new development. It is here that his ineptitude clearly reveals itself. Using his mother's failing health as a pretext, and accepting Annetta's self-serving suggestion that he leave Trieste for a short while so that she can sort things out, he returns to his village. He does so in spite of Francesca's frantic but well-founded admonition that by leaving the city he will lose forever the opportunity of marrying Annetta.

When he arrives home, he discovers that his mother is really ill, that in fact she is dying. He patiently and affectionately tends to her needs until her final moments. His return to Trieste is further postponed when he himself falls seriously ill immediately after his mother's death. Upon his recovery he sells his property and finally returns to Trieste, only to learn that Annetta has become engaged to Macario. He is secretly relieved by this development because he no longer feels responsible or guilty about having abandoned the girl. At the office, however, he is now regarded as persona non grata by his supervisors and in particular by Maller who suspects him of being an unscrupulous adventurer. Alfonso is demoted and transferred to another department. In an attempt to exonerate himself in the eyes of Annetta, he invites her to a rendezvous. Instead, her brother shows up and, after some vulgar insults, challenges Alfonso to a duel. In the solitude of his room Alfonso ponders his fate and his miserable life. When he realizes that there is no escape for him and that the Maller family is out to kill him, he takes his own life. We learn about his death from a cold business letter written by Maller to the notary of Alfonso's hometown.

A Life, which originally had the title *Un inetto* (The failure), is a disquieting book, difficult to classify because the author did not yet have a precise idea of what he was doing and consequently did not follow rigorously any literary school.[1] He seems to have been intuitively led toward certain themes and forms. Italo Svevo began his literary career when romanticism was waning, although it still retained considerable influence. His first dramatic attempts—particularly *Ariosto governatore* (Ariosto the governor)—were inspired by the romantics and featured romantically Hamletic characters. But this was only a transitory phase. Soon after, he radically changed his literary creed. Under the influence of Zola and the programmatic lessons of naturalism, the young Svevo tried to present, as frankly and objectively as possible, the problems and conditions of contemporary life; he also tried to show the debilitating effects of an unfavorable environment.

When Svevo began to write the novel, he did not have a congenial Italian model to guide his literary aspirations. It is for this reason that the chief influence came from France and primarily from Zola's formula for the novel: "the human problem studied in the framework of reality."[2] Generally speaking, the literary tradition to which *A Life* belongs is that of the realistic and objective nineteenth century novel. But in absolute terms Svevo was not a realist, nor a romantic nor a naturalist, but a writer sui generis whose works were born out of his own experience. He sought, rather, to include all these partial views of life and art in his first novel. A naturalist more in theory than in practice, he nevertheless tried to follow two of its principles: accurate observation and documentation, and impersonality of style and treatment. But unlike Zola, he did not stress the animal in man—*la bête humaine*—nor did he emphasize determinsitic theories or the lower and coarser forms of life. The book abounds in minute detail. Even minor characters are sharply individualized in appearance and temperament. Physical details at the bank and at the Lanucci and Maller residences add to the sense of reality; the novel is rich in descriptions of furniture, rooms, dress, and social customs. In particular, the descriptions of illness—Fumigi's spinal meningitis and mental deterioration, and Alfonso's mother's heart ailment—show the influence of the naturalistic movement, although Svevo does not offer these details merely for their shock value. Mrs. Nitti's death is described at great length in the clinical manner of a medical textbook, though the effect is mitigated by Alfonso's filial love and anguish.

Even more important than the realism of its physical details is the novel's social realism. It is an exhaustive study of three social classes at a particular time and place in history, at work and in public life, in society and at home. Their existence of complete artificiality and hypocrisy affects all who come in contact with them. Even within the Mallers' own circle, we note certain social distinctions between the rich and the less affluent, between those who may be invited to Annetta's salon, and those who may come only for business-related reasons.

Couterbalancing the banker's family, Svevo describes in great detail the "natural history" of the Lanucci family, much like Zola had done in his Rougon-Macquart series of novels. The Lanuccis are represented by Svevo as victims of forces and circumstances beyond their control. We see how they have fallen on hard times, how the wife is virtually the sole breadwinner, and how the husband's efforts to earn a living are unrealistic and fruitless. Svevo likewise presents a detailed, though gloomy and depressing picture of life at the Maller Bank, where the ill-paid and overworked employees are treated with indifference and contempt by their bosses. It is not simply an exploitation of labor but of emotion as well. The repeated use of the word *disaggradevole* (disagreeable) highlights Alfonso's feelings of monotony, fatigue, tedium, exhaustion, and tension. His experiences at work have an autobiographical component, since they reflect Svevo's own long employment at the Trieste branch of the Viennese Unionbank.[3]

> Tired? Nauseated, rather. From day to day his work slowly increased, but varied little . . . and his attention would stray, for lack of stimulus; sometimes he was forced to fling down his pen and abandon work out of nausea, like someone who has eaten too much of one dish. He never quite caught up with this work, and worry was now added to his malaise.[4] (69)

By and large, the dark mood of the novel and the crystallization of the social and economic problems of the Triestine middle class are naturalistic. Naturalistic too is the author's detailed and dispassionate analysis of the character's behavior. However, Svevo fails to maintain his stance as a severe and impartial recorder of society's maladies. He is frequently too sympathetic and emotional in his attempts to present things with scientific realism. Indeed, the patent compassion he shows for the misfortunes of the Lanucci family, and the subjective manner with which he dwells on Alfonso's consciousness while depicting his gradual downfall and final degradation, indicate that naturalism was too limited and restrictive a literary technique for Svevo; that his intention was to focus primarily on Alfonso's most intimate and profound feelings.[5] Simply put, Svevo adheres to the rules of objective representation only in the descriptive parts dealing with the city, the bank, and the Lanucci family. Whenever he centers on Alfonso, his perspective and style change drastically; he becomes more verbose, subjective, and psychological. Naturalism is no longer enough to bridge the gap between the inner and outer realities. The impersonality of the author is further compromised by the rival claim of autobiography, which, with its inherent subjectivism, inevitably leads to contradictory results. Because of this, Svevo must create for himself an "aesthetic that adapts itself perfectly to the spiritual uneasiness and psychological incoherence of modern man."[6]

From the very beginning of *A Life* the description of Trieste—never specifically named but recognizable through the names of its streets and the description of its port—sets the tone of the novel, and the city becomes an essential part of the story, providing a sense of cultural dignity and a vibrancy of commercial activity that contribute much to the novel. At the same time its panorama is always painted impressionistically with gloomy colors because Alfonso is repelled by the hostile environment of the city. He finds it joyless, gray, congested, polluted, and airless. Upon his arrival and entrance into the Maller Bank, he writes home to his mother: "And I feel such a need to breathe some of our good pure air straight from its Maker. . . . The other men here are all or nearly all quite content, not realizing one can live so much better elsewhere"(4).

Alfonso has a love-hate relationship with the city and is constantly perturbed by the clash between his country boy's temperament and the urban environment. He regards townsmen as "physically weak and morally lax" and despises "their sexual mores, their womanizing and easy love affairs" (74). The protagonist persists in contrasting the decadence of the city with the virtues of rural life, seen as a refuge from a corrupted world, almost an Arcadia from which harsh reality is excluded. Upon his return home, his expectations of an unspoiled and authentic life are quickly dashed when he realizes that rural life is not necessarily better than city life. He is finally convinced that the people among whom he had grown up are corrupt, sly, avaricious, hypocritical, and far less peaceful and a good deal more ugly than expected. All their motives are reduced to one: possession of money and land. Both in the city and in the country Alfonso is dissatisfied with the world around him. He is always contrasting his actual surroundings with the world of his imagination. He writes to his mother: "Now mother, you mustn't think it's bad here; I just feel bad here myself" (4)! Unsuited both for city and country life, his only happiness lies in his daydreams.

Like Zola in *La terre (The Earth)*, Svevo too apparently wanted to show the falseness of rural society, regarded by the romantics as the exemplar guardian of moral and social values in an era of decadence. Nature could no longer be seen as a refuge from a changing and declining world. Ironically, although Alfonso comes from the country and for the most part extolls its virtues while condemning the city, nevertheless what emerges is a strong and vivid image of the city rather than the country. It is Svevo's Trieste that stands out and not Alfonso's hometown.

Octavio Paz, Mexico's leading poet and essayist, believes that writers do not have a biography, that their work is their biography. For Paz, poetry and literature are a way of reinventing the self: "I am the shadow my words cast."[7] *A Life* can be seen as a spiritual autobiography inasmuch as Alfonso experiences the same problems of identity, frustration, anxiety, and timidity encountered by young Ettore Schmitz while working at the Unionbank, when he still was "unprepared for the serious business of living."[8] Literature and writing are the only redemption from the bank's daily routine of mindless tedium, and in Alfonso's case from his debilitating feelings of inferiority, especially as regards Annetta and her circle: "He found happiness partly in study itself, partly in a swollen ambition, a hunger for glory. He felt himself superior to others, and though he did not yet know how he would gain this glory, fortified his hopes by a love of study which had become a passion" (78).

Literature has become an escape, a panacea for the ills of the individual and of society. Its role is similar to the relief Alfonso gets from his frequent walks in the surrounding hills, where he can breathe freely the fresh and clean air, away from the social and physical claustrophobia of the city. It is only when he discusses literature that he forgets his "organic defect" (70) and can feel equal, even superior to those who cause him to feel inferior. Yet, Alfonso fails to make the best of his talent and fight for what he wants because he lacks the necessary determination, aggressiveness, and sense of worth and purpose; he prefers to sit back and wait for justice to be done, for the coming of the Messiah.

Alfonso Nitti is typical of Svevo's antiheroic characters, the *inetti* (the inept)[9] who lack a capacity for action, who cannot make bold decisions because they find themselves in a world where decisive action is only possible on blind impulse. In general, Svevo's male protagonists are always portrayed as weaklings who, due to their continuous self-analysis and self-searching, become impotent, inept, and finally complete failures. While Verga's *vinti* (defeated) are undone by a fate over which they have little control, Svevo's *inetti* bring about their own demise by remaining withdrawn from reality, and, as Amato points out, "nailed on the calvary of their inaction, confined within the narrow limits of a desperate loneliness."[10]

The portrait that emerges of Alfonso is that of the angst-ridden talented young man as a bungling bank clerk, an outcast who senses that there is something in his character that condemns him to be second-rate in spite of all his struggling and all the good fortune in the world because, as he is warned by Macario

You study, you spend hours at a desk nourishing your brain uselessly. Anyone who isn't born with the necessary wings will never grow them afterward. Anyone who can't drop like lead on prey at the right second by instinct will never learn, and there'll be no point in his watching others who can, as he'll never be able to imitate them. (107)

When Alfonso loses Annetta to the successful but unprincipled Macario, he realizes that he lacks his rival's practical disposition, and that his inferior status as a hired hand is an insurmountable block in a society where money is stronger than personal feelings and even family ties.

Debenedetti ascribes this ineptitude to Svevo's Jewish origin and cultural formation. He sees in his characters the temperament of the Jew of the Diaspora who is incapable "of being like others in the face of his daily existence." He compares Svevo's characters to Weininger's stereotype of the Jew, whose inherited identity prevents him from exhibiting any positive instinct for life or opening himself up to it, unlike his opposite, the Aryan model.[11] According to Weininger's anti-Semitic theories[12] the Jew is also "gifted with an unstable multiplicity of moral backgrounds which allows every shock to shape, influence or deform him."[13] Debenedetti suggests also that, as a Jew, Svevo followed through his characters the suggestions and demands of his race. He concludes by saying that if Svevo had accepted more openly his Jewishness and had made use of his people's plight, then his artistic creation would have found more readily its just note and would have been more successful and better understood. Unfortunately, Debenedetti (a Jew himself) failed to see that the traits displayed by Svevo's characters are not exclusively Jewish, but rather those of modern man; that in this gloomy portrayal of human frustration, man is depicted as a puppet living in a Kafkaesque world inhabited by *all* races; that we are all suffering from loneliness, isolation, uncertainty, and doubt; and that we are all caught in a nightmarish tangle from which we cannot free ourselves and determine our own destinies. Svevo's characters are "creatures belonging to no particular age" and to no determined world, suffering from the same uneasiness, "the same unresolved and unresolvable dramas" that afflict modern man.[14] However, there is some truth in Debenedetti's findings inasmuch as Svevo *never* allows the reader to glimpse his Jewish identity and almost goes out of his way to hide it. Indeed, Alfonso's condition reveals a profound feeling of alienation from the world—a feeling that is typical of many other assimilated Jews.

Svevo stated frequently to his friends that during his life he had written only one book and that its theme had remained unchanged and constant; only the external structure had been changed.[15] Renato Poggioli points out that the only theme in Svevo's works is the bourgeois soul "who tortures himself in his free time."[16] Alfonso's milieu, his nature and outlook on life, are a crystallization of Svevo's unchanging theme and, if we are to understand what the author was trying to convey, it must be appreciated that the terms *borghese, borghesia* have overtones that far transcend their social or political connotations. For Svevo the "bourgeois" represented a *forma mentis,* a particular outlook on life, a frame of reference, a psychological conditioning which he felt within himself at all times, just as Montaigne claimed that "each man carries within himself the entire essence of the human condition."[17]

This, perhaps, may explain why Svevo, instead of attacking and denouncing his society openly, preferred to do so in more subtle ways.

All of his characters are dissatisfied, unhappy people leading dreary and uninteresting lives, searching for an impossible change. There is a tragic failure in them, and in their irresoluteness they wander from one misdirected ambition to another, from one unsuccessful venture to another. Svevo portrays these antiheroes as being oppressed (as he was) by the commonplace qualities of a petty, dull, and provincial bourgeois environment from which there is no escape. They are fully aware of their failings and Svevo leaves them raw and naked, with no beliefs and no meaningful set of values—except the profit motive. However, they are conscious of being victims of their times; they suffer from *bovarysme,* according to Montale,[18] because they know ahead of time what the reality of life will be. Alfonso, like all other Svevo characters, exudes the painful knowledge of his inevitable defeat as predicted by Macario's admonition that he lacks the necessary "wings."

On the surface, the typical Svevo protagonist seems to lead a "normal" life, but within he is tormented and torn by "disquieting instability, anxiety, torturing self-analysis and hesitation . . . endless preoccupation with reason and causality."[19] Unlike Greek heroes, he is defeated not only by Fate[20] but also by chance, trivialities, insecurities. They could all save themselves if there were not in them "a malicious force pushing them to act contrary to their good sense and self interest."[21] In these contemplative individuals we find the crisis of twentieth-century man: they are complete misfits in the world they inhabit, unable to keep in step with society, Triestine Charlie Chaplins[22] who bungle all they attempt.

Alfonso's only occasional companions are Macario, Annetta's cousin and soon to be fiancé, and Gustavo, the good-natured son of the Lanucci family. Together they represent the extremes of the spectrum of Triestine society, while Alfonso, who falls somewhere in between, is, as Brian Moloney remarks, the "odd man out rather than the representative of a social class."[23] Macario and Gustavo are foils for Alfonso's antiheroic qualities insofar as they are more able to determine their own destinies. Their actions are not hampered by constant introspection. They are "survivors" who do not have Alfonso's "hang-ups"; they are realistic about their situation in life and have made peace with the world by accepting it as it is; they have no dreams, no illusions.

It would, however, be erroneous to assume that Svevo's intention was to imply that people such as Gustavo and Macario are better human beings than Alfonso.[24] Though both characters give the appearance of being "natural" and even relatively "happy" with their lot, they still have their own weaknesses, frailties, and faults. Gustavo is a failure and when he tries to resolve his sister's problems, he inevitably ends up drunk. We can predict that eventually he is going to turn out like his father, drifting from one menial occupation to another. On the other hand, will Macario be happy with his tyrannical cousin, knowing that she had given herself to Alfonso, his inferior rival? And, given the fact that he shares Weininger's misogynous ideas, will he ever be happy with any woman? The principal difference between these characters and Alfonso is that he is not indifferent to life as they are; they do not have his anguished sensitivity, his intelligence, nor his weltanschauung. We are left with the Pirandellian questions: who is sane and who is insane, who is normal and who is not?

Svevo considered the love motif to be the nucleus of *A Life*. We have it in his own words: "Certainly, for the author, the relationship between Alfonso and Annetta, the daughter of the rich banker Maller, is the important part of the novel. . . ."[25] This, however, would appear to have been only a pretext, for, by focusing on this theme, he was able to dwell at length on Alfonso's neurotic personality and to show the anxieties suffered by him as a consequence of this unhappy romantic involvement. Annetta and Alfonso are fundamentally incapable of loving, no matter how hard they try to pursue false images of love, but for quite different reasons. Annetta—arrogant, ambitious, insensitive—toys with him contemptuously. He, like Emma Bovary, is a romantic more in love with the idea of being in love than with the girl he is courting. He is never happy away from her, but once in her presence, he is as unhappy as before because her confession of love is never forthcoming. He needs and wants to love her, yet he does not really like or respect her. He wants Annetta because he suspects he can't have her. Once he has seduced her, or better made love to her—which he eventually does in a very crude manner—he quickly loses interest in her.

It is interesting to note that whenever Trieste is described, it is always in gray tones and colors that reflect Alfonso's negative feelings toward the city. He is ambivalent too toward Annetta—always "firmly enclosed in her favorite gray material" (115)—the example par excellence of the high Triestine middle class. Throughout the novel this twofold ambivalence remains unresolved.

Following the grand seduction scene, Alfonso's attention is drawn to the unpleasant smell of glue permeating the room. Symbolically, from this moment on he will try, consciously and subconsciously, to extricate himself, to "unglue" himself from this new dimension in his already entwined relationship with Annetta for which his personality is unprepared. He returns therefore to what Roditi calls his "passive listlessness."[26] In spite of his neurotic compulsion to cling to what he risks losing, once he has obtained the object of his desire, Alfonso begins to doubt once again his feelings, does she love him etc., and succumbs to only one impulse: to flee.

There are two puzzling, unresolved questions in the novel: First, why does Alfonso leave Trieste after Annetta's seduction, knowing that in doing so he is throwing away every advantage that he is on the verge of gaining: respect, money, a better career, high society, and a handsome woman? And second, why does he finally kill himself? Did he have no alternatives?

The morning after spending the night in the girl's boudoir where the ambiance must have been far more pleasant than that of the library, one might have expected the young man to feel elated, satisfied, and, perhaps, even happy,

> But on waking he found himself with the same malaise. As he went over in his thoughts all the events of the night before, his revulsion grew. He disliked everything about the evening, from his first stolen embrace to the last greeting which he had answered by forcing himself to a pretense that had been an effort, however easy. He did not want to face up to the conclusion which he should evidently draw from this feeling; in spite of all his delight in possessing Annetta, he disliked the way he had won her. He did not believe Annetta loved him; she was bowing to the irrevocable. (230)

Alfonso's return home becomes more understandable if we consider it not in an amorous context, but in existentialist terms. The fact that he has obtained favors does not bring happiness to Alfonso because paradoxically his very search for happiness prevents him experiencing it. Like the romantic poet Leopardi, "He never attained the reality of love, because he was not seeking for it: he preferred his own illusions."[27] After having reached the object of his desire, Alfonso finds that there is no such thing as real pleasure and that the expectation of pleasure is far greater than pleasure itself. Similarly, his malaise winds its way into the very core of his emotions, leading him to introspective self-torment, anguish, and ennui.

The solution to the second puzzling question, namely, why does Alfonso kill himself, may be found, in part, in Schopenhauer's theories. Although in the novel the philosopher is never mentioned by name, there are several references to his ideas: the contemplative life, Nirvana, moral philosophy. Indeed, Svevo insists in several of his writings that the novel was written under the influence of Schopenhauer. In his autobiographical sketch he writes that at an early age Schopenhauer became his favorite author, and it was due perhaps to the great German philosopher that he chose the pseudonym Svevo (Swabian), which appeared for the first time on the cover of *A Life*. According to Svevo's wife, he was a lifelong member of the *Schopenhauergesellschaft* of Frankfurt am Main, and he owned all of the philosopher's writings from which he used to quote long passages from memory.

Some scholars have refused to accept fully the author's explanation that *A Life* was written entirely under the influence of Schopenhauer. Several, in fact, have seen the question of Alfonso's suicide as a demystification or an unmasking of the philosopher's beautiful theories and noble programs.[28] Along a similar line, Poggioli views the whole novel as a parody of Schopenhauer's ideas, just as *Confessions of Zeno* may be regarded as a parody of Freud, inasmuch as Svevo "psychoanalyzed psychoanalysis itself."[29] Similarly, Furbank sees it as an ironic commentary on Schopenhauer, in particular on the concluding section of *The World as Will and Idea*, dealing with "The Assertion and Denial of the Will to Live."[30] In fact, years after having written the novel, Svevo himself intimated that the final part of *A Life* did not turn out the way he had originally intended. Alfonso, he says, *"was supposed to have been [doveva essere]* the very personification of the Schopenhauerian affirmation of life so near its negation."[31] This implies that his first design was not carried out fully. It would appear, then, that Svevo had intended to follow Schopenhauer's schema by allowing Alfonso to retire to his village and there follow the philosopher's doctrine of salvation through aesthetics, ethics, and religion; not by rejecting life, but by repudiating desire and thus gaining salvation from the will and passing into the state of Nirvana, where peace and tranquillity were to be found. However, as in the case of Augusto Pérez in Unamuno's *Niebla,* the character acquired, as it were, an independent existence, taking on additional characteristics not envisioned by the author.

However, things did not quite work out as Alfonso had expected because he realized that life in the country was as bad, if not worse, than in the city. Thus he returns to Trieste where he still intends to adhere to the ascetic concept of renunciation of earthly things, by trying to experience acts of compassion, of selflessness, of human kindness, and of participating in the sufferings of others as if they were his own, by withdrawing from active engagement in the world of Will and by transforming it from *voluntas* into *noluntas*. Of course, for poor Alfonso it is easier said than done. Once again he fails to achieve the desired "turning of the Will" which, alas, continues to be as active as ever, regardless of his serious attempts. For example, he submerges himself in work and for a while succeeds in becoming calmer than ever before: "He was, he thought, very close to the ideal state he dreamed of in his reading, the state of renunciation and quiet. He no longer even felt enough agitation to work up energy for more renunciation. No one ever offered him anything: by his last renunciation he had saved himself, he thought, from the depths to which he might have been dragged by [the] urge for enjoyment" (342).

When he is transferred to a less important job at the Maller Bank, he forgets about the state of renunciation and falls prey again to his self-torments, pathologically obsessed by the snubs he has to endure. He yearns to be generous and participate in the suffering of others, and so he gives away his entire inheritance to Gralli, Lucia's seducer, who would otherwise have refused to marry her. Yet Alfonso cannot be totally altruistic: "every cold word from the Lanuccis gave him a little stab of satisfaction because as soon as they realized how unjustly they had treated him, their gratitude would be all the greater" (370). Alfonso prides himself in having given up all his desires, and yet whenever he thinks of Annetta, jealousy gnaws away at him. At the very end, when he is about to fight a duel with Annetta's brother and contemplates suicide as a way out and as a means of regaining her affection, he feels that he had never loved her as much as at that moment: "He did not want to live on and appear to her as a contemptible enemy whom she suspected of trying to harm her and make her pay a high price for the favors she had granted him" (397). In a Petrarchan fantasy, he romantically imagines Annetta rekindling her love for him one day, visiting his grave to scatter tears and flowers on it.

Clearly, there is a gap between Alfonso's inner and outer reality. Svevo must have reached the conclusion that Schopenhauer's ideas are valid in theory, but that in *real* life they are unrealistic and impractical; that the philosopher's "appalling universe is more an intellectual exercise than a real heart-breaking discovery."[32] Alfonso knows that he will be no match for his opponent in the duel and that he will play a miserable and ridiculous part. He sees suicide for the first time without the prejudices of others, and he calmly reviews all the arguments against it, from the moral ones to those of the most modern philosophers (like Schopenhauer). Smilingly, he concludes that they are not valid arguments against suicide, but expressions of the desire to live:

> He, though, felt incapable of living. Some feeling which he had often tried and failed to understand made it an unbearable agony for him. He knew neither how to love nor how to enjoy; he had suffered in the best of circumstances more than did others in the most painful ones. He was leaving life without regret. It was the one way to become superior to the suspicions and hatreds of others. That was the renunciation of which he had dreamed. He must destroy this organism of his which knew no peace; while it was alive, it would continue to drag him into the struggle because that was what it was there for. (397)

Thus Alfonso repudiates Schopenhauer's tenet that suicide is a "vain and foolish act, for the thing-in-itself—the species, and life, and will in general—remains unaffected by it,"[33] since suffering continues even after death as long as the Will is dominant in man. Suicide, therefore, according to the philosopher, does not deny the Will but rather asserts it, it wills life. Alfonso accepts only Schopenhauer's major and minor premises and refutes the conclusion. He can never be indifferent to life, nor can he deny and eradicate the impulses that constantly urge him to take part in the world of existence. Stoically, death becomes a harbor for Alfonso whose anguish is more than he can suffer. In this bildungsroman, the protagonist had set out to find the truth about love, life, and to acquire a philosophy on the "art of living," but discovered instead infinite ambiguities. Once Alfonso realizes that he has the power to end his plight and gain freedom from care and pain, suicide inevitably follows.

When Svevo was writing *A Life* he still showed a certain hesitancy about the direction the novel was to take.[34] At the completion of the novel the author realized that it was quite an achievement for a first novel. Had it received the expected acclamation from the critics, it is very possible that Svevo would have abandoned his ill-paid job at the bank and devoted himself fully to a literary career. Although, as he was writing it, he claims to have felt that his work was "mere rubbish"; later on, in spite of its lukewarm reception, he became very fond of *A Life*. It always remained his favorite novel, perhaps because of its autobiographical elements. He was wont to say that he had written only one novel. In 1925, in a letter to the French critic Larbaud, Svevo wrote:

James Joyce always said that in a man's heart there is room for only one novel (at the time he had not even considered writing *Ulysses*) and that when more than one is written, it is always the same thing, artificially masked with words. In this regard my only novel would be *A Life*. Except that it is written so badly (far worse than the other two) that I ought to rewrite it.[35]

The originality of *A Life* is not to be found in the overworked themes of disappointed love and the discovery of the world's ills, but rather in Svevo's inspired manner of presenting his vision of life; in the force of its expression and the perspicacity of his observations on human nature and suffering; and, apart from a few lexical and stylistic aberrations, in an almost absolute control of language. Granted, he did not always use *le mot juste* nor did he show the beauty and linguistic precision of a Flaubert. In fact, Svevo's style is characterized by total disregard for literary rhetoric. He used only the unadorned everyday language of common conversation; that allowed him, however, to be extremely communicative. His functional prose, although severely criticized by his purist and highly literary contemporaries for its artlessness, lack-luster, and its "spiky commercial jargon translated from the German with provincial idioms,"[36] is indeed quite modern and is used with great resource and inventiveness. His nimble and nervous style underscores the tension and mental subtlety it expresses.

Unfortunately, the severe criticism Svevo received for the "poverty of the language filled with grammatical and dialectal expressions"[37] resulted in a linguistic inferiority complex that was to plague him throughout his life. Never again did he feel secure about standard "Tuscan" Italian, and regarded it as almost a foreign language.[38] The linguistic objections are analyzed by Devoto who identifies the following faults: lack of grace, barbarism, antiliterary style, a-syntactical and archaic forms, improper usage of antecedent tenses.[39] This entire linguistic polemic was justly disposed of by Carlo Bo who called it stupid.[40] He points out that Svevo's language is powerful and effective since it has the capacity for critical observation and it achieves the "interior documentation" sought by Svevo. Even Devoto admits that literary Italian would have been insufficient for the exigencies of Svevo's art. This is why, as has been pointed out by O'Brien,[41] Svevo was intuitively compelled to create his own language in order to express more fully the torment of analysis, the inner tensions, and the meanderings of the subconscious. His characters would not have been able to narrate their inner conflicts without such linguistic inventions. Svevo's language has dramatic vigor and reflects the need of the individual to express himself without ornamentation.

Throughout the novel the omniscient point of view allows the author to shift freely from the external to the internal worlds of Alfonso. From this vantage point, Svevo reveals the character's innermost thoughts and occasionally comments upon them, without openly sitting in judgment. The narrator's role, though, is not limited to selecting events and translating them into language. Given the autobiographical nature of *A Life,* to a large extent born out of Svevo's own closely observed experiences at the Unionbank, it is difficult at times to differentiate between the consciousness of the author and that of the protagonist. This problem stems from the paucity of dialogue in the novel, almost entirely written in indirect discourse, including Alfonso's frequent and extensive inner monologues. In the course of the narrative we never know with certainty who is seeing and experiencing the events and emotions present in the text. Is there more than one consciousness, or do we merely see in both author and character a refraction of similar attitudes and feelings, given that Alfonso is a kindred soul of the author? To some extent, Alfonso's crisis is that of Svevo, who not only defines himself through him, but frequently presents a scene not as his characters see it but as *he* would see it. This is so, except for the concluding parts of the novel where Alfonso gains a degree of independence by breaking away from his maker, Svevo, who is compelled to alter the course of events leading up to the inevitable suicide.

The only time the point of view shifts from that of the omniscient narrator is in the case of Mrs. Lanucci, who, as an interested mother, carefully observes Alfonso's behavior, eager to promote her daughter's well-being with her eligible boarder. Svevo's narrative technique works well with Alfonso who is carefully put together and set in motion. Yet it does not work with Annetta who is not fully developed as a character. As already indicated, we never know what she is thinking and never see things through her eyes. What we do know about her character comes not only from the perceptions of the narrator, but also from the biased views of Alfonso, Francesca, and Macario.

The structure of *A Life* seems to correspond almost to perfection to

Gustav Freytag's pyramid of the "well-made play," as outlined in his *Technique of the Drama*—at that time the standard German drama reference work and one that Svevo must have been familiar with, considering his passion for the theater.[42] Alfonso is always the focal point and is never out of the picture, even when the author dwells on the two principal subplots (the Lanucci family and Mrs. Nitti's death), which are skillfully handled in their direct relationship to the main story as inciting forces to the interest and development of the narrative. Many of the secondary characters (Macario, Gustavo, Miceni) emphasize the isolation and superiority of Alfonso.

The leitmotiv that pervades the whole atmosphere of the novel gets its timbre from the ubiquitous presence of the key adjective *disaggradevole* (today *sgradevole*)—meaning unpleasant, disagreeable, uncomfortable, unsuited, and even offensive—that usually defines Alfonso's mental and emotional states resulting from his maniacal practice of observing himself.

Architectonically, *A Life* opens and closes with letters: the first, highly emotional and full of foreshadowing elements; and the last, announcing Alfonso's death, written in the curt and impersonal language typical of business correspondence. This structural device is to be expected since both Svevo's and Alfonso's job was to write letters. Indeed, all the significant events of the novel hinge on the numerous letters that play an important role in the development of the narrative.

The controlling hand of the artist is also apparent in the carefully manipulated contrasts and parallels that add unity and form: Alfonso pursues Annetta, Francesca pursues Maller, and Lucia wants Alfonso; life at the bank, life at the library; the Maller residence contrasted with the Lanuccis'; urban and country settings; characters born with "wings" and those without them; life and death, health and illness; the seduction of Francesca, of Annetta, and of Lucia; the abandonment of Lucia by Gralli, and of Annetta, Rosina, and Maria by Alfonso. The plot of the novel written together by Alfonso and Annetta reflects Alfonso's life; Alfonso's demise equals that of Francesca whose fortune is tied to his; and arranged loveless marriage is the proposed remedy for Annetta's and Lucia's seductions; Alfonso's agony parallels his mother's; the extinction of the entire Carli family presages that of the Nittis.

The publication of *A Life* did not bring Svevo his hoped-for success, and he gave away to friends and acquaintances most of the one thousand copies printed at his own expense. There appeared two favorable reviews in Trieste and one mixed review in *Il Corriere della Sera* by

Domenico Oliva, who criticized Svevo not only for having taken the title from Maupassant (Svevo had not yet read Maupassant), but also because the novel covered only part of Alfonso's life, his youth, unlike the Frenchman's novel. Oliva, nevertheless, recognized Svevo's potential talent as a writer, concluding that "in spite of its lack of interest and very limited technical value, this novel reveals the true spirit of an artist endowed with a clear vision."[43] *A Life* was soon forgotten and it was not until 1926 that it received a proper evaluation in the Italian and international press. It has been faulted for its language, its prolixity, and its lack of focus and direction. According to Furbank,

> The novel is half a dozen things at once, the study of a milieu and a profession, an *éducation sentimentale*, a tragedy of 'urbanisation' and a case-history, in the manner of Stendhal, of the bourgeois Napoleon-cult. It is an unconscious attempt to go beyond Zola, and it fails in its aim because it only fulfils one of the two conditions of the modern novel; it is centrifugal without having a centre. Svevo has not yet found the 'single thing' which is the corollary of the attempt to attain totality.[44]

On a more positive note, Eugenio Montale, winner of the 1975 Nobel Prize for Literature, remarked that *A Life* is Svevo's most ambitious work and that we have to read it "as one would read or look at a great fresco on which we have worked together with the master as collaborators or helpers. The master has painted the most vivid scenes, while others have been outlined by him, leaving the task of completion to the apprentice. Both the apprentice and the master coexist in him [Svevo]."[45]

Most modern critics tend to agree with Pampaloni who sees in Alfonso "the archetype of the Svevo character already representing the full expression of his world. His presence is an almost absolute novelty in the tradition of our late nineteenth century novel."[46] Although *A Life* may lack the force, cohesion, brilliance, and maturity of Svevo's later writings, it endures as a significant work of art, whatever its defects may be. In recent years the problem of the language seems to have become less significant even in Italy where the modern reader, no longer nurtured under the influence of aesthetes such as D'Annunzio or Croce, appreciates the propriety of Svevo's style and language which complement and are consistent with the characters, the setting, and the subject matter of his novel.

Chapter Three
As a Man Grows Older

Senilità (As a Man Grows Older), like *Una vita*, is the story of an unhappy love affair: this time between Emilio Brentani, an inexperienced thirty-five-year-old bachelor employed in a Triestine insurance company, and the young and beguiling Angiolina Zarri, a far more knowledgeable working-class girl of doubtful respectability. With his meager earnings Emilio leads an uneventful and desolate existence with his devoted unmarried sister Amalia. Brother and sister are full of the bitterness of unfulfilled desire as they try to come to terms with a life that is slowly and inexorably passing them by. The only bright light for Emilio is his lingering reputation as the author of a novel written in his youth, a novel praised by the local press, but soon forgotten even by the local artistic community. Since then, he has written nothing else because of sheer inertia. Still, he longs for what might have been and deludes himself into thinking that perhaps, one day, he will write again and perhaps even experience love. In contrast to his own celibate life, he would prefer to be like his intimate friend Stefano Balli, a sculptor and notorious ladies' man, whose artistic failure is more than compensated by his remarkable success with women. Stefano, who is over forty and less cultivated, exerts a paternal influence over Emilio, who readily accepts it and admires his friend's experience and outlook on life.

It is at this juncture of his sorry but placid existence that Emilio meets Angiolina and cautiously embarks on an affair with her. At first, he envisions only the possibility of enjoying himself without risk, considering her no more than a plaything. But, in spite of his intentions, he falls utterly in love with Angiolina and suffers many indignities and is tormented by jealousy. At first, he naïvely imagines himself to be the defender of her innocence—he never goes beyond kissing Angiolina—and hopes Pygmalion-like to raise her to his level, in spite of her reputation as a flirt and her equivocal past—aspects of her that he refuses to recognize. In his idealization, he translates her name into French and calls her "Angèle" or, even more romantically, "Ange."

Stefano, on the other hand, who sees her for the slut she is, coarsely calls her "Angiolona" or "Giolona." Yet, each time Emilio discovers a new deceit, he becomes more entrapped by the girl. He debases himself to such an extent that he lends himself to a proposal of hers that he allow her to become engaged to marry a tailor from a nearby town, so that she may give herself totally to Emilio without worrying about getting pregnant. In the meantime, reassured by his willful blindness, she continues to give herself freely to other men about town. Finally, when Stefano accidentally sees her flirting openly with another man, and informs him of this, Emilio unconvincingly breaks off their relationship. Inevitably, he regrets this action, reflecting that he was the only loser, seeing that all her admirers had possessed her except himself.

Several weeks later, when he meets her on the street, he immediately forgets his misgivings. She invites him to spend the night with her, explaining that there are no more obstacles because she is already the lover of the tailor Volpini, who had made it a condition for their engagement. Emilio finally satisfies his senses, possessing only "the woman he hated, not the woman he loved" (143).[1] The effects of this affair with Angiolina arouse a craving for love in Amalia too. She falls desperately in love with Stefano who finds her totally unattractive and treats her simply as the sister of his friend, entirely unaware of her feelings for him. Emilio accidentally finds out about her secret passion when he overhears her talking in her sleep. She recoils strongly when he, trying to console her by pointing out his own unhappiness, asks her to confide in him. Apparently, she refuses to consciously acknowledge her own emotions. Without saying anything to his sister, Emilio feels it is his duty to distance his friend from her and succeeds in doing so by falsely accusing him of compromising Amalia's reputation. When Amalia begins to wonder why the sculptor is staying away, Emilio tells her that someone had asked Stefano whether he intended to get engaged to her. When the poor girl hears this, she grows more and more despondent and, in desperation, becomes addicted to scented ether.

Meanwhile, Emilio continues to get more involved with Angiolina, frequently meeting her at a sleazy rooming house, where she became a "complacent mistress and divined all his desires with exquisite intelligence; in that bed at least he need not complain of the quickness of her intuitions. There all was pure pleasure and delight" (149).

The tragedy reaches its climax when frail Amalia falls gravely ill with pneumonia and in her delirium speaks of Stefano as her husband.

The attending doctor holds out little hope because her condition has been made worse by her use of alcohol. The incredulous Emilio finds in a closet several bottles of scented ether, which he realizes she must have taken to escape from her dreary destiny. Feeling guilty for his neglect and for having distanced his friend from her, Emilio asks Stefano to come and visit again. As she lies dying under the caring hands of a neighbor and the watchful eyes of Emilio and Stefano, Amalia is admired by the sculptor who is fascinated and moved by the drama of her agony. Emilio, fully aware that he has brought about Amalia's sad fate, resolves to give up his mistress for good and to devote himself totally to his sister. He goes to his last appointment with Angiolina and discovers another of her infidelities. They argue violently and for the first time he calls her a whore, and finally leaves her. He returns home, and the morning after Amalia dies. After this traumatic experience Emilio's life resumes its monotonous course. In the novel's closing fantasy unhappy sister and beautiful mistress (who has run off with a bank thief) blend into one feminine image that he will always cherish.

Svevo began to write *Senilità* in 1892 shortly after meeting Giuseppina Zergol, a beautiful young woman belonging to that "indefinable category between a seamstress and a store clerk."[2] The story was born out of this stormy affair. At first, the author had not planned to publish the novel because he intended it only for his lover's education. In fact, she was the first person to read several of its chapters: "Six years before [its publication] many chapters had been written with the purpose of preparing Angiolina's education that is so much spoken of in the novel. Angiolina was the first to read the novel of which she was the protagonist. Moreover, the names of all the four protagonists are known in Trieste."[3] It is interesting to note the confusion of reality and fiction by which the name of Angiolina is substituted for that of Giuseppina. This substitution underscores the autobiographical elements of the novel and Svevo's difficulty distinguishing between the persona and the anima of his inspiration. Apparently, the narrative flowed easily out of his personal experience, as he himself attests: "The novel practically wrote itself effortlessly for him."[4]

On 20 December 1895 Italo Svevo became engaged to his cousin Livia Veneziani whose mother, Olga Moravia Veneziani, was a first cousin of his own mother, Allegra Moravia Schmitz. He was thirty-four years old and she only twenty-one. This is an important event for the author and hitherto confirmed bachelor. During his engagement, and even after, it was clear that he was not proud of his amorous past, from which he had not yet fully recovered: ". . . the love I have known had an entirely different countenance! If you only knew what kind! I shan't describe it otherwise I couldn't even hand you this letter."[5] He felt extremely unworthy of Livia's pure and innocent love for him.

Throughout the *Diario per la fidanzata* (Diary for my fiancée), written during the engagement, Svevo shows his determination to forget his past, become a new man, and start a "new era."[6] In Livia, he found a contagious health and energy that would help him overcome life's obstacles and eventually allow him to redeem himself. And yet, the violent emotional shock suffered with Zergol produced a long-lasting emotional effect on Svevo that manifested itself in his constant doubts, groundless exaggerated fears, and an almost paranoid jealousy brought about by what he imagined to be the flirtations of Livia.

After Giuseppina Zergol had left Trieste sometime in 1893,[7] Svevo no longer saw any reason for not publishing this novel, which had eventually been expanded to include, alongside the two protagonists of the original draft, Balli and Amalia. The first documented reference we have to this narrative is found in a letter written to Livia on 14 May 1897, in which Svevo excitedly informs her he has finally found a title: "Il carnevale di Emilio" (Emilio's carnival).[8] Oddly enough, the manuscript had remained without a title for five years and one did not occur to Svevo until the book was more or less completed. Only later, between May of 1897 and 15 June 1898, when the novel first appeared in serialized form in *L'Indipendente,* did the author settle on *Senilità* as the final title for it.[9]

Why did Svevo consider "Il carnevale di Emilio" as a possible title? No doubt he associated the idea of the Carnival with his own experience with Giuseppina, as well as Emilio's affair with Angiolina. For Svevo the affair was a prelude to his own commitment to Livia, as Carnival (still a very popular holiday in Italy) is a carefree and even licentious prelude to the spiritual rigors of Lent. For Emilio it symbolized his one and only fling, since from the very beginning of the narrative he knows his affair with Angiolina cannot last. An interlude between a past of self-denial and a future of total resignation, its real usefulness is as a warm and colorful, if fading, memory, a transfigured past, which can be called upon as consolation for his resigned and humdrum existence:

His love of images led him to see his life as a straight, uneventful road leading across a quiet valley; from the point at which he had first met Angiolina the road branched off, and led him through a varied landscape of trees, flowers and hills. But only for a short while; after that it dropped to the valley, and became again the straight high road, easy and secure, but less tedious now because it was refreshed by memories of that enchanting, vivid interlude, full of colour and perhaps too of fatigues. (30–31)

The novel indeed begins at Carnival time (1892) and ends, one year later, with the conclusion of the Carnival season—though the final curtain does not fall until the summer. The key for an understanding of this original title and its implications is to be found at the beginning of chapter 6, when Stefano Balli, walking alone, notices two *pierrettes* (female clowns) on their way to a Carnival ball, in which he himself will take part later that evening. The sculptor is conscious of

. . . assisting at the prelude to a tragi-comedy. The whirlpool was beginning to form which would swallow up the factory-hand, the sempstress, the poor bourgeois, and withdraw them for a moment from the dreary round of common life only to fling them out again into greater suffering. Some would return bruised and ruined to take up their old burden and find it heavier than before; there were some who would never find their way out at all. (76)[10]

The tragicomedy Svevo had in mind was no doubt that of Emilio who, at the prophetic age of thirty-five—the age of Dante at the beginning of the journey narrated in the *Divine Comedy*, "half way through our life's course"—had gone "cautiously through life, avoiding all its perils, but also renouncing all its pleasures and all hope of earthly felicity" (1). When he meets Angiolina he immediately becomes aware, with a sense of bitterness and regret, of what he has missed in life and "the desire for pleasures he had never tasted, for love he had never known surged up in his heart" (1). At this point he becomes cognizant of "a great mistrust of himself, and of the weakness of his own character which hitherto he had had occasions rather to suspect than to prove by actual experience" (2). Willingly or unwillingly, in his desperate quest for happiness and passion he allows himself to be drawn into the vortex of the Carnival. The Carnival theme marks also a turning point for Emilio who cannot withstand its consumptive force. When he finds out that Angiolina is openly deceiving him with other men, Emilio decides they must split up. Ironically, this separation will result in sexual intimacy between the two lovers. The Carnival also corresponds to Balli's so-called interference in the affair and ushers in Amalia's tragic end.

The title finally arrived at, *Senilità,* captures practically all the sad and negative qualities of Emilio Brentani, who, being only thirty-five, is still in his physical prime. The title conveys rather premature old age as a *forma mentis,* a psychological attitude toward life. This "senility," a normal condition for Emilio, is interrupted when he meets Angiolina. She takes him into an allegorical Carnival that temporarily brings back his youth, which "coursed powerful as ever through his veins and annulled whatever resolution his *senile mind* [my emphasis] had made" (146).[11] It is not a physical deterioration of the body, but a stunting *progeria* (premature senility) of the spirit and of the will. Emilio is a kindred soul of Alfonso Nitti, only somewhat older and more experienced. He is without willpower—far more passive than active, even in bed with Angiolina—and lacks the stamina, the ambition for love and success manifested by Alfonso. Indeed he exhibits all the classical signs of senility except those of physical and mental deterioration.

Svevo was always preoccupied with old age, and in fact it appears throughout his writings as a constant theme both in a figurative and literal sense. Indeed, this preoccupation appeared in his first play *Ariosto governatore* (1880), wherein the protagonist laments not only his real and physical age, but, more important, his spiritual and mental state of "senility" as well. In Svevo's works we constantly find what Giorgio Luti calls "the incurable contrast between youth and old age,"[12] which became more acute when he married a woman much younger than he. This sensitivity and vulnerability, compounded by extreme jealousy, was noted by the author during his engagement: "Last night . . . I felt I was old, old and you young, young. I had never felt such a disparity in our ages before, and I began to beg you violently to tell me that although you found me old, old, always old, you would love me just the same. Actually, little devil, you didn't give me this satisfaction! You told me that you did not understand. . . . "[13]

It could be argued that Svevo, during the period of *Senilità,* probably felt very much like his protagonist. In fact, years later, in 1927, when he was revising the novel for a second edition, he steadfastly refused to change the title, notwithstanding the reservations of his friends and particularly Valéry Larbaud, who had translated parts of the novel into French, for the special issue of *Le Navire d'Argent* devoted to Svevo. In the Preface of this revised Vram edition, Svevo wrote:

Now that I know what real senility is all about, I too, at times smile when I think that I regarded it with such an overabundance of love. Nevertheless, I must have very strong reasons for not agreeing even with the opinion of Larbaud. . . . For me it would appear to be mutilating the book to deprive it of its title; for me it seems to explain and justify something. I was guided by that title and I actually lived it.[14]

And so it is with Emilio who, at the very end of the novel, when he has re-created a new Angiolina, thinks back on that period that had been the most important in his life and "lived on it like an old man on the memories of his youth" (232).

We have already seen in chapter 1 the importance Veruda's friendship had for Svevo, personally and artistically. He was for Svevo a combination of emotional confidant, intellectual model, and artistic mentor. Though the painter was seven years younger than Svevo, they were inseparable friends and saw each other several times a day, meeting at his studio, and in coffee houses and clubs frequented by the Triestine intelligentsia. Silvio Benco who knew both Svevo and Veruda gives a vivid description of the two friends:

They were always to be seen together, passing remarks on women in the streets, or frequenting fashionable drawing-rooms (which they were both fond of); Svevo always very correct and bourgeois, with a look of a clerk *à la mode,* his twinkling eyes set flat in his huge, yellowish, Buddhist philosopher's head; Veruda immensely tall and spectacular, wearing fantastic clothes with imperturbable gravity.[15]

Veruda dressed and lived the part of a true Bohemian, blatantly disregarding the conventional standards of behavior of the local bourgeoisie. Svevo was a moderating influence for his friend, tempering the "impetuousness of his bizarre personality and bridling his sharp tongue."[16] Though the two men's "spiritual agreement was complete and for many years they lived in a profound mutual understanding,"[17] eventually, their intimacy suffered when Svevo married Livia who, together with her mother, apparently resented the painter's way of life.

Veruda the painter is in part the model for Balli the sculptor. Svevo himself tells us this, quoting from Benco's review of the novel in which the critic stressed the similarities between the model and the copy as well as the decisive influence that Veruda had had on Svevo. According to Benco,

The figure of the sculptor Balli (who in the novel to a certain degree represents the legendary symbol of art) is self-assured, adventuresome, skeptical, rebellious against the moral conventions of society, but capable of kindness, compassion, and even absolute discretion. . . . The book does not merely include Veruda's robust description, but it reproduces as well his way of seeing things, a certain correctness and integrity of pictorial awareness. Whereas Svevo received from the painter the great gift of the art of laughing at life without succumbing to it, Veruda too, profited from that great intimacy: in fact, Veruda's masterpiece *Ritratto dello scultore* [A portrait of the sculptor], clearly recreates a scene from *Senilità*.[18]

This, of course, does not necessarily mean that the model and the copy were exactly the same. Nine months after this review, in a somewhat contradictory letter to a friend, Svevo tried to set things straight, pointing out that when they first met, Veruda at nineteen was already struggling to support his family with his paintings and at that time his personality was radically different from Balli's.

. . . the young man had already experienced life's perils and approached women with the same caution one uses with things that burn. . . . He was therefore totally different from the self-assured and not-too-artistic Balli. Unlike Balli, he obtained artistic success from the very beginning. Likewise, success with women who adore men with a certain reputation. However, we never spoke about love and for many years there were no women in our lives. Then I had that adventure and shortly after he too had a similar one which ended, however, with his departure for Vienna, without any regrets or any other excitements. . . . He certainly resembled Balli in certain things that Benco has expressed so well: his great loyalty, but also a certain indifference for things in this world that are not so beautiful. . . . It was always said of him that he was a great fighter. Yet, he preferred the company of insignificant writers like me. . . .[19]

Notwithstanding the liberties that an author has to take in the creation of a character, Veruda and Balli clearly manifest remarkable similarities in their physiognomy, deportment, and personality. Though the friendship between Svevo and Veruda was warm, intimate, comforting, full of affection, mutual respect, based on a bond rooted in an affinity of thought, reciprocal esteem, and appreciation between two equals, and above all nonantagonistic, the love-hate rapport between Brentani and Balli, however, is ambiguous from the very beginning. It is based on an imbalance weighted down by the imperious figure and personality of the sculptor, projected by Svevo as the natural man; the juxtaposition of the inept, senile, and antiheroic Brentani, totally dominated by the older man who comes to stand for all that Emilio and Amalia have missed in life. The major difference is that in the novel Balli functions at first as a father figure for Emilio and then, when Angiolina enters the picture, the sculptor becomes also his rival in love.

Balli not only wields power over Emilio, but dominates all the other principal characters of the novel. The sculptor is somewhat suggestive of Gabriele D'Annunzio's "superman," who, unfettered by the bourgeois ethic, sets no limits for himself in his hedonistic aestheticism. Balli is always in control of his emotions and the love affair that proves fatal for Emilio would certainly not have grazed him in the slightest. Still, there is something disturbing about this man. He is seemingly unsuited for a "normal" family life, capable of loving only beauty "which [is] shameless" (61); and yet a man unfulfilled in spite of his charm and apparent success with women. Hearing him speak so serenely about love, "which for him had never been a sin" (65), Emilio nevertheless finds that he has "an odd way of being in love with women; he loves them very much and all equally, supposing they please him at all" (49). Balli's contempt for women and drive for mastery remind us not only of Don Juan's insatiable desire for sexual conquest, but also of his unconscious fear of getting close to women on an emotional level. Balli, according to Spagnoletti, with his "conquering impetus" and "explosive life force" gets what he wants, thus serving as counterpoint to Emilio's unrealistic and useless plans.[20] Surrounded by his subdued entourage of friends, Balli dissolves reality for the benefit of his own egotistical will. Thus he dismisses his artistic failure and is insensitive to Emilio's and Amalia's plight, to which he has contributed.

From the very beginning, when he first meets the flirtatious Angiolina, Emilio is tormented by the premonition that she will eventually betray him. His jealousy is at first ill defined because his rivals are many and no one in particular stands out in the notorious gallery of photos she keeps in her room. The first serious crisis occurs when he obtains proof that she has been seen in a compromising situation with an umbrella maker. Emilio's feelings and reaction are not those of simple jealousy but rather of indignation for the humble social background of the tradesman. Eventually, when he returns to Angiolina after a short-lived separation, they both can laugh at this when she mockingly reproaches him with "You jealous thing . . . fancy being jealous of that wild man of the woods" (141). Balli, however, constantly looming in the background as a potential and superior rival, is kept at a distance from Angiolina by Emilio.[21] And even after Balli has been introduced to her, Emilio still shields her, trying his very best to hinder the artist's plans to use her as his model for a sculpture. This competitive drive for Angiolina expresses itself also in resentful and hostile behavior on the part of Emilio, which becomes aggravated when Balli turns into a "real" rival, since Angiolina openly shows great interest in him, and even submits willingly to his brutal barbs: "It was terribly painful for him to see how lightly and easily the sculptor carried off the prize which he could not win even at the cost of so much suffering" (75).

It is ironic that Emilio is constantly defeated and overpowered by Balli who, though perhaps meaning well, frequently relegates him to an inferior position, unaware of the pain he is causing. When he tries to teach Emilio how women should be handled he forgets his intention and instead flirts with Angiolina, enjoying himself thoroughly at Emilio's expense. The only person Emilio controls and feels superior to is, of course, his sister Amalia, who is entirely dependent on him materially and emotionally. When she too succumbs to Balli's charm, as Saccone perceptively writes, she no longer belongs to him and he cannot use her any more as an alibi or justification for living as he had stated at the beginning of the novel.[22] Therefore it becomes clear why Emilio distances Balli from Amalia when he finds out that she is secretly in love with him. He does not do it merely to protect his sister, but rather as an aggressive response aimed at his rival who has caused him to lose "his only possession, his only superiority," and "has kept in check" all his enterprises.[23]

Bruno Maier writes that *Senilità* is a "Verudian novel" inasmuch as Svevo's intimacy with the painter and admiration for his work influenced the author's own artistic expression.[24] What the narrator says of Emilio's and Stefano's "complete agreement" in artistic matters regarding "the necessity of discovering afresh for ourselves the simplicity or naïveté of which the so-called classicists had robbed the arts" (10), was also true of Svevo and Veruda. No doubt, there is something of Svevo, the artist who had not yet received the recognition he thought he deserved, in the portrait of Balli: "His very originality must prevent him from having a wider and more popular appeal, and he had continued to pursue an ideal of spontaneity, a certain wilful ruggedness, a simplicity, or, as he preferred to say, perspicacity of idea, from which he thought his artistic ego must emerge purified of all that was not original either in form or idea" (9).

Svevo learned from his friend how to see things differently, with the understanding and imagination of an artist, and to transfer to the written page the actual visual experience of the painter[25]—similar to that of Balli when his imagination becomes fixed on Angiolina because "he had detected in the extraordinary purity of line, though quite independent of it, an indefinable expression of vulgarity and coarseness which Raphael would no doubt have repressed but which he, on the contrary, wanted to copy and to accentuate" (164). In writing this novel not only did Svevo go beyond the veristic conventions and stylistic limitations of the period, but he also learned how the artist's pure imagination and intuition must not be subverted by his academic training, which inevitably would "intervene to destroy all that was personal in his art, all his first impressions and feelings, so that only impersonal dogmas and old prejudices remained" (67). In the description of the sculpture exhibit in Milano Balli is able to see in a piece of unfinished marble the concept of his artistic inspiration and expression. Svevo is echoing if not anticipating here the critic Benedetto Croce's aesthetic ideas on art as "pure intuition and pure expression"; as an inseparable unity of feeling and imagination, of impression and expression, of form and content.[26] Thus, when Balli is sculpting Angiolina at his studio and Emilio, visiting, observes the rough and shapeless mass of clay, the artist explains: "'You see how the thing is coming out. . . . The idea is not all there yet; it lacks form.' But the idea was only visible to him, something delicate and intangible. A prayer was to rise from that clay, the prayer of someone who believes for one moment and perhaps never will believe again" (168).

What stands out, above all, is the lesson of impressionism that Svevo, under the influence of Veruda, puts into practice in the descriptive pages of the novel, particularly those concerning Angiolina and Trieste, always presented in a jubilant exultation of color and light. Unlike *Una vita* with its subdued, drab colors, in *Senilità* Svevo employs color with charm, spirit, and a sensuous warmth, showing a facility for invention in coloristic terms unprecedented in his previous writings. As Svevo presents Angiolina, she is unabashed nature, unafraid, without any mental reservation, simply beautiful in her healthfulness, and like the sun of which she has the resplendent colors, she too is a source of life, energy, and desire: "She was a tall, healthy blonde, with big blue eyes and a supple, graceful body, an expressive face and transparent skin glowing with health. As she walked, she held her head slightly on one side, as if it were weighed down by the mass of golden hair . . ." (2–3). By his subtle use of color intensities rather than a more linear perspective, Svevo's descriptive pages are worthy of comparison with the great masters of impressionism in beauty and intensity. The same iridescent beauty does not change in the darkness when she is illuminated by a match that lights up her rosy face: "Lit up thus in the darkness it seemed to shine with an adorable brilliance: the small yellow flame pierced her pale eyes like the clear waters of a pool and they shone back at him with their sweet, wild, bewitching lustre" (50).

The same chromatic technique is used in the description of the city, seen more as a vision, a sensation rather than a cognition. Here again he is intoxicated by color, surface reflections, and by changing light. It is an atmospheric study in light and shade, in whites, yellows, and silver: "The city . . . seemed one vast expanse of colour, mysterious, undefined. Motionless there in the silence, city, sea and hills seemed to be all one piece, as if some artist had shaped and coloured all that matter according to his own strange fancy, and dotted the intersecting lines with points of yellow light which were really the street lanterns" (18). As we can see from this luminous nocturnal "canvas" and the other impressionistic passages we have cited, Svevo's attention is drawn to the outdoors just like the impressionists, who were the first to take their easels out *en plein air*.

Although the novel centers on Emilio's psyche and "senility," it is Angiolina with her luminous and genuine vitality who brings life to the novel, functioning as an unchanging catalyst in the lives of Emilio, Amalia, and Stefano. This unforgettable character is regarded as "the first fully drawn creature of Svevo's fantasy" and, in her breathtaking beauty, the "first beautiful person" in Svevo's writings.[27] According to Pampaloni, this "stupendous invention . . . like all truly living characters, is both carnal and metaphoric and at the same time real and paradigmatic of a way of life."[28] Angiolina, all instinct and cunning, tall, blonde, healthy, beautiful, tempting, like a feline capable of tearing to pieces all those exposed to her danger, represents the quintessence of the primitivist view of the feminine in all its ambivalence and multivalences. From her coloring emanates a joyous warmth representative of a constant outflowing of a boundless vitality. This luxuriantly endowed creature is the classical *hembra* (female), the embodiment of earthly sensuality and the source of the ultimate wholeness of man.

Still, in view of her flamboyant sex appeal and success with men, one can't help but wonder why she perseveres with Emilio who is always jealous, cerebral, shy, consumed by nagging doubts about her whereabouts, by obscure scruples and coy anxieties—a distressingly ordinary man indeed! It is clear that she is interested in him but does not really love him. Most likely she is charmed and flattered—perhaps even excited—by his attentions, ardor, and sentimentality which other men fail to give her. Apparently, he is the only man who truly courts her in a romantic way and treats her like a lady, and not merely as the "female" she is. She likes the French names he has given her, and it pleases her vanity to be like her namesake, the bewitching heroine of the *Orlando Furioso,* whose presence sows discord among the paladins. Charles C. Russell seems to imply that it is a matter of professional pride, that Emilio is just another client, and that the "photographs around her bed of the men she has known are like merit awards for superior achievement, and she is proud of them."[29] It is also possible that because of her inferior social and cultural status, Emilio's poetic tendency and literary reputation may bolster her sense of self-esteem. Finally, it is rather obvious that she is the dominant member of the liaison and that she derives satisfaction by controlling him. Unconsciously she may also be getting pleasure from the pain, indignity, and embarrassment she causes him to suffer.

In the story there are two Angiolinas and Emilio shuttles back and forth between them—the one who lives inside himself, the idealized "Ange," and the other, "Giolona," who exists in the real world. Since the woman he has created in his imagination is more an impression, a momentary sensation, it is quite fitting that Svevo chose to describe her in impressionistic terms, since the word "impression" itself implies an effect produced upon the mind, a vague notion or remembrance, an opinion arrived at instinctively rather than through reason, something unfinished, an affair of the moment. The real Angiolina Emilio is loath to admit to—the one he eventually calls a whore, the one "spoilt by her base, perverse soul" (137), the seductive figure every man in the street thinks of going to bed with, someone who even "flirts with God" (168)—still remains charming and forgivable because of the impassioned way the author presents her. Above all, she is honest in her dealings with Emilio who, unlike her, with his bourgeois complacency and prim propriety cannot even contemplate making a long-term commitment to the girl. She, however, earnestly tells him that she would be quite happy to live with the man she loved, no matter how poor. Ironically, instead of appreciating her frankness, he complains that she is not calculating enough and that a girl in her situation should look after her own self-interest. She listens in bewilderment as he counsels her that an "honest woman was one who looked out for the highest bidder and took care not to fall in love unless she could make a good thing out of it. . . . If you are not honest you must at least seem to be so. . . . It was better to do wrong than look as if one were doing it" (16–17). Although she is deceitful, particularly when it means safeguarding her independence and freedom of action, she never intentionally hurts her vulnerable suitor. Her blatant lies are indeed more for his benefit, since he refuses to see her for what she really is. She follows Emilio's educational program with great zeal, and, given her background, she is most logical in all her actions. We find her in different situations as she sells herself to the various men in town including Emilio, too naïve and blind to realize that he too has been paying her with gifts and money. In either case it is always clear that she is merely trying to survive, to profit from the circumstances at hand, and at the same time, accommodate herself to his wishes.

In contrasting this novel to *Una vita,* Svevo wrote that there "are no philosophical intentions, nor are human weaknesses—especially those of Brentani—sublimated by any theorems."[30] Although Svevo was breaking away from the programmatic lesson of naturalism by making use of what Giacomo Debenedetti calls "the corrosive element of the narrative fabric,"[31] and by a far greater psychological depth, particularly in the characterization of Emilio, and furthermore by a very artistic and personal descriptive language in the impressionistic canvases of city and characters, still, the literary tradition to which *Senilità* belongs is that of the realistic nineteenth-century European social novel. The principal characters are all artfully individualized in action and temperament; and the physical descriptions of Angiolina, Stefano, and Amalia add to the sense of reality. Emilio, however, is not described by the author in physical terms. No doubt, he is a projection of Svevo himself who must have identified with him to such an extent that he overlooked providing a description of him.

The detailed and objective descriptions of Amalia's illness and death are good examples of the naturalistic style. The accuracy of Amalia sinking into a deep sleep and awakening comparatively clear mentally but physically exhausted and with total amnesia for what has happened, is clinically accurate. The naturalist who still lay hidden in

Svevo could not help being revived, in particular, when he subjects the Zarri family to critical scrutiny. They are doomed to their condition by determinism and atavistic forces, just like the Lanuccis in *Una vita*. In the naturalistic description of Angiolina's home and milieu Emilio seems to cry out against the law of nature and to exonerate her, showing how difficult it is for her to escape her background: "Why revolt against the law of nature? Angiolina was a lost woman even in her mother's womb. This complicity between her and her mother was what revolted him most. It was useless to punish her: she did not even deserve it; she was only the victim of a universal law" (91). At the end, after his mistress has fled from Trieste and Emilio visits the Zarri home, he finds Angiolina's very same sensual traits in her younger sister when she flings her arms around him and covers his face "with kisses that were by no means childish" (231). Thus, the cycle continues in the Zarri family.

Stefano Balli is, to a large degree, Emilio's opposite and Angiolina's counterpart; similarly Amalia Brentani is Emilio's counterpart and Angiolina's antithesis. Just like the other three major characters of *Senilità*, the figure of Amalia was also based on a living person. She was inspired by Maria Rossi, the spinster sister of Svevo's friend Cesare Rossi, who lived with her two bachelor brothers and apparently was addicted to ether.[32] Like her brother, Amalia too has gone cautiously through life, renounced its pleasures and "all hope of earthly felicity" (1). She suffers from the same maladjustments, inertia, and "senility" that afflict Emilio, though her own pathetic condition is far more sad and tragic than his. She senses the hollowness of her existence far more than Emilio, who, after all, has a secure position, friends, and even a somewhat respectable reputation among his peers. She, on the other hand, is an unmarried woman, homely, with no dowry, no talents. Her life revolves only around the petty affairs of the household and the care of her only brother.

In the description of Amalia, Svevo shows again a mastery of psychological observation and analysis. The abject and submissive sister is hopelessly bound by her appearance: ugly, colorless, small gray eyes, a weak body with a long neck and drooping shoulders, legs as thin as spindles, and the body of an ill-nourished boy. Unlike Angiolina's sparkling blonde hair which stands for energy—the *élan vital*—the feeble Amalia has "curiously shaded hair of which it would have been hard to name the colour" (69). She always dresses in the color of "grey like herself, and like her destiny" (135). Balli, who feels pity for her and is uneasy in her presence, can't understand why such a creature was ever created. For him she is an obvious "mistake on the part of Nature" (60). She has resigned herself to the grayness of her life, settling into the role of sister and mother to Emilio, the only emotional depth in her life. She reminds us of Laura, the shy and crippled figure in Tennessee Williams's *Glass Menagerie,* who uses her menagerie as an escape from the world. Defensively, Amalia makes up for her frustrated spinsterhood by repressing her natural needs, scoffing at love, and talking about it with "intolerance, as if something outside the pale" (65).

Ironically, the harmonious involvement of brother and sister endures not only because of their similar nature, but also because of their failures with love. When Emilio, however, falls in love with Angiolina and confides in Amalia his new joy and happiness, feeling no longer needed, she has second thoughts about her way of life. In Svevo's own comments, "she is disturbed seeing her brother who shamelessly devotes himself to the dangerous and forbidden game of love, and soon following her brother's example and Balli's theories, she is convinced that she has been deceived and that love should be everyone's right."[33] She becomes fascinated by "her own fate which suddenly assumed for her a new and vivid interest. Love had entered the house and was there beside her, restlessly at work. A single breath had sufficed to dissipate the stagnant atmosphere in which she had lived blindly up to that moment and she was astonished, when she came to examine her own feelings, that being made as she was she could have been content to live like that, without being conscious of any desire to suffer or enjoy" (11). A tremendous change occurs in the homely girl: she becomes alive as her face lights up and turns radiant with a rosy glow and dancing gray eyes. When Balli, in his vain attempt to cure Emilio's illness, becomes a frequent visitor to their home, she succumbs to love and desperately tries to escape from her "menagerie." Nevertheless she has no illusions about him, knowing full well that her love is unrequited: "She was living solely in the present, rejoicing in the one hour in which she felt herself important and an object of desire" (69).

Unable to admit even to herself her love for Balli, she reacts by repressing her emotions and taking refuge in erotic dreams in which her forbidden wishes find fulfillment. She dreams of being married to Balli and of her honeymoon when "everything can be allowed" (88). When Balli is distanced from her by Emilio, who offers only feeble excuses, she patiently continues to hope that he may return, and even lays an extra place for him at the table. In one of the most beautiful and poignant scenes of the novel Amalia puts Balli's cup back in the cupboard when she finally acknowledges that he will not come back and that her dream will not be fulfilled. It is at this point that she finds refuge in ether. Unlike Emilio, who at the end returns to his initial inertia, she instead secretly procures an escape in the hallucinatory chemical.

There follows a long and gripping description of Amalia's illness and death. Svevo, apparently, having witnessed the illnesses and deaths of so many close relatives, was fascinated if not obsessed with death scenes, which are prominent in his three novels. In *Una vita* we saw the prolonged illness and death agony of Alfonso's mother. In *La coscienza di Zeno* there is the death scene of Zeno's father which is fraught with psychological meaning. Here, the prolonged segment dealing with Amalia's death is somewhat out of proportion to the rest of the novel. Furbank thinks that Svevo was "trying, in a covert fashion, to put in the conventional decent feeling that his hero is so lacking in."[34]

To a degree, *Senilità* is a sequel to *Una vita* inasmuch as Emilio seems to be an older extension of Alfonso, who though retaining the same psychological traits and antiheroic qualities of the *inetti,* has at the same time matured somewhat and has even become more aggressive in his resolve. For example, when Alfonso meets Maria on the street, a woman who clearly is a prototype for Angiolina in their physical resemblance,[35] he lacks the courage to develop a promising relationship and loses her by failing to show up for a rendezvous, never to see her again. Emilio, to the contrary, upon meeting Angiolina, allows himself to be befriended by her and undertakes a relationship he knows full well is fraught with danger. Emilio Brentani stands between Alfonso and Zeno, who, as we shall see, is far wiser and more philosophical than his two predecessors. Among the three, one critic finds Emilio "the most authentic character, in a narrative sense, because for the first time the summing up of memories succeeds in giving us a true feeling of the real."[36] Unlike Alfonso, Emilio's conflict is no longer with society or with his work, but rather with his own personality and the dual reality of his life, being and appearance. Emilio feels rather secure at his job and, save for his poverty, he does not have any conflicts with the social circle he frequents.

Once again, as in *Una vita,* the point of view is always that of the protagonist. There are occasional lapses, particularly in Balli's case, when the point of view shifts to other characters. Even so, it is always in agreement with Emilio's perception of reality.[37]

The novel is constructed along traditional narrative lines, with a proper introduction, exposition, conclusion, and a well-defined central theme. Unlike *Una vita,* there is no profusion of minor characters to detract from the story, nor does Svevo dwell on describing all the people or things the protagonists encounter. In his second novel the more skillful and disciplined author never lost control of his material, concentrating on the theme and on the four principal characters. The narrative unfolds with clarity and simplicity, with an economy that still gives the essentials of character and situation, yet with discerning and colorful details. Except for the parts dealing with Amalia's illness, the story moves swiftly, logically, grippingly. Many years after the publication of *Senilità* Svevo wrote in his diary:

> A person reading a novel must feel he is being told something that really took place. However, the one who writes a novel must believe in it even more, notwithstanding that he knows that it never really happened as depicted. Fantasy is a true adventure. Take care not to categorize it too soon, otherwise in stifling it, you will render it unsuitable for your painting. It must remain fluid like life itself which it is and is becoming.[38]

Upon the publication of *Senilità,* Svevo's hopes of being recognized as a writer were dashed once again by the almost total absence of "either praise or censure"[39] by the critics. Save for Benco's review in *L'Indipendente,* which had already printed the novel in serialized form, the Italian press barely paid any notice to Svevo's second novel.[40] Even the German novelist and 1910 Nobel Prize winner Paul von Heyse (1830–1914), who had praised *Una vita,* wrote that, although he found again the same acumen for psychological analyses and observation, Svevo had nevertheless wasted his time and talent writing about a subject as "repugnant" as Emilio's dismal life and his fascination with Angiolina. He reproached Svevo for seeking his material in such pathological situations and not choosing stronger and healthier individuals.[41] Heyse's judgment shattered Svevo's hopes and dreams. He resigned himself to what he called "a unanimous judgment (there is no more perfect unanimity than silence) and for twenty-five years I abstained from writing. If it was a mistake it was mine."[42] Again, Svevo tells only part of the truth. What he meant was that he no longer wrote for publication. Yet, he continued to be active with his pen because literature was his fate, as well as his *pharmakon.*[43]

Chapter Four
Confessions of Zeno

La coscienza di Zeno (Confessions of Zeno), often considered Svevo's best book, is the first Italian psychoanalytic novel. As a seminal work in the development of contemporary narrative fiction, it is comparable in importance to the artistic contributions made by Joyce and Proust. At the time it was written, *La coscienza* was an original experiment in form, technique, and content. It is looser in structure and the simple linear plot of his earlier novels is supplanted by a flexible chronological collection of incidents in the life of Zeno, which are recorded retrospectively in the form of a diary. It is constructed on two levels of action, one external, the other internal.[1] The first is a loosely knit sequence of interconnected and overlapping events, in which the narrated facts are not always in perfect chronological sequence, but are arranged thematically into the five logical episodes that are most crucial in Zeno's life and most revealing of his character. The second level of action is to be found in the meandering realm of the subconscious with its hidden springs of motivation. As Zeno tries to come to terms with life and his neuroses, he probes deeply into the human mind and explores the profoundest recesses of his unconscious.

There is in *Confessions of Zeno* a temporal coexistence of both diachrony and synchrony because it presents a succession of events in the past (memory) and the ongoing present, as well as the atemporal and entropic flux of Zeno's subconscious. It consists of both memory and the present where, in Bergsonian terms,[2] time works as a continuous flow in which past and present are inseparable from consciousness and memory. And in this new coherence of time and duration of reality, referred to by Joyce as the "continuous present tense,"[3] true reality is a continuous becoming and unceasing flow and flux that can be understood by intuition rather than by intellect. In other terms, as has been pointed out by Sandro Maxia, two distinct temporal planes are at work: one of actuality, "of the present (Zeno's 'Now as I write') in which the writing of the recollections and the psychoanalytic cure occur contemporaneously," and the other level that concerns the recollected events that go back twenty-five years.[4]

Zeno Cosini, a fifty-six-year-old well-to-do Triestine businessman, is beset by various complexes and psychoneurotic disorders characterized by an obsessive preoccupation with real and imagined pains and physical malfunctions. Above all, he is concerned with an obsessive addiction to nicotine. In a last attempt to find a cure, he decides to subject himself for treatment to a newly discovered therapy: psychoanalysis. The analyst, Dr. S., suggests that to facilitate the cure it would be helpful for the patient to keep a diary that will constitute an essential part of the therapy. Thus, *La coscienza* is a book of remembrances recorded without conscious control, and under the summoning up of repressed memories and impressions. For six months the patient, using the technique of free association, succeeds in producing material from his unconscious. He records his dreams, impulses, memories, emotional feelings, and reactions—in short, everything that comes to mind. Thus, we are provided with an autobiography narrated by the patient who functions simultaneously as actor and narrator of his own life and actions.[5]

The book proper, consisting of five principal episodes in the life of Zeno, is preceded by a "Preface" (chap. 1) and a "Preamble" (chap. 2), one written by the analyst, the other by his patient Zeno Cosini. In the "Preface" the vindictive and somewhat unprofessional Dr. S. informs the reader, by way of an apologia, that he has decided to publish the memoirs of a former recalcitrant patient as a punishment for his having suddenly stopped his therapy just when the treatment was beginning to show promising signs of success, thus cheating Dr. S. of the fruits of his labor. Though brief, the "Preface" gives us a glimpse of Zeno, described as an old man of intense curiosity about himself, and manifesting the classical signs of hostility toward his analyst. The "Preface" functions also as a caveat for the reader, who is warned that in view of the patient's hostility and the mass of truths and falsehoods contained in the memoirs, he should be careful in the interpretation of the material. Still, notwithstanding the falsehoods, many surprises lie in wait if someone were to analyze these memoirs. It is unclear whether Dr. S. stands for Sigmund, Svevo, Schmitz, or Samigli. Quite possibly the doctor represents Svevo's good friend Edoardo Weiss, the renowned Triestine psychoanalyst.[6]

In the "Preamble" Zeno describes his first attempts at reevoking his early childhood memories. At first, he succeeds only in seeing his thoughts at a distance from himself. The present is too strong and the past is blotted out. Finally, while in a half-waking state, he dimly sees a locomotive puffing up a steep incline and pulling an endless number of coaches. Each coach represents a memory or an image that evokes another memory related to the former. Suddenly, Zeno sees himself as an infant in a cradle, exploring his tiny body in search of pleasure. The child does not resemble him at all and Zeno thinks that it is his nephew, born only a few weeks before. He warns the child not to repeat his mistake; that it is essential for his health not to forget anything about his early experiences because one day he may be called upon to recollect every event in his life, even those he would rather forget. What Svevo is actually saying is that personality is strongly influenced by the infantile environment and the parents' rearing practices. Zeno also muses on Freud's theory of the influence of psychosexual development: "Meanwhile, poor innocent, you continue to explore your tiny body in search of pleasure; and the exquisite discoveries you make will bring you in the end disease and suffering, to which those who least wish it will contribute" (4).[7] The child is obviously in the initial "polymorphously perverse" stage of its psychosexual development. As it explores its own body, it learns that the stimulation of erogenous zones arouses pleasure. Here is an anticipation of Dr. S.'s diagnosis for Zeno who, at the end of the book, will be told that he suffers from the Oedipus complex. The words "those who least wish it will contribute" signify that the child's sexual drive is directed toward the mother who unwittingly contributes to his conditioning.

Smoking

The novel proper begins with chapter 3, entitled "Il fumo" ("The Last Cigarette"). In it, Svevo describes Zeno's vain attempts to give up his lifelong addiction to nicotine and free himself from the allure of the last cigarette. His entire life is presented as a succession of continuous attempts and failures to break this compulsive habit. The whole chapter consists of uncommonly vivid images reconstructed from past experiences revolving around smoking, as though Zeno were reliving these experiences again. Being convinced that his physical and emotional ills are the result of his addiction, the very first thing Zeno mentions to Dr. S. is his "weakness for smoking." The analyst recommends that Zeno begin his analysis by tracing the growth of the habit from the beginning. Thus, sitting at his desk with cigarette in hand, Zeno begins to flush out minor and major events connected with cigarettes and his quest for conquering them. He traces his vice to his childhood and to the money he used to steal from his father to buy cigarettes. At first, these images are fragmentary and isolated, told as vaguely as if seen by a little boy, but soon, just as the madeleine's flavor evokes a rush of memories in Proust's work, Zeno's past suddenly rushes back in its entirety, enabling him to re-create his early attempts at curing himself from this *sozza abitudine* (filthy habit).

The realization that he hated cigarettes occurred when at age twenty he suffered for a long time from a violent sore throat. Although the family doctor ordered him to give up smoking "entirely," and his father with his ubiquitous cigar in his mouth kept admonishing him to obey, Zeno, nevertheless, continued to smoke, rationalizing: "As it's so bad for me I won't smoke anymore, but I must first have just one last smoke" (8). Thus his days became filled with many cigarettes and with as many resolutions to give them up, giving birth to Zeno's "dance of the last cigarette"—the last always tastes better, says Zeno. Consequently, tricks, bets, and resolutions became a necessary and integral part of any crisis or turning point in Zeno's agitated life, forever marked by last cigarettes. Ironically, at first cigarettes were a habit, but now *last* cigarettes have become a habit. Like an alcoholic in need of the perennial one last drink, required to garner enough strength before withdrawing from his addiction, Zeno goes from one precious last cigarette to another resolution and back again. As a student he devised a system of choosing a significant date for his ephemeral last cigarette, which he used to write on the walls of his apartment. Once he had to have the walls repapered because they were covered with dates. He was partial to certain symmetrical numbers, such as "Ninth day of the ninth month of the year 1899," or "First day of the first month in the year 1901." All entries were punctuated by "U. S."[8] which stood not, the narrator tells us, for "United States" but for *ultima sigaretta* (last cigarette).

Finally, chapter 3 ends with the novel's most humorous part, worthy of Boccaccio's best wit and earthy revelry. Zeno's desperate quest for health climaxes with the suggestion of his wife, who, by the way, had never taken his disease seriously, that he be detoxified in a local sanatorium where he will be confined to a small suite with a special nurse to supervise him and make sure that he does not smoke or escape. Zeno, however, using his ingenuity, not only manages to bribe his guard into supplying him with cigarettes—he has told the lecherously inclined woman that tobacco excites him sexually—but he does not even stay for one night because he is obsessed with jealousy, thinking that his wife may be betraying him with Dr. Muli, the young and handsome director of the sanatorium. Zeno escapes by getting his guard drunk, and returns home where his homely but faithful wife greets him with understanding and bemused laughter.

Smoking is paradigmatic of Zeno's illness and establishes from the very beginning a perspective on his character. His inability or unwillingness to free himself from this addiction reflect the neurotic characteristics of his personality, as well as the jumbled, distraught existence of a man in modern times. Smoking (and smoke) spans both Svevo's and Zeno's lives. It moves in time from Zeno's childhood to the present moment of writing; it culminates with the poisonous gases (fumes) of World War I and, finally, it concludes with an apocalyptic explosion that will cause the earth to return to its "nebulous state" (398).

In his diary, essentially, Zeno asks the reader to comply with the popular logical paradox: "this statement is false." What is remarkable is that the statement is not paradoxical, but in fact true. In giving the character the name of Zeno, the author was obviously evoking Zeno of Eleas, the inventor of dialectics, who taught by paradoxes. The assumption of the Eleatic School was that commonsense notions of reality on which most of us depend, are always in error. In fact, the whole notion of the "dance of the last cigarette" in *La coscienza di Zeno,* reflects the paradoxes of the Eleatic philosopher, who believed that the universe is static, that there is no motion or change, and that we need to distinguish appearance from reality. The paradoxes postulate the infinite divisibility of space and time, raising problems about the nature of space, time, and motion. In one of his paradoxes the philosopher Zeno stated that it is impossible to cross an infinite number of points within finite time because in order to go from point A to point B we would have to pass all the intermediate points. But since the distance from A to B can be divided into an infinite number of intermediate points, it is impossible to travel an infinite number of spaces within the limited time, and arrive at point B. In another paradox the philosopher shows how it is impossible to pinpoint the precise moment that separates past time from future time because when we say "now" time has already moved onward. Zeno of Eleas concludes that it is impossible to catch up with time as it is impossible to hold fast to the present moment.

Zeno Cosini has been trying all his life to avoid point B of his trajectory, and the mass of cigarettes he has consumed, particularly all the "last" ones, represent the infinite intermediate points one has to travel before arriving at any destination. But since there always are "last cigarettes" or intermediate points, Zeno will never reach the absolute last smoke. This inability to reach a particular point or goal is evident also in other aspects of his personality, particularly his chronic procrastination, which is not limited to cigarettes, but is pervasive in all his undertakings. Zeno first studies chemistry, then changes to law, and then back to chemistry without ever obtaining a final degree. He cannot decide what he wants to do in life, and even when he decides to get married he places himself in a situation that is problematic, to say the least, as we shall see further on. Even his repeated attempts to find a cure for his ills are symptomatic of these paradoxes. Indeed, every cure is interrupted by him before its completion. Breaking off his psychoanalysis is only the last example of his unwillingness or inability to reach point B, namely, to be cured.

The fact remains that Zeno Cosini does not really want, nor does he intend, to stop smoking. It is not smoking that causes him personality and physical disturbances, but rather the *idea* of having to smoke and the anguished frenzy resulting from his vain attempts to keep his resolutions. It is the principle, the obsession, his dependence that torment him. Zeno knows that these failures are symptoms of a serious aberration of his will. Smoking complements Zeno's personality traits and symbolizes the philosophy of "hopeless hope" that permeates all of Svevo's novels. Cigarettes are a crutch, a pretext that allows him to do and act the way he wants, no matter how odd or bizarre this might be. Zeno is like a bedridden patient who enjoys certain privileges, advantages offered him out of consideration by his family and friends. If he were to stop smoking, become cured and healthy, he would obviously lose his advantage and have to behave like the rest. Cigarettes have become for Zeno an alibi, a shield behind which he can hide: "Did I really love cigarettes so much because I was able to throw all the responsibility for my own incompetence on them? Who knows whether, if I had given up smoking, I should really have become the strong perfect man I imagined? Perhaps it was this very doubt that bound me to my vice . . ." (10).[9]

Like Alfonso Nitti, Zeno is also undone by his doubting, indecisiveness, and equivocation. He is a procrastinator tormented by guilt and tortured by his narcissistic tendencies, of which smoking is but one manifestation. Still, unlike Alfonso, he seems to accept his destiny, and he plays the role of the neurotic to the hilt. By procrastinating, Zeno is postponing the inevitable recognition of life's reality for man and all his obligations inherent for survival. Deep down Zeno knows that the *last cigarette* is the one he will smoke just before facing his Maker. "I was always thinking about death," he remarks "and so I had only one sorrow: the certainty that I must die" (71). Thus, his ploy is to postpone the inevitable out of fear and anxiety. Zeno wants to delay the encounter with death, to put off indefinitely, if he can, this moment of truth. The ploy, or game, of the last cigarette, the interruption of the succession of countable intervals that lead in only one direction, permits him to slow down the countdown, to create as in the Eleatic paradox, a duration, or better a stasis, where there is no count—or a false count such as the dates on walls marking a last cigarette. This retardation affords him the assurance that he alone controls the count. Furthermore, his procrastinations permit him to explain away things ad infinitum, and to concoct an endless series of reasons telling why and wherefore, but leaving the deed undone. One is reminded of the popular one-liner attributed to Woody Allen: "I am not afraid to die, I just don't want to be there when it happens."

Although Zeno claims that nicotine causes all his ills—abnormally heightened libido, insomnia, indecisiveness, difficulty with his studies, and absentmindedness—he nevertheless clings to the protection of this addiction because it not only enables him to rationalize his incompetence, but also permits him to engage in a behavior that turns an observer's attention away from his deficiencies, which, if noted, would cause him embarrassment and guilt.

Perhaps the most significant theme of the novel is Svevo's dialectic on illness, which is introduced early in this propaedeutic chapter. Zeno declares: "Ill-health is a conviction, and I was born with that conviction" (11). However, he detects symptoms of disease where others, particularly the medical profession for whom he has a great distrust, see instead health. The electrotherapist regards Zeno's troubles with women—"I was not satisfied with one or even with many; I desired them all" (12)!—as something quite normal and healthy for a young man in his early twenties. When Zeno explains to him his perverse appreciation of women: "I was not in love with women as a whole, but only with parts of them. I was always attracted by small feet, especially if well shod, by a slender and well-rounded neck, and by very small breasts," the doctor interrupts him with: "All those parts make up the woman as a whole" (14).

Even Zeno's wife fails to see any abnormality in his smoking and other behavior, in spite of his blatant quirks and neurotic idiosyncrasies. In fact, she plays along with him in a jocular manner, as she makes all the arrangements for his confinement in the sanatorium. Svevo himself characterized Zeno as someone "who considers himself an exceptional invalid suffering from a prolonged illness. The novel is the history of his life and of his cures."[10] While illness is presented in this chapter under a humorous guise, subsequently it will be developed by Svevo as "the condition of existence." As Richard Gilman points out, "what Svevo promised to cure us of was precisely our desire to be cured."[11]

Charles C. Russell notes that "the principal source" of *La coscienza* is "always Svevo himself."[12] In fact, there are various autobiographical elements that Svevo interweaves in chapter 3: both the author and Zeno are more or less the same age; both are absentminded and easily distracted; both have had a younger brother who died some years before; both are extremely jealous of their wives; both have had a fat friend[13] "who employed his leisure in reading and writing" (14); and finally, both have had experiences with psychoanalysis. Svevo was first introduced to Freud's work in 1908 by Edoardo Weiss, the prominent Triestine psychoanalyst who was Freud's friend and disciple. Svevo took an interest in psychoanalysis because his brother-in-law, Bruno Veneziani, was contemplating treatment. At first, Svevo read various books on the subject "intent on understanding what perfect moral health consisted of. Nothing else!"[14] In 1910 Bruno Veneziani was sent to Vienna so that he could be treated by Freud himself. But the treatment failed, and in 1912 Bruno returned to Trieste worse than before. He reported that Freud had judged his neuroses and homosexuality incurable. This failure caused Svevo to become skeptical as to the efficacy of Freud's methods. But in 1918 Svevo collaborated with his nephew, Dr. Aurelio Finzi, on the translation of Freud's *On Dreams*. It was at this time, Svevo tells us, that he experimented with self-analysis "fully aware that it was totally against Freud's theory and practice. The technique of procedure remained unknown to him, a fact of which all can become aware by reading the novel."[15] Nonetheless, it would appear that Svevo knew far more about psychoanalysis than he is willing to admit in his "Profilo autobiografico." He seems to be echoing here some of the criticisms that greeted the novel upon its publication, in particular that of Dr. Weiss who refused to review the book because, in his opinion, it had nothing to do with psychoanalysis. It is interesting to note that as a young man, while he was undergoing electrotherapy, Zeno had spoken to the doctor about psychoanalysis, "for I was one of the first, though timidly, to dabble in it" (12). It would follow, then, that Zeno first experimented with self-analysis when he was twenty and eventually returned to psychoanalysis at the age of fifty-seven.

In addition to the unorthodoxy of self-analysis, Zeno's method of free association is just as invalid because it is a persistently controlled process. In psychoanalytic terms, free association is a voluntary recalling of repressed memory. The analysand reports to the analyst whatever comes to mind, regardless of how painful or irrelevant it might be. There are absolutely no restrictions on the nature of this summing up. Usually the directions of the analyst lead the patient toward a verbalization of his unconscious, with no limits or restrictions. The analyst facilitates this by offering the analysand access to speech, which does not center on a particular subject. When things are summoned up, they are usually expressed immediately and spontaneously, without time for reflection or correction. The mind wanders freely providing connected and disconnected thoughts, feelings, and emotions. The mere act of writing requires reflection, organization, stylistic perfection, and the necessity of a continuous sequitur that presents the material in a logical manner. The fact that all the memories found in chapter 3 revolve around one central motif—smoking—is further proof that Zeno is not really practicing free association. In recording his memories on paper Zeno keeps his thoughts under the strict control of the ego that fosters Zeno's concept of himself, the way he would like to think and appear to others. As he writes, he does not have to confront directly the scrutiny of Dr. S., nor his proddings when he reaches points of resistance, when his inner censor tries to prevent some repressed material coming to consciousness. In the relaxed atmosphere of his study Zeno faces hardly any duress and little motivation. This explains why he frequently falls asleep during self-analysis and also why he gets carried away by his verbal incontinence. The freedom to say or write anything is simply too satisfying to Zeno.[16] Of course, there is more to psychoanalysis than just free association. Zeno fails to talk about analysis; he shields us from this, keeping us in the dark about the other aspects of his therapy.

It is clear that both Zeno and the analyst are extremely unreliable. The former on account of his exaggerations and blatant lies,[17] to which he openly admits, his negative transference with regard to Dr. S., and his general contempt for and mistrust of all doctors. The latter for asking Zeno to write a diary and then publishing it as an act of revenge, betraying the confidence of his patient. Since Zeno concentrates primarily on self-analysis, we do not know much about the analyst. We do know that Dr. S. seems to take no interest in his patient and fails to use his skills in helping Zeno find out *all* that lies buried in his unconscious. He appears aloof, distant, and as we shall see, more interested in proving his Freudian theories than in helping Zeno get rid of his neuroses.

Also Zeno's (and Svevo's) linguistic problems with Tuscan Italian prevent him from fully deploying the language and saying exactly what he wants to say. In the last segment of the book Zeno muses that such confessions cannot be complete or sincere: "If only [Dr. S.] knew how we tend to talk about things for which we have the words all ready, and how we avoid subjects that would oblige us to look up words in the dictionary! That is the principle that guided me when it came to putting down certain episodes in my life. Naturally it would take on quite a different aspect if I told it in our own dialect" (368).

No doubt, smoking is more than an addiction, more than a scapegoat that Zeno can blame for a whole panoply of neurotic behavior and his obsessive-compulsive fretfulness. Each cigarette marks an end and a beginning for Zeno. All cigarettes in their serial form are related to one another, and their image recalls a series of long-forgotten associated incidents. The eidetic images thus evoked are intricately and symbolically coded. They are windows that open on Zeno's early experiences that predisposed him to various anxieties. His early compulsive smoking as a child, before any addiction had taken hold of him, may be seen both as a substitute for breast suckling as well as a sign of sibling rivalry with his younger brother whose birth caused Zeno to be weaned prematurely. The brother appears just once, only to reappear in a dream at the end of the novel. Zeno seems to blame *him* for stealing money and for his addiction. In fact, the earliest image that comes into focus is that of his brother and a boy with a rather hoarse voice, named Giuseppe, who provides them with cigarettes but "he gave my brother more than me, and . . . I was therefore obliged to try and get hold of some for myself. And that was how I came to steal . . . So now I traced my bad habits back to the very beginning" (5–6). The second recollection of cigarette smoking occurs in a dark cellar. There are two other boys with whom Zeno competes to see who could smoke most in the shortest time. Zeno wins in spite of feeling sick. When he boasts about his victory, one of the boys says: "I don't care about losing. I only smoke so long as I enjoy it" (8). This episode shows the difference between compulsive smoking and normal indulgence. Young Zeno's determination and need for gratification can be seen as a compensation for his lack of virility, his sense of personal deficiency and inferiority. These feelings lead him to strive for a positive situation of superiority that he achieves by smoking far more than the other boys. The Pyrrhic victory presages the rivalry Zeno will have later with his brother-in-law Guido, as well as his future bets and broken promises.

Perhaps the most plausible psychoanalytic interpretation of Zeno's smoking is that of mastery over and equality with Zeno's father, whom Wilden calls "the central master-figure."[18] The oral dynamism (which includes his prolixity), the stealing of money and cigars, all reflect Zeno's oedipal anxieties, hostility, and ontological rivalry with his father. By smoking he overcomes his guilt feelings and his apprehension (castration complex) regarding his forbidden desires toward the mother, and for wanting to get rid of the father. Cigarettes permit the child to redirect his unconscious sex instinct into a more acceptable form or outlet. The incident in which Zeno's clandestine smoking is discovered by his parents explains why the boy persists in his habit even though it makes him violently ill. He remembers one summer day, when his mother undressed him and made him lie down next to her on a sofa. He recalls "the delicious sensation" one has at that age, when one is able to rest after being tired and "lying there close to her body" (7). Suddenly the pleasurable experience was interrupted by his father who was searching for a cigar he had left in the room. Zeno recalls his mother's smile which "made such a deep impression on me that I immediately recognized it when I saw it one day long afterwards on my wife's lips" (7). Clearly the identification of wife and mother, or better their sublimation, reveals the true feelings of Zeno, whose unacceptable instinctual demands are channeled here into a more acceptable form of gratification. The association of his wife's smile with that of his mother is further proof of the sexual overtones of this scene.

Svevo tells us that Zeno is an obvious older and wealthier brother of Alfonso Nitti and Emilio Brentani. Not engaged as they are, however, in a daily struggle for survival, Zeno can contemplate the toil of others, as he himself alternates between heroic intentions and not surprising defeats.[19] In *Una vita* Svevo's resolve was to treat Alfonso's gray life grayly; in *Senilità* his intent was to make it almost perversely humorless. What distinguishes *La coscienza* from the previous novels is the inclusion of humor that becomes the moving force not only of the novel, but of all his subsequent writings. Zeno is fated to be different, and beginning with chapter 3, he gets himself constantly into the most absurd scrapes; the tour de force of the sanatorium is particularly amusing given the fact that he is willing to forgo his own freedom in order to be free of his nicotine habit. As Zeno recounts his life, he himself is surprised and amused at his own eccentricity and penchant for self-satire. Svevo writes that Zeno comes close to being a caricature.[20] Zeno's humor—typical of many Jewish comedians such as Woody Allen—prevents him from despairing and shields him from the terrible ridiculousness of life and from his ambiguous position in society. We are reminded of Heinrich Heine's words: "I cannot relate my own griefs without the thing becoming comic."[21] It is safer for Zeno to mock himself before others do; this way he always has the upper hand, and as Freud points out, people are apt to favor us when they laugh at something with us. Although Svevo never allows his readers to glimpse his Jewish identity, Zeno fits quite well Ruth Wisse's description of a schlemiel, the loser in practice who wins only an ironic victory of interpretation.[22] According to Albert Goldman, the power of the schlemiel "rests on his daring to lay bare his own weakness and to acknowledge his own limitations. Although he may appear pathetic or absurd, the schlemiel conceals behind his mask a hidden strength: a shrewd sense of self-preservation."[23] This hidden strength of the schlemiel is precisely what Zeno will reveal as he plays out his role in life, that is, his ability to succeed by failing.[24]

Death

In chapter 4 of *Confessions of Zeno,* entitled "The Death of my Father," Svevo deals first with Zeno's rebellion as a son, and then with the trauma Zeno suffered during and after his father's illness and death. The story begins with the following entry found on one of his philosophy books: "*15.iv.1890—4.30.My father died.L.C.* For whoever it may be of interest . . . the last two letters stand for 'last cigarette'" (27).[25] Up to this tragic moment Zeno had always felt that he and his father had nothing in common and therefore he had never made any attempt to get close to him. The events surrounding the parent image as remembered by Zeno twenty-five years later need not necessarily correspond to reality. Yet, Zeno tells us that he remembers every detail of the death and of his grief, but that he understands nothing (28). In Zeno's account, the father's perception of his son is that he is irresponsible, insecure, obsessed with his health, absentminded, aimless, inept in business, unable to take anything seriously, a mocker, irreligious, lacking strength of will, and even crazy. Although Zeno is rebellious, shows typical hostilities toward his parent, and is eager to assert his individuality and authority, he is, nonetheless, obedient, respectful, and even caring. He even senses in his father a superior force and virile strength: "my father's head was covered by a great mane of curly white hair, whereas mine, at thirty, was already very thin" (40). He knows that his father is disappointed in him, and that he "was one of the human beings who gave him most cause for anxiety" (30). Still, in spite of their perceived differences, father and son are very much alike. They are both unsuited for business, resentful of doctors, inveterate smokers, womanizers; they marry women with similar characters, and are absentminded, and inept. The principal differences are that the father is at peace with himself, has firm beliefs and faith. Zeno, instead, cannot take anything seriously. When he changes his course of study and the father good-naturedly says that he is mad, Zeno goes to a doctor for a thorough examination and obtains a certificate of sanity. When he presents it in triumph, his father exclaims with agony: "Ah, then you really are mad" (31)! Unlike his father, Zeno is determined to enjoy his suffering. There is no question that the intensity of his existence, a result of his suffering, is a source of enjoyment.

This chapter is memorable for the much-discussed slap suffered by Zeno moments before his father's death. The evening his father fell ill—he had difficulty in speaking and was short of breath—they had discussed religion at dinner. The father, thinking that Zeno was mocking religion, became agitated by his contention that it was merely a phenomenon to be studied like any other. Later on, his condition worsened and he lost consciousness. Zeno spent that night in his father's room, feeling remorseful for having neglected him for so many years, and terrified that he would die with such a negative opinion of him. As Zeno now recalls those anguishing hours, his father's irregular breathing reminds him of the sound of a locomotive drawing a string of coaches up a hill. Suddenly Zeno understands the significance of all these images that have been flowing through his conscience, all related to smoke, and the part they have played in his analysis: "How curious that is! My first real effort to remember had carried me back to the night that was the most important in my life" (41). On the night of his death his father had been sitting on the edge of the bed gazing out of the window. Suddenly with a supreme effort he tried to stand up.

Zeno tried to restrain him and his father's hand came crashing down on his cheek, as if he wanted to curse him for his transgressions. He then collapsed and, shortly after, died. Zeno was overwhelmed by the shock and by the realization that he would never be able to prove to him his innocence. When he at last returned to the death chamber, "His beautiful white hair had been brushed. . . . Death had already stiffened the body, which lay there proud and menacing. His large, shapely, powerful hands were livid, but were disposed so naturally that they seemed ready to grasp and punish" (53). Zeno then became good, and for a long time he returned to his belief in religion. The father's image changed with time, turning into a weak, but good and understanding man.

Much has been written about the significance of this scene. To begin with, Svevo took this event from the life of Umberto Veruda, whose mother had died under similar tragic circumstances. It was her death that actually precipitated Veruda's own demise one year later. Veruda's mother, who suffered from a heart condition, had been warned not to drink liquids, yet she continued to do so. One day, when Veruda came to visit her at a clinic, the doctors asked him to speak to her. In her room he pretended to be angry with her. However, he got carried away by his emotion, and his gestures and tone of voice terrified the poor woman who suddenly suffered a heart attack and died in her son's arms. Veruda was horrified and for a while was on the verge of taking his own life. His state of nerves grew worse, his physical condition deteriorated, and one year later he died racked with guilt and remorse.

Critics have offered various explanations for this episode in Zeno's life. Furbank thinks that Zeno's trauma is caused by the fact that he wanted to kill his father (oedipal complex). He also sees the father's curse as an irreversible judgment on his talents for business and practical life.[26] Bouissy doubts whether it was a real slap. He thinks that it may have been involuntary and regards the episode as a remembering of a humiliation suffered by Zeno.[27] Robinson sees it as proof that Zeno never really wanted to kill his father, and that all his actions at the sick bed are logical and proper; and that "Zeno is innocent in fact, but in unconscious fantasy he is guilty."[28] Saccone sees it as a form of resentment Zeno experiences when he realizes that with the death of his father he has lost the shield that has protected him against death.[29] Fonda's interpretation is based on Freud's theory that memories of incidents that have given rise to hysterical phenomena are frequently absent from the patient's memory during a normal psychic state.[30]

These repressed memories do, however, come alive during hypnosis, trance, or spontaneous attacks of hysteria. This explains why Zeno is only able to remember the immensity of his pain at his father's death, and why he has to rely on a dream to recall the details. Fonda views this episode an an oneiric allegory in which the protagonist relives the trauma experienced following the death of his parent, "to have hated his father and not loved him enough."[31] Because they are distorted, the scenes and images related by Zeno are not real, but rather conscious or unconscious alterations. In order to find an explanation we must follow the advice of Dr. S., "discern truth from falsehood, reality from dream." Fonda concludes that the blow never occurred; that it symbolizes feelings experienced by Zeno during the traumatic moment of the father's death. Russell, who echoes in part the Marxist view of this scene, writes that symbolically it is a blow "struck by the bourgeois world against his volubility, his wackiness and his nonconformity. It is a reminder to him that life can be more serious than he had thought and that it is difficult to rebel."[32]

As one can see, even the most perceptive critics, who never fail to point out the importance of this episode, fail to agree on its meaning. I suggest another possibility that may perhaps shed some light. It hinges on Svevo's Jewishness, more specifically on his apostasy: the rejection and betrayal of his father's religion and the resulting penalty. We have already seen how Svevo's conversion to Christianity did not sit easy with him. Indeed, he harbored not merely feelings of guilt but outright hostility toward the Church. "The Death of My Father," with its numerous religious references, allows us to glimpse the Jewish aspect of Svevo's experience. The key to this enigmatic chapter, full of ambivalence and contradiction, lies precisely in the inner life of Aron Hector Schmitz the man, rather than Italo Svevo the author. For a long time critics have argued whether Aron Hector Schmitz is Italo Svevo and whether Zeno is purely a fictional reflection of the former or the latter. Some have taken exception to the traditional identification of author and subject, refuting the opinion that Svevo/Schmitz universalized himself in his fiction, and that Zeno is indeed a self-portrait of Svevo. Still, others agree that there are many elements, incidents, characters that have a definite basis in Svevo's own life. In this regard, Montale wrote: "The businessman Schmitz is the one who provided the material for Italo Svevo's novels."[33] In discussing the Svevo-Schmitz autobiographic question Tullio Kezich writes that "between Svevo and Zeno there exists a kind of sly complicity," and that "Zeno the character is always one step ahead of Svevo as he accompanies him" from infancy to the wisdom of old age. He concludes that we must consider the biography of Schmitz and Zeno as "parallel lives."[34]

There are similarities between Ettore's father and Zeno's. In fact, they seem to be made out of the same mold. Both are authoritarian and impose their strict will on their sons. They are particularly severe when it comes to their son's future. Ettore always resented the practical outlook of his father who objected to his interest in literature and his wish to pursue his academic studies. The senior Schmitz was totally absorbed by his business vicissitudes, and failed to understand both Ettore's and Elio's sensitive natures. In comparing his parents Ettore said: "The mother is the one to whom we owe our life, the father *idem*, but in him we also find the master of the mother and everything that is around us."[35] In order to understand the meaning of the various religious references, we must view them as part of a compulsion to be punished by reliving an unpleasant experience whose story pattern may convert latent content into manifest content—a process similar to dream work in psychoanalysis. Zeno suffers from reminiscences, from a past that has not been dealt with, from a mourning process that has not reached its term. At thirty he buried his father and now at fifty-seven he must bury him again, making sure that he remains buried! Indeed, the father has been and continues to be a powerful guiding force in Zeno's behavior. Therefore, the relationship with the father is the axis around which Zeno's life, as well as the novel, revolves. The death of his father is a rite of passage that subverts Zeno's philosophical reasoning; it makes him aware that his paradoxes do not work in practice, only in theory; it forces him to accept the fact that he no longer can afford to be the careless child; that he has to assume certain responsibilities in life; and that he too is mortal, no matter how many cigarettes he is going to smoke and use as a protection.

I realized for the first time that the most important, the really decisive part of my life lay behind me and would never return. But my grief was not so purely selfish as this would seem to suggest. No! I mourned for him and for myself, but for myself only because he was dead. Up to that moment I had passed from cigarette to cigarette. . . . His death destroyed the future that alone gave point to my resolutions. (28)

Zeno tells us that at fifteen, when his mother died, he was still religious. We must assume, then, that his faith grew weaker as he grew older and that by the time of his father's death he had lost it completely. The evening his father fell ill Zeno was delayed in coming home by a "learned friend" who had insisted on "treating" him to "his ideas on the origins of Christianity" (33). Zeno, who had never before thought about the subject, submits to the long lecture only to please his friend. If Zeno were a Christian, would it not be strange for him to be in the dark about a subject that all children study in their catechism? Does his father get angry at him because he treats religion as a phenomenon, or is it because he recognizes here the image of a Jew subjected to a typical proselytizing technique that stresses the communality of both religions? Later on, the ailing man keeps searching for the words that will express his feelings to Zeno: "I know a great many things but, alas, I don't know how to make you understand them. How I wish I could! I feel that I can see the meaning of things to a certain extent and can also distinguish between what is *true* and what is *false*" [my emphasis] (35). What are these things that Zeno is to understand? What truth and falseness does his father refer to?

In my opinion, it is quite possible that the dying man may be searching for the biblical verses known as the Shema ["Hear, O Israel: The Lord is Our God, the Lord is One"], proclaimed by Moses shortly before his own death. The Shema is Israel's confession of faith, a proclamation of the existence and unity of God. It occupies the central place in Jewish religious thought and is recited during the morning and evening prayers; it is the first prayer learned by children and the last utterance of the dying, as they prepare themselves to meet their Maker. The Shema commands Jews to teach these truths to their children: ". . . and thou shalt teach them diligently unto thy children." The verses contain also the promise of reward for those who believe in the true God and fulfill His laws, and of punishment for their transgression.[36]

The father, knowing that he is about to die, may be desperately searching for this prayer; and at the same time he may be making a final attempt to teach Zeno its truth. According to his wife, as he grew older, Svevo himself acquired a certain pose with his right hand, very reminiscent of Zeno's father's last gesture: "Sometimes he would raise his right arm as if he were protecting himself from an invisible enemy, and he would say pantingly: 'I hear it coming!' And if I asked: 'What?,' he used to reply 'The blow.'"[37] The raised hand of the father in both cases may be a reminder of David's raised hand and famous invocation concerning Judaism and Jerusalem, its living symbolism: "If I forget thee, oh Jerusalem, may my right hand forget its cunning and wither." This popular saying became the inspiration and cry of hope for the Jews in the Diaspora. In the presentation of the death scene Ettore through Zeno relives his own experiences of guilt, and his father like a biblical prophet seems to be visiting a horrible curse upon him. At the same time, he may be pointing out to his son that, according to Jewish law, despite his actions, an apostate may return without any ceremony back to the Jewish religion. Indeed, Svevo did precisely that when he asked to be buried in a shroud, in accordance with Jewish custom. At this extreme moment Svevo merely put into practice what he wrote at the end of chapter 4: "It is the essence of true religion that one does not need to make a loud profession of it in order to get the consolation which at certain moments one cannot do without" (54).

Ménage à trois

We have seen how in "The Last Cigarette" Svevo used the comical element in presenting Zeno and his neuroses revolving around his nicotine habit; in "The Death of My Father" we noted a dramatic shift from comedy to tragedy. In chapter 5, "The Story of My Marriage," a lengthy chapter and perhaps the best part of the novel, there is a convergence of drama and comedy. Zeno dominates the action throughout and reveals to the full all his antiheroic schlemiel qualities. He becomes a truly Chaplinesque character, constantly tripping over his own feet, finding himself in the most bizarre situations.[38] And yet, like the amiable "little tramp," he bounces back with resiliency to spare. Zeno has spent thirty years of his life alternating between one resolution and another, without ever making any lasting commitments in life. Now that his father is no more, he has to fill the void left by him. He makes two resolutions: a career and a wife.

At the stock market Zeno meets Giovanni Malfenti, a smart businessman, who becomes his business mentor, friend, surrogate father, and eventually future father-in-law. Though their relationship is based on rivalry and some hostility (just like with his father), and despite their cultural differences, Zeno is drawn to the overweight man. Malfenti was "an important business man, ignorant and pushing. But his ignorance gave one an impression of quiet strength which fascinated me" (56). Zeno is mesmerized and clings to him, hoping to enrich himself with sufficient knowledge to enable him to take charge of his own business, which had been entrusted by his diffident father to an administrator named Olivi. From this business world, the city of Trieste emerges as the indispensable port and marketplace for the Austro-Hungarian Empire. In observing its citizens engaged in various commercial and cultural activities, we sense the vitality of the city. Zeno learns that Malfenti has four beautiful daughters whose names all begin with the letter *A*. He is fascinated by this and dreams of "those four girls linked together so closely by their names. I almost felt they were a bunch of flowers. But that initial meant something else too. My name is Zeno, and I felt as if I were about to choose a wife from a far country" (62). He is invited into their home where he first meets Anna, who is still a child; then Augusta who disappoints him because she is crossed-eyed and homely (actually she's the one he will eventually marry); Alberta, attractive but only seventeen and still at school; and finally beautiful Ada, whom he selects as the only qualified candidate who "was to guide me to moral and physical health in the holy monogamy of marriage" (66). Ironically, Zeno does everything in reverse order: first he chooses a father-in-law, then the bride, and finally he decides to fall in love. The whole affair smacks of a commercial transaction, whereby deals are made at an exchange without any direct contact with the merchandise.

The Malfenti girls become Zeno's only interest as he sets out to win Ada's affection. He tries to make himself likable by making everyone laugh at his jokes and amusing stories. He succeeds with Alberta and Augusta, but fails miserably with Ada who is outright hostile toward him. He makes such a fool of himself that little Anna constantly tells him: "But you're mad, you are quite mad!" Mrs. Malfenti, much to his surprise, warns him that while he is trying to impress Ada, he is actually compromising Augusta who has fallen in love with him.

This tragicomedy reaches its funniest moment when Zeno participates at a séance conducted by Guido Speir, a rather dapper and socially at ease young man who has begun to court Ada. While they are all seated around the table in the dark room, Zeno touches what he thinks is Ada's leg; he then puts his arm around her waist and declares his love to her. Much to his surprise, he soon finds out that it is Augusta sitting next to him. Later on in the evening, being determined to bring the agony of his courtship to an end, Zeno first proposes to Ada, then to Alberta (Anna is too young), and finally, having been turned down by both, he proposes to Augusta, who readily accepts. All this in the span of about fifteen minutes! When it is too late, Zeno realizes that he has been outmaneuvered by the sly Mrs. Malfenti who had deviously guided him in this direction, reserving Ada for Guido. And so Zeno becomes engaged to the homeliest of the three sisters, who, however, will become in time a most affectionate, ideal wife for him, and will bring order and stability into his irregular life. He will discover eventually that Augusta is after all a rather attractive and desirable woman. Besides, he rationalizes, it is better to be Ada's brother-in-law than a total stranger to her.

Why is Zeno so enthralled by the four girls bearing names beginning with the letter *A*?[39] And why does he persist in a futile and ridiculous courtship, knowing full well that Ada despises him as a suitor and has given her heart to Guido? The answer is to be found, once again, in Zeno's paradoxes. He sets up for himself a goal that is both unreachable and unrealistic. The letter *A,* so distant from *Z,* stands for a resolution that cannot be kept: unconsciously Zeno is not ready for marriage. He therefore creates for himself obstacles that will prevent this from happening. However, he trips himself up and becomes a victim of his own making.

Before the death of his father Zeno had suffered primarily from personal and emotional aberrations. In "The Story of My Marriage" these disturbances grow worse and manifest themselves in several psychosomatic disorders stemming primarily from the frustration of not being able to conquer Ada and from his rivalry with Guido, which goes beyond the amorous question. Zeno's real and imaginary complaints of pain are employed, consciously or unconsciously, to attract attention to himself and thereby gain satisfaction through recognition. They also express unconscious emotional conflicts, frustration, sense of inferiority, low self-esteem, and sheer ineptitude. When Zeno realizes that the Malfentis want him to marry Augusta and not Ada, his disappointment is almost unbearable. It is precisely this blow to his ego that triggers all his imaginary hypochondriac illnesses.

One night, in a café, Zeno meets an old school friend by the name of Tullio, who is crippled in his right leg due to rheumatism and obsessed with his illness. Zeno listens in bewilderment as Tullio speaks of the anatomy of the leg and foot, pointing out that, when we walk, no fewer than fifty-four muscles are set in motion. When Tullio inquires about his life, Zeno finds it difficult to relate his unhappiness with Ada. Instead "he had to find an outlet somehow" for his suffering. And so Zeno gives Tullio such an exaggerated account of his bodily symptoms that tears come to his own eyes. Zeno, who has always had a fascination with illness, soon becomes intrigued by his own limbs, and when he walks out of the coffee shop, he limps feeling as "if the whole machine needed oiling" (95). Thereafter Zeno limps [like Oedipus] whenever his ego suffers a blow.[40] The second event that causes Zeno to "fall pray to disease" occurs the evening of the proposal, when he squares off in a duel of ability with his rival Guido, who seems to have all the qualities that Zeno lacks: he is attractive, debonair, has a full head of curly hair, is sure of himself, and to Zeno's eyes appears to be the epitome of masculine success. Most important, he is liked by Ada, and he plays the violin to perfection. Zeno experiences a sharp pain in his hip and arm when Guido ridicules him in front of Ada by drawing two caricatures of Zeno that poke fun at his absentmindedness. From that moment on, in spite of all the doctors and cures, Zeno will never be able to get rid of this pain that will afflict him during moments of stress and conflict.

When the two men leave the Malfenti house, Guido invites Zeno to go to the very café where he had met Tullio. Later on, as they walk up a hill, Guido stretches himself out on the wall that separates the upper road from the one below. Zeno first wishes fervently that he might fall, and then he almost pushes him to his death. He is stopped by a sudden sharp pain that forces him to crouch to the ground and scream out of frustration for not being able to get even and, of course, out of guilt for harboring such violent thoughts. Zeno's underlying conflicts of affection and rivalry with Guido are reflected in the organic symptom of pain that pierces his side: Guido has taken Ada away from him, though he does not really love her;[41] Zeno has been caricatured by him; and Guido has shown his virtuosity with the violin which Zeno plays badly. According to Fonda's reading of this chapter, Zeno's feelings of sibling rivalry are transposed to his matrimonial adventure: "Zeno relives in his transposed relationship with Ada, the anger and suffering experienced when he believed he had lost his mother's affection with the birth of his brother."[42] This accounts for Zeno's expression of both anger and love toward Ada (the mother) and in particular Guido (the brother), as well as his erratic behavior in their presence. "Zeno is like a child, who, torn by conflicting emotions, tries to become the center of attention, but ends up making a nuisance of himself instead."[43]

The violin with its characteristic shape and symbolic meaning, becomes a dueling weapon for the two antagonists. Before Guido's appearance on the scene, in his frenzied attempts to woo Ada, Zeno used to play the violin, however badly, with the piano accompaniment of Augusta. At the end of the séance, after Guido's beautiful and passionate rendition on the violin of Bach's *Chaconne,* when he steps out of the room in order to find out why Anna is crying, he entrusts "his precious violin" to Ada. When Zeno offers to hold it, she refuses holding "her violin" still closer as she sits down. It is at this peculiar and inopportune moment that Zeno makes his first declaration of love to Ada. She sits there staring at him in horror and amazement, without giving him an answer and still holding the violin tightly. Zeno insists: "Surely you must have understood! You couldn't have thought I wanted to make love to Augusta" (117)! At first Ada is angered by Zeno's cavalier attitude toward her sister, but after she has calmed down she suggests to Zeno that Augusta is a fine woman and would make him a good wife. In essence, Ada is telling Zeno that Guido's virtuoso playing of the violin suits her, and that Zeno should continue to play his for the willing Augusta. The musical instrument and the manner in which it is clasped by Ada are clear symbolic expressions of sexual and rivalrous feelings. It is interesting to note that Ada holds "her" violin and that the bow is not referred to, which means that Guido has it with him. In Freudian terms, any pointed or elongated object represents the male organ, while receptacle-like shapes, such as small boxes, chests etc., correspond to the female organ.[44] In the present case, the characteristic shape of the violin and the movement of the bow on its strings are clear symbolic references to the sexual act.[45] When the two young men are at the coffee shop, upon hearing from Guido that he is going to ask for Ada's hand, Zeno viciously replies: "Now I understand why Ada liked your travesty of Bach so much. You played well, but you remember there used to be a notice up in the streets of medieval Florence: '*Gli Otto proibiscono di lordare in certi posti*'" (129). [Roughly translated: It is forbidden to dirty in public places, public lewdness is forbidden.] The blow strikes home and Guido turns red in the face. What Zeno wishes to convey with these cryptic words, is that Guido should not have played his violin so erotically as to have made a fool of himself.[46]

One can say that, at the end of this chapter, the dueling has resulted in a draw—though only Zeno shows any wounds. Guido has been victorious with his caricatures of Zeno and his amorous music; Zeno has won at the séance and at the coffee shop. Hence, the two future brothers-in-law will be friends and will no longer show conscious hostility to each other. Guido, who harbors no animosity, will treat Zeno like a brother, but the latter will continue to struggle with his unresolved and contradictory emotions.

Wife and Mistress

With the multiplicity of episodes that have taken Zeno almost "midway of the journey of his life," Svevo has successfully brought forward the narrative by making it fluctuate in a harmonious rhythm between past and present, the conscious and unconscious, reality and memory. Most remarkable has been the presentation of a gallery of characters, all masterfully interwoven and dramatically depicted with bold brushstrokes that reveal their idiosyncrasies. Now that the "transaction" has been completed, and Zeno has become part of Augusta's bourgeois household—which stands for health, order, and stability—Giovanni Malfenti, the businessman par excellence, is slowly displaced in importance by Guido, to whom more attention will be paid than any other character except Zeno. Towering over them is Zeno whose life is like a "seawave, which from the moment it is born until it expires is in a state of continual change" (55). In chapter 6, "Wife and Mistress," Zeno, who suddenly finds himself pleasantly married, gives us an account of how "Mother Nature guided [him] mysteriously . . . and with what violence she imposed her commands" (61). Actually, being married is not difficult for Zeno after the ordeal of becoming engaged. He is elated not because he has made a fortuitous right choice, but rather because he no longer has to go from one resolution to another: "Everything was decided for me. At last I had obtained certainty" (123).[47]

During their honeymoon trip Zeno becomes even more appreciative of Augusta's qualities as companion and wife. Their relationship is happy and Zeno smiles, though he is in constant pain. For him, Augusta is the personification of health. He feeds on it. He is fascinated by her physical and emotional well-being and tries to arrive at its source. He fails, however, "for directly I start analyzing it I seem to turn it into a disease" (142). It is as if he were placing her perfect health under a microscope, where, due to the intense magnification, various imperfections become visible. He is irresistibly fascinated by illness and almost takes pride in his own suffering. He finds in it a masochistic gratification, a certain sensuality and moral freedom for his actions. He cannot understand health, life, or himself, unless these are approached by way of unconventional paths of sickness and death. He is convinced that healthy people like Augusta have "no conception of what health really is. Health cannot analyze itself even if it looks at itself in the glass. It is only we invalids who can know anything about ourselves" (146).

At this time he becomes jealous of his wife and is attacked by "a slight illness" from which he will never recover: "the fear of growing old, and above all the fear of death" (145). He fears that upon his death Augusta will immediately replace him with another man, for whom she will provide the same sane and regular world as she is now providing for him. In Venice, in a scene reminiscent of Thomas Mann's *Death in Venice,* Zeno envisions his own death: his "legs, in which the circulation was already poor, would become gangrened, and the gangrene would spread and spread till it reached a vital organ" (146). In spite of Augusta's sincere protestations, Zeno continues to be obsessed by the ever-advancing and "terrifying specter of death" (147). Actually, it had always been present in his subconscious, but now it has become manifest to him. Perhaps, like Gustav von Aschenbach, he too is afraid that by surrendering to love and life he will surrender to death.

Upon their return to Trieste, Augusta makes Zeno's life as comfortable as possible. He, however, is far from being the ideal husband. First he betrays her in thought, and then in practice by acquiring a young mistress. One day he runs into an old school friend, Enrico Copler, who suffers from a chronic kidney ailment. Zeno immediately becomes fascinated by Copler's illness—the very same that killed Elio, Svevo's younger brother—and a polemic ensues: what is better, a real or an imaginary illness? Copler prefers having a real illness because an imaginary ill person, like Zeno, "is ridiculous and pitiable: and then nothing can cure him, whereas in the case of a real invalid like me there is always some drug that can be found to meet the case" (154). Eventually they agree that one sort of invalid is as good as the other. This conclusion will be developed further by Svevo when he will point out that we are all diseased; that there are the real sick, the imaginary sick, and the imaginary healthy.

One day Copler introduces Zeno to a poor but beautiful aspiring young singer by the name of Carla Gerco. The similarity between Gerco and Zergol, the name of Svevo's lover and model for Angiolina, is striking, since in the Triestine dialect the two sound almost the same. Zeno helps her out with money and begins to visit her on a daily basis. In order to have a legitimate excuse for his escapades and appease his guilty conscience, Zeno becomes Carla's self-appointed voice teacher. In recompense for her docility and application to her music lessons, he gives her large sums of money. Of course, there is an ulteri-

or motive: her dependency gives him increasing control over her. When he finally kisses Carla, he suffers from the usual physical pains. And when he seduces her, he is quick and brutal (as Emilio had been with Angiolina), as if he were punishing her for his own unfaithfulness. When Zeno tells Carla the story of his marriage, she finds it difficult to share him with Augusta and feels responsible for having taken him away from her. Carla, the opposite of "Giolona," accepts Zeno's magnanimity with great reluctance and sincere embarrassment. He becomes so involved in her music that he even hires a voice teacher for her, who, alas, falls in love with her too. Ironically, Zeno is able to control his feelings of remorse toward Augusta by devising various stratagems that help him overcome his pains of guilt; Carla, on the other hand, truly feels guilty and responsible for his infidelity.

Wanting to show his mistress what a beautiful woman he is sacrificing for her, he leads her to believe that Ada is his wife. When Carla sees her walking along the street, she is struck by her beauty and by the visible sadness caused by Guido's unfaithfulness, and can no longer bear to harm this woman, who appears to her like a goddess. She breaks off with Zeno and marries the music teacher. In doing so she shows a remarkable determination to act honorably: she marries not because she is in love, but because she no longer wishes to harm the woman she thinks is Zeno's wife.

Zeno's relatively successful ménage à trois lasts for almost two years. During this time he alternates between wife and mistress, always returning home to the sanctity of matrimony, without ever arousing the least suspicion in Augusta. The affair ends only because Zeno's machinations backfire on him. The whole episode can be read on different levels. He embarks on this adventure because he is bored, and because it permits him to escape from the traditional restrictive environment to which he has irremediably tied himself down. It is too stable and regular for someone like Zeno, constantly under stress and in a frenzied state of agitated animation. Subconsciously, Zeno may be engaging in substitutive behavior that makes up for his frustration with Ada who is about to be married to Guido, his archrival. At the same time the affair covers up his awareness of an undesirable impulse toward Ada and Guido: the former represents his mother, the latter, the rival sibling brother. This explains Zeno's irrational anger when he is told of Guido's infidelity; besides Ada, Zeno seems to be the only one who is really concerned about this. According to Mario Fusco, Zeno's behavior with women results "from a neurotic fixation brought about by an ill-resolved Oedipal stage."[48] In fact, practically all the female characters in Svevo's writings, except the mistresses, have distinct maternal characteristics. Their main task is to take care of the home, the children, and to fulfill for their husbands the multifarious roles of mother, wife, lover, and comforter; they must always be ready to soothe the husband whenever he is overburdened by the hardships of the business world or by emotional distress. Zeno always turns to Augusta for comfort, "as children hold out the hand they have hurt to their mother to be kissed" (147).

Zeno's affair may also be a reaction to his feelings of inferiority vis-à-vis his father and the other men who inevitably become father figures for Zeno; or a means of counteracting the fear of growing old and dying. All the other men have had mistresses, so must he.

The most intriguing and interesting part of "Wife and Mistress" is the way Zeno deals with his feelings of guilt, as he tries to juggle his passion for Carla, his domestic tranquillity, and his own irreconcilable conscience. During the liaison he has to deceive all three in order to maintain a balanced existence. Life at home is boring, so he goes to Carla where he finds passion and excitement. Once he has had his fill, he eagerly returns to the tranquillity of his home and "the sphere of health and respectability wherein Augusta reigned supreme" (222). Whenever his conscience is vulnerable or wounded, it immediately sends painful signals to the side of his body that are like "a sympathetic pain, an echo of the great wound" in his conscience (173). Whenever these signals occur, Zeno lavishes the tenderness he feels for Carla upon Augusta! He justifies his infidelity by disguising it and by convincing himself that the affair is good for his marriage: "I was going to Carla to kindle my passion for *her*" (189). He conjures up various rationalizations that permit him to disguise his transgressions and make them conform to his moral standards. He toys with the idea that he is a perfect husband, seeing no reason "why that husband became less perfect by having committed adultery" (206). Although it would be possible to seduce Carla immediately, Zeno decides to do it in phases, not out of concern for the poor girl, but out of concern for his unrelenting conscience, which can take only so much at a time. When he finally decides to possess Carla totally, his body reacts like that of a child feigning sickness because he doesn't want to go to school: "It was not death I desired, but an illness, which would serve as an excuse for doing what I wanted or which would prevent my doing it" (186). Zeno must maintain at all times a balance between these conflicting forces.

As long as he sees Carla in the morning, when Augusta is busy and thinks that he is occupied with business, and provided he returns home on time for lunch, then he feels innocent and bears no pain. However, if he stays longer with Carla, or something negative is said about his wife, then he has to pay the penalty. This explains why he refuses to spend the night with his mistress. When he is compelled to do so, he leaves her in the middle of the night and seeks shelter in Augusta's arms.

It is in dreams that Zeno's repressed emotions and anxieties are given free rein. Most interesting from a narrative and psychological point of view is the one he has after having kissed Carla in a most passionate way. According to Zeno, this is what happened to inspire the dream: "I drew her to me, pushing away with my nose the great lock of hair in her neck, so that I could touch her skin with my lips and even with my teeth. It seemed quite a playful kiss and she ended by laughing too, but only when I had let her go" (172). In the dream, however, Zeno adapts his unconscious or repressed wishes into an acceptable form; by condensing and displacing the actual occurrence of the kiss, he finds a release from the tension and anxieties associated with his infidelity. This is the dream:

I was not only kissing Carla's neck, I was positively devouring it. But though I was inflicting terrible wounds on it in my mad lust, the wounds did not bleed and the delicate curve of her neck was still unaltered under its soft white skin. Carla, prostrate in my arms, did not seem to suffer from the bites. It was Augusta, coming in unexpectedly, who suffered. To calm her I said "I won't eat her all up: I will leave a little for you." (174)

The manifest significance of this dream is that Augusta is the victim of the ménage, that he is the victimizer and Carla a mere participant. Still, with some effort, we can discover other oneiric dimensions as we reach further into Freud's "laws of the illogical" and examine what Teresa de Lauretis calls the "deep-seated unconscious motivations of such behavior, which can only be communicated and understood in the symbolic language of the science of the unconscious."[49] It is clearly understood that the dream is an aggregation of sexual symbols, and so is its stimulus. First of all, it is remarkable that Zeno after so many years is able to remember in great detail both the oneiric inspiration and the dream itself. The basic difference between the two scenes, of course, is the presence of Augusta and the absence of Carla's "great locks of hair" in the dream.[50] Carla's hair represents the pubic area which loses some of its erotic appeal once sexual intimacy has been achieved. This explains its absence in the dream. Instead of being disturbed by this dream, Zeno wakes up savoring a sense of satisfaction. This pleasurable experience results from having two women in his power, both eager to please and satisfy his sexual aggressiveness.

The dream could be classified as an anxiety dream or even a wishful dream—Freud tells us that all dreams are an attempt at wish-fulfillment. Therefore, the situation is modified in order to adapt Zeno's unconscious wishes into an acceptable form. In the dream Zeno manages to keep both women happy and his conscience in check. He vents his mad lust on Carla and, at the same time, when Augusta sees them together, he manages to calm her down. In fact, his wife profits repeatedly from his guilt feelings by receiving expensive gifts and greater love from him. Thus we have a complete wish-fulfillment in the dream: Zeno wants to make love to Carla, he wants Augusta to know about it and accept it, and finally his conscience is clear. Carrying the decoding of the dream a step further, we can say that by means of condensation, Carla represents Ada (Mother) and Augusta Zeno's younger brother whose interference could reflect Zeno's unhappiness at being weaned when his sibling was born.[51] The terrible wounds he is inflicting upon Carla's neck reveal Zeno's sadistic attitude toward women and a possible overcompensation for his sense of inferiority. At the same time, the fact that Carla does not seem to suffer would indicate a possible repudiation of his potential sadism.

Of course, when the dream occurs, Carla has not yet been seduced and, therefore, her wounds do not bleed and her neck remains unaltered. This could mean that Zeno feels no guilt toward his future mistress because he has not yet possessed her; and even when he does so, he will pay well for her services. This being the case, why does Zeno call the dream a nightmare? Is it because Augusta suffers in spite of his attempt to calm her? Both he and Carla obviously seem to enjoy themselves. Augusta suffers because Carla is a transformation of Ada, as we have already indicated, and she is jealous of her sister who always looms important in Zeno's thoughts and dreams. The dream seems to repeat Zeno's oedipal conflict where all women are syncretized in the person of Ada, who symbolizes the mother figure, a child's first erotic object and first seducer, who, in Zeno's case, presents herself as a principal performer in his life conflict.

The way Zeno approaches Carla's skin, both with his lips and teeth, is an obvious infantile regression, very similar to the way a child being nursed approaches (or attacks) the mother's breast. Although he bites the nipple, rarely does he harm it or make it bleed. He suckles with the same frenzy with which Zeno devours Carla's neck. The image of the suckling child is carried a step further when Zeno fully awakens from the dream. He realizes how dangerous his affair may be not for his marriage, but in particular for the child he suspects Augusta is carrying. At the end of the novel Zeno dreams that he is a child dreaming that he is possessing a woman seated in a cage "in the strongest manner: he was convinced that he would be able to eat little bits off her at the top and the bottom" (373). The biting in the first dream and the eating of the mother's flesh in the second suggest a carnal pleasure that ought not to be indulged in because it is forbidden. Obviously, this strong oral fixation ties in with Zeno's libidinal gratification; he seems to be carrying over into adulthood early infantile experiences related to the oral stage. His oral dependency—this includes smoking—indicates a desire to return to an earlier stage of development that permits him to incorporate his mother into his self. In longing for his mother's breast, he makes use of an innocent desire as a screen for a more serious one.

A Business Adventure

In chapter 7, the longest in the novel and bearing the title "A Business Partnership," many of the themes and events already presented in previous episodes converge. The action as always is retrospective and at the same time ongoing. Until now Zeno has been both actor and observer in the events surrounding his life's experiences. In this chapter, however, there occurs a shift in the action: Zeno will be primarily an observer, albeit an active one, of Guido's ups and downs as he goes into business, betrays his wife, and accidentally commits suicide. After Guido's untimely death, Zeno will become once again the principal actor; his actions, however, will no longer be those of the antihero, but rather those of someone capable of decisive conduct. The axis of the action will be Guido who, after the death of Giovanni Malfenti and Copler, will become the focal point of the narrative and Zeno's main concern. Guido will precipitate the events and entangle all the other characters, old and new. As Zeno will try to be of help in Guido's life—still tripping occasionally over his feet—he will, nevertheless, reveal a new dimension to his character: that he has, after all, common sense and a relatively good and practical knowledge of life; and that he can be successful in business in spite of his family's skepticism. It is precisely in this chapter that Zeno will triumph over his rival, for whom he still harbors ambivalent emotions of anger, jealousy, and love. Subconsciously there is a strong and deep resentment toward his brother-in-law, for taking away Ada from him [mother and object of his desire], and then betraying her. Indirectly, he has also caused Zeno to lose Carla, since she broke off the affair after having been distressed by the suffering she saw on Ada's face, caused by the knowledge that Guido was having an affair with his secretary. Here Zeno's good qualities will stand out, while Guido's mediocrity and vulnerability will become more and more evident to his friend.

Guido, who has been given a large capital sum by his father, asks Zeno to help him set up a new commercial undertaking in Trieste. The underlying reason for Zeno's acceptance is that he wants to prove to himself and to Augusta that his close relationship to Guido is a sign of his absolute indifference to Ada. At first, both are totally unprepared to run the business. Zeno is put in charge of the accounts, while Guido, who has studied commerce at an English school, is eager to reject common business practices and "strike out a new path" (247). Guido quickly shows a lack of seriousness in the selection of an office and its furniture, and by introducing a sporting dog into the premises. He is more intrigued by the intricacies of a business proposition than by mere profits. For him the business of buying and selling is a game, an adventure, and a toy to be played with. When Augusta asks, "But when are you going to begin to make money?," Zeno replies that the thought had not yet crossed their minds (254). Guido hires a young apprentice named Luciano, who gets "as excited about business as other lads of his age do about women" (253). And finally he hires the beautiful Carmen as his secretary, in spite of her lack of clerical abilities—Zeno immediately recognizes her as someone meant to be a mistress and not a secretary. Carmen's coming gives a new animation to the office, but especially to Guido who is anxious to show everyone that the new member of the staff is essential to the business. He and Carmen soon become lovers and eventually everyone finds out about it, including Ada, who has just given birth to twins and is naturally overcome with jealousy and anger. Even Zeno is jealous of his friend's good fortune and looks "on Carmen as Guido's Carla, a gentler and more submissive one. He had had better luck than me with his second woman, as with his first" (265).[52]

Carmen becomes a source of contention between the two rivals, who fight for her admiration the way they had done over Ada. Trying to outdo each other, they invent fables in which they ridicule each other's faults. Although very little of the business invented by Guido bears any fruit, the losses are rather minimal until they speculate to buy sixty tons of sulphate of copper. Unfortunately, the price of the mineral falls drastically and the business suffers an enormous loss. When its collapse is imminent, Guido asks Ada for financial help, but she refuses. To convince her how desperate he is, he fakes a suicide attempt, making sure that the dose of morphine he takes is small and not lethal. Ada is frightened, she gives in, but begs Zeno not to abandon Guido and to go on helping him.

Instead of putting Ada's money to good use, Guido begins to speculate dangerously on the stock market. When all his capital is lost, Guido improvises a second suicide attempt intended to convince Ada to give him more money. This time, however, due to a combination of unforeseen circumstances—there is a storm, the doctor is late in coming—Guido's plan misfires and he dies. Zeno is the only one who is aware of the tragic mistake. Feeling partly responsible for this tragedy, he begins to play the market in Guido's name and recuperates some of the losses. Zeno gets so involved in this gambling frenzy that he forgets to be on time for Guido's funeral. When he finally goes to the cemetery, he follows the wrong cortege and misses his friend's funeral. He is so excited at being successful where Guido had failed that this blunder does not seem to bother him. Zeno returns to the Bourse where fortune continues to smile at him. Finally, he manages to recuperate half of Guido's large loss. Although, prior to the suicide, Zeno had become very intolerant of Guido and had upbraided him for the weakness and conceit that were causing his ruin, now that he is dead a metamorphosis occurs, one similar to that of Angiolina in Emilio's memory: "He had had many faults, but I saw at once that now he was dead nothing remained of them. . . . Guido was pure now. Death had purified him" (351). Ada is the only one who understands the underlying reasons for Zeno's *lapsus* and her anger passes all bounds: "What good would you have done beside his grave? You, who never loved him! Kind as you are, you might have wept to see my tears, but you would have shed none for him. You hated him! Poor Zeno! My poor brother!" (361).

Indeed, Zeno is fully aware of the fact that he loved, but also resented Guido; that he could have done much more to help him and that he could have saved him, had he wanted to. He should have guessed that something serious was going to happen to Guido when he repeatedly inquired about the barbiturate Veronal. Ada's reproaches will continue to torment Zeno for a long time. She too feels guilty for her own failings and leaves Trieste to live in Argentina with her husband's family, "leaving [her] pangs of conscience behind" (365). Zeno weeps, knowing that he will never be able to prove his innocence to her. He avoided following the right funeral cortège because of a Freudian *lapsus memoriae,* that is to say, unconsciously he cannot accept Guido's death because as Fonda points out, "once Guido is dead, Zeno's best part becomes extinct: the ideal one."[53] Furthermore, Zeno must face the disappearance not only of Guido, but also of Ada (the mother figure) who sails away, never to be seen again. We can assume that Zeno consults Dr. S. at this point in his life.

It is during their financial and marital crisis that Ada falls ill with Basedow's [Graves'] disease. There is a change in her voice, her face becomes disfigured, and her eyes "seemed to have grown bigger, to have grown almost out of their sockets in their effort to see more clearly" (284). Zeno is horrified, but at the same time fascinated. Basedow virtually becomes an obsession for him; he reads various monographs on the subject, thinking that he has discovered the secret of life:

But I alone lived by Basedow! He seemed to me to have penetrated to the roots of life, and shown it to be as follows: all living beings are ranged along a certain line, at one end of which is Basedow's disease. All who are suffering from this disease use up their vital force recklessly in a mad vertiginous rhythm, the heart beating without control. At the other end of the line are those wretched beings, shriveled up by native avarice, and doomed to die from a disease that looks like exhaustion but is really cowardice. The happy mean between these two maladies is to be found in the middle of the line, and is called health, though it is really only a suspension of movement.[54] (286–87)

He uses the symptomatic characteristics of Graves' disease—hypoactivity and hyperactivity—to formulate a vision of life and man's place in it. Zeno can never resist a theory! The thyroid's hormonal over- and under-production is seen in terms of social and economic productivity. The balance between the active and inactive—the hero and the antihero, the sick and the healthy—makes society survive and move forward: "I still believe that at whatsoever particular spot of the universe one settles down one ends by becoming poisoned; it is essential to keep moving. Life has its poisons, but counter-poisons too which balance them. It is only by moving about that one can avoid the first and profit from the second" (287). Illness loses its particularity as it pervades everyone in its universality. "What makes Italo Svevo a major author," writes P. N. Furbank, "is the generality and universality of his handling of disease."[55] The author begins to unravel here a painfully acute and pessimistic view of European society, before and after the Great War—indeed, he makes this experience into an object of consciousness. "What Svevo . . . tells us," writes the French critic Robbe-Grillet, "is that in our modern society, nothing is any longer *natural*. And there isn't even any reason to grieve about it."[56] Both mental and physical illnesses become a metaphor for the pernicious *mal du siècle*: Europe was sick, its social classes were out of kilter, there was turbulent political and social unrest, the Russian Revolution, fascism—in short, society was on its way to destruction. At first, Zeno pokes fun at the illusions of bourgeois life, but then becomes serious as he shows it to be the victim of a vicious urban and commercial world; he brings out its contradictions, as he catches for us the culture's sense of oppression. He calls society's values into question and registers the dilemma posed by European society. Guido's financial and marital failure is reflective of this malaise.[57] The exaggerated insecurities of Zeno and Guido incarnate those of a competitive society with its terror and hopeless expectations, its members consumed by desire, ambition, pleasure, and even work. Illness in all its manifestations—smoking, neuroses, limping, nephritis, etc.—is an existentialist metaphor of Europe's sickness, and the Basedowian axis is dialectically related to an inordinate expectation of life. Zeno, as an interpreter of this era, shows a lack of trust in man's rational abilities, and a detachment of the intellectual from the masses. He destroys the myth of a greater, united, and democratic Europe. Health (progress) loses its meaning and its equivalent becomes disease. As Spagnoletti aptly points out, "life leads us to death by way of the mystery of health."[58]

Italy had hoped that, from the bloodbath of the Carso, Piave, and Caporetto, there would have emerged a more trusting and self-confident generation. Instead, the ensuing nationalism in Italy—and in the rest of Europe—proved to be vacuous folly, totally unsuited to mankind's true needs. Shortly after the war and the euphoria of Trieste becoming part of Italy, the realization that the meager results were unworthy of the great sacrifices suffered during the conflagration, utterly discouraged those who had harbored hopes for a better world. They lost heart, became restless, convinced that life was empty, absurd, pointless. Man's inability to change society, his impotence and alienation, as well as an awareness that the power, wealth, and dishonesty of the privileged classes were completely at odds with the ignorance and poverty of the lower classes, all these things appeared to many as unjust and immoral. Added to this, the discoveries of Freud and Einstein further confused and disheartened those who still retained some hope. It was in this climate that Svevo was shaping his novel and interpreting his lost generation. "Life is hard and unjust," exclaims Zeno, and "man has found his way into it by mistake and does not really belong there" (299). In a Darwinian view of evolution, or even better declination, Zeno demystifies Trieste's merchants, underscoring with biting irony the absurdities of their business practices often conducted in a foolish manner. Of course, Zeno himself and his partner, two amateurs par excellence, typify this capricious world of business. What is remarkable is that Zeno is the only one to see behind the façade of commercial success, just as he is the only one to see clearly the illness that is everywhere. When he tries to make Guido stop speculating at the Bourse, he is told by the Malfentis that his father-in-law had made large sums of money on the market, and that they all look "upon gambling just as if it were any other kind of business" (324). We have already noted that health cannot analyze itself and that any attempt to analyze it converts it into disease. This is why Augusta and her equals see order and normalcy where Zeno with his introspective and perceptive nature sees illness. For him health is but an illusion.

Of course, we must take into account the apocalyptic ending of the novel in order to grasp the full meaning of life, disease, and death. Svevo, a truly modern visionary who would be ranked today among the ecologically minded conservationists, depicts the damage man has caused to his habitat:

> Our life today is poisoned to the root. Man has ousted the beasts and trees, has poisoned the air and filled up the open spaces. Worse things may happen. That melancholy and industrious animal—man—may discover new forces and harness them to his chariot. Some such danger is in the air. The result will be a great abundance—of human beings! Every square yard will be occupied by man. Who will be able then to cure us of the lack of air and space? The mere thought of it suffocates me. (397)

The patient is no longer Zeno, Tullio, or Ada. The patient has become modern man, capable of great but also horrible things. Man, as a rational and excitable being has lost the ability to be natural, spontaneous, and instinctive—thereby losing any hope for happiness. Zeno exemplifies "the tragic sense of life" of the Spanish philosopher Unamuno, whose sad comment on life is that "to live, is to suffer."

Chapter 7 includes the famous dream that has attracted so much critical attention. When Ada leaves Trieste for treatment in a nursing home in Bologna, Zeno has a very disturbing two-part dream: *Part 1*: Zeno, Augusta, and Ada are looking out of Mrs. Malfenti's kitchen window. Its frame is so narrow that Ada, who is standing between them and holding their arms, presses against Zeno. She has recovered from her illness and her features are normal again, though her eyes are cold. Her neck is covered with light curls [just as in Zeno's dream about Carla]. In spite of her coldness, she clings to Zeno who wonders why she is doing so. He is happy about her recovery and in an attempt to pay some attention to Augusta, he asks her where Basedow is. Augusta points to Basedow and they see him on the street being chased by a menacing crowd, shouting "Kill the charlatan!" [in Italian, *untore*].[59] Basedow appears as "an old beggar man, dressed in a stiff brocade cloak that was all in rags: a mane of untidy white hair, blown about by the wind, covered his massive head, and his eyes were starting from their sockets with fear, a look I had seen in wild beasts at bay, a menacing, fearful look" (290). *Part 2*: After a brief interlude, Zeno finds himself alone with Ada, on the steep stairs that lead up to the roof of his house. She faces him as if she intended to come down while he is going up. Zeno puts his arms around her legs and she bends toward him. Momentarily he thinks that she is ill again, but looking at her anxiously he succeeds in seeing her again healthy and beautiful. Ada tells him to go on in front of her, that she will follow him directly. As he turns eagerly to go down, he notices that the trapdoor to the roof is opening up and Basedow's head is peering through with a fearful and threatening face. Zeno runs away, but cannot remember if he was running in front of Ada, or trying to flee from her. At this point Zeno wakes up and narrates the dream to Augusta who is jealously pained by it, thinking that her husband is unhappy because of Ada's departure. Zeno tries to humor her, explaining that Basedow was the significant figure in the dream, and not Ada.

It is clear that his dream was inspired, in part, by some of Freud's own dreams, as reported in *The Interpretation of Dreams*. Basedow is the significant figure in Freud's two-part dream, which he titled *"My friend Otto was looking ill. His face was brown and he had protruding eyes."* In the dream Otto suffers from Basedow's disease and has precisely the same symptoms as Ada. Both, however, fail to develop a goitre which is typical in such an illness. In Freud's writings there are also numerous examples of "Staircase Dreams" that Svevo, no doubt, became familiar with when he translated the psychoanalyst's book into Italian. In one of these dreams we have an almost identical scenario: Freud walks up the stairs of his home and a woman comes down toward him.[60]

It is a highly dramatic dream that displays the conflicts Zeno has with his impulses and desires. On the whole, I tend to agree with Fonda's interpretation that the dream represents the unconscious telescoping of several experiences: Augusta symbolizes Zeno's brother, Ada his mother, and Basedow his father, sex, and evil, since it was he who had sex with the mother, resulting in the birth of the sibling brother. What characterizes the dream is anguish stemming from the presence of incestuous desires that come to the surface demanding satisfaction, and from the ensuing censure.[61]

Basedow clearly represents Zeno's father: the white hair, the large head that reflects the swelling caused by the cerebral edema that brought about his death. The menacing crowd is symbolic of Zeno's tumultuous and incestuous desires for his mother, as well as his resentment toward the emasculating parent—feelings he is unable to control. The narrow window frame and the need to squeeze (penetrate) into a narrow space are, according to Freud, among the commonest sexual symbols.[62] The neglect of Augusta reflects Zeno's feelings of sibling rivalry that he alone experiences without the others' awareness. He believes that he has been rejected by his mother—that is why Ada appears cold and detached—who, in fact, has no such feelings but, on the contrary, continues to love all her children. This explains why Ada (the mother) is holding onto both Zeno's and Augusta's (sibling) arms, and why she clings to Zeno's body.

In the second sequence are the three currents of sexuality: father, mother, and child—the classical oedipal triangle. Unlike the first oneiric segment, this one is clearly an Oedipus dream, the kind that Freud called "a disguised dream of sexual intercourse."[63] The climbing and the shape of the staircase, Ada's and Zeno's movement toward each other, the opening of the trapdoor, Zeno's embracing of the woman's legs, and finally her leaning toward him, are all clear indications of the sexual nature of the dream. Most notable is Augusta's absence in the dream [she is sleeping, however, next to the dreamer]. In both segments it is Ada who is making the advances on Zeno, it is she who leans on him at the window, holds his arm, and tells him what to do. He follows her command eagerly, although there appears to be a momentary reluctance when he thinks that she might be ill again. In this oneiric segment Basedow chases Zeno, who is discovered in a very compromising situation with the mother. This takes us back to another dream, when Zeno was a child and his mother undressed him and made him lie down next to her on a sofa. The animalistic image of the old beggar typically symbolizes the dreamer's interdicting father. According to Wilhelm Stekel (1868–1940), one of the founders and theoreticians of the psychoanalytic movement, wild beasts, beggars, and the "man all tattered and torn" are some of the symbols of "parapathy" [neuroses] and indicate a "judgement of moral depreciation."[64] When Basedow shows himself through the trapdoor, Zeno is obviously frightened and runs away. However, it appears that he is not running away from Basedow, but rather from Ada. The old man's "feeble legs and his poor thin body" (291) show that he could hardly run after Zeno. Saccone indicates that Zeno's intentions are not to make love to his mother, but that he wants to be stopped.[65] This explains why Zeno does not object and also why the dream comes to an end.

Basedow, as Zeno admits, is the significant figure in this dream. With his white hair and threatening look he is a projection of the father figure, both emasculating and vengeful for the son's transgressions and failure to meet the parent's expectations. He represents the same prophetic man who smote the famous blow on his son's cheek. Therefore, when we try to identify the etiology of Zeno's illness, we must go beyond the oedipal question since everything seems to revolve around the father figure and the night he died which "was the most important in [Zeno's] life" (41). Saccone is convinced that "the crisis of the father, of the law of which he should be a guarantor, this is the sickness which is the central point of the novel."[66]

A Psychical Adventure

Chapter 8, composed of three dated diary entries, and bearing the title "Psychoanalysis," brings to a conclusion this rather lengthy but always intriguing novel. It is primarily an indictment of psychoanalysis because it has been a failure as a cure for Zeno's conscience—and whatever else he may be suffering from. Zeno has been led on a hopeless search for the roots of his difficulties, and after almost two years with Dr. S., he finally concludes that he is no better off than before; in fact, his condition has gotten worse. Zeno has given up psychoanalysis because the doctor has at last diagnosed his illness as the Oedipus Complex: "I was in love with my mother and wanted to murder my father" (367). Zeno is certain that the doctor is wrong because he has not been cured of it. He is fully aware of Freud's theory that sexual trauma is the basis of our neuroses. He also knows that Freud treated in the main hysterical women with problems. Zeno is quite the opposite. There is absolutely nothing wrong with his sex drive and its gratification. On the contrary, he seems to do rather well! Zeno quits because there is nothing more to be gained from Dr. S. and his analysis. Furthermore, he is no longer able to make new discoveries and experience fresh sensations during analysis. But above all, war has broken out and has brought to a stop all of Zeno's activities. Although he is no longer seeing the doctor, he resumes keeping a diary because he thinks that it "may help to work off the mischief that the treatment has done" him (366). It is an ultimate attempt to cure himself and make some sense out of life. Zeno recounts two dreamlike visions dealing with his brother and his own competitive feelings toward him. Another deals with his attachment to his mother and his father's resentment.[67] Unable to find any relief for his ailments, he goes to a medical doctor who analyzes his urine. Zeno is elated because at last he is "going to have a true analysis after all this psychoanalysis," which he thinks should be called instead a "psychical adventure" (379). After two weeks of such recollections, Zeno decides to avoid dreams and memories, fearing that by "dint of studying my psyche, I only infected myself with new diseases" (380).

War has finally reached Zeno and he is separated from his family who has found safety in Italy. Olivi is away and Zeno must take charge of the business, which takes up his whole day. One year has passed since he last wrote in his notebook. Dr. S. has written him from Switzerland, asking to send him what he has written up to this moment. Zeno does this gladly so that the doctor will know what he thinks of him and of his treatment. Zeno tells us that these are not confessions of weakness and ill health, but an account of "perfect health":

I am cured! I not only have no desire to practice psychoanalysis, but no need to do so. . . . I really am well, absolutely well. For some time past I have realized that being well is a matter of conviction, and that it is a mere day-dreamer's fantasy to try and get cured otherwise than by self-persuasion. Of course I have pains from time to time, but what do they matter when my health is perfect? . . . Pain and love—the whole of life, in short—cannot be looked on as a disease just because they make us suffer. (396)

And so, notwithstanding his father's mistrust of his son's business abilities, it is Zeno's business that finally cures him. As he watches the convulsion of the world, he suddenly begins to buy anything that is available and sells it at a great profit, making a fortune for himself. In essence, Zeno concludes that there is no cure for life. To live is to suffer. The only remedy for our suffering is death, and he is not yet ready. Therefore, he declares himself cured. In this resolution to life he follows in the footsteps of another Zeno, Zeno of Citium (ca. 336–264 B.C.), the founder of Stoicism. He and his followers believed that man conquers the world by overcoming his own impulses; that man gains self-control by showing indifference *(adiaphora)*[68] to pleasure and pain. True happiness can be achieved only if we have a state of inner tranquillity, a state of mental composure. If health is not possible, then we must despise it. The secret of Zeno's inner peace is not to equate his successes with his desires, but rather to lower his desires to the level of his successes. Zeno Cosini, however, is ready to give up the suffering in life, but not the pleasures.

The merits of psychoanalysis remain inconclusive. Even though Zeno is determined to prove that it is not a science, and that it is a failure in his own particular case, the fact that he continues to write in his diary and submits it to the analyst is sufficient proof that it has, indeed, some merit for him. The fact that Zeno—war or no war—is able to make peace with himself and with life, that he gains sufficient confidence and self-esteem to face life and its adversities—these circumstances indicate that his analysis has not been a waste of time and energy. For Svevo's assessment of psychoanalysis, we must make use of his correspondence with Valerio Jahier, an admirer who was considering undergoing psychoanalysis and eventually committed suicide. In one letter Svevo writes: "Freud was a great man, but more for us novelists than for the ill." In another, he points out that Freud himself had doubts about his therapy and that "in literature Freud is far more interesting. I only wish I had undergone a cure with him. My novel would have been more complete."[69] Fonda sums it up best when he writes that psychoanalysis is both a success and a failure, inasmuch as "it explains the causes of our suffering, but a failure because it cannot cure us."[70] True, psychoanalysis is a failure because Zeno continues to suffer from his daily toils and afflictions. Indeed, he cannot be considered clinically cured because he consciously refuses to accept or understand the analyst's final diagnosis. Yet, success can also be measured by the degree of insight Zeno has gained into the unconscious motivations for his behavior and thoughts, but above all, by his ability to apply this newly gained experience to solving his life problems. Zeno is not cured, he has only gotten better. At the end of his analysis he emerges as a whole and authentic human being, fulfilled and even contented, able to work and function in society as well as anyone else—perhaps even better, because of his capacity to laugh at life.

What did Svevo wish to convey with the title of the novel? The English title, *Confessions of Zeno,* is appropriate, but does not quite capture the full essence of the Italian *coscienza*. True, Zeno confesses his past memories and the most intimate details of his life with an amazing candor, even when they are contemptible and revolting. Anyone else would have taken the greatest pains to conceal them. Of course, we never know when he is telling the truth, lying, or just simply creating fiction for us and the "ignoble" doctor. At times, his confessions are strange mixture of unflattering self-revelation and pretentious justification for his actions. The idea of "confessions" is appropriate inasmuch as Zeno deals with hidden and highly private matters, intensely personal and introspective experiences. They are revelations, disclosures, admissions of fault, and declarations of guilt. Indeed, Zeno confesses to his analyst in person and in his diary.

In Italian the word *coscienza* (conscience, consciousness) has a multiple meaning. Not only does it give a sense of right and wrong, an awareness of moral values, but also an awareness of oneself, of one's actions and goals. It also expresses an inner awareness, a perception of psychological and spiritual matters. Actually, any of these definitions could easily be applied to Zeno who is constantly striving to know himself. The answer lies, perhaps, in Freud's theory of psychoanalysis: "The whole of psychoanalytic theory is in fact built up on the perception of the resistance exerted by the patient when we try to make him conscious of his unconscious."[71] Obviously, in this psychoanalytic confession, Zeno becomes conscious of his unconscious. The diary makes visible the invisible inner life of Zeno as he searches and discovers the circumstances to which he is reacting and, to a lesser degree, his own motivations. The diary is an account of the nonverbalized and subconscious life of Zeno, its unreliable author, whose statements we question, but whose unconscious, nevertheless, peeps through the gaps of his fabrications.

The novel ends with an apocalyptic prophesy which today, after Hiroshima and Nagasaki, has a far more immediate and terrifying impact on man living in the atomic age, than it did when first written. Man and his horrible machines and inventions have caused such a degeneration in life that "we need something more than psychoanalysis to help us" (398). In a desperate cry of rage at human folly, Zeno wonders if civilization ought not start anew, with a clean slate. Perhaps a cataclysmic explosion produced by man's inventions will lead us back to health:

When all the poison gases are exhausted, a man, made like all other men of flesh and blood, will in the quiet of his room invent an explosive of such potency that all the explosives in existence will seem like harmless toys beside it. And another man, made in his image and in the image of all the rest, but a little weaker than them, will steal that explosive and crawl to the center of the earth with it, and place it just where he calculates it would have the maximum effect. There will be a tremendous explosion, but no one will hear it and the earth will return to its nebulous state and go wandering through the sky, free at last from parasites and disease. (398)

Chapter Five
Svevo's Secret Passion: The Theater

Although Svevo finally obtained his rightful and long overdue recognition as a novelist, as a dramatist he failed to gain any notice except for a short-lived performance of *Terzetto spezzato (Broken Triangle)* in 1927. Considering the absolute indifference of critics and friends alike, one wonders why Svevo continued to write plays [fifteen extant works] throughout his life.[1]

For Svevo, literature was both his vice and his fate. Through his writings he felt that he could learn to understand himself better and achieve therapeutic benefits.[2] In his plays he hoped to analyze and reveal the drama of the individual and of his society, to understand the complicated and baffling aspects of human nature. He thought that through the theater he could communicate more directly the themes that interested and haunted him. Svevo remarked to his friend Silvio Benco that "the theater is the form of forms, the only one in which life can be transmitted through direct and precise channels."[3]

Svevo's theater, contrary to the opinion of many critics, was neither sporadic, occasional, secondary, nor marginal to his novels.[4] Nor was it a mere pastime or exercise, if we consider that he persevered in playwriting from 1880 until his death in 1928, and that he wrote his novels and short stories only after he had experienced continuous disappointments with his plays. The theater was his first authentic love and nothing appealed to him as much as the mastering of this literary genre.

Under the influence of Zola and the programmatic lessons of naturalism and verism, young Svevo attempted to present, as frankly and objectively as possible, the problems and conditions of contemporary life, and to portray the debilitating effects of an unfavorable environment. He firmly believed that his "scene di vita borghese" (scenes from middle-class life) must be true to life in the minutest detail, and that everything which happens on the stage must give the impression of reality. The plots of his early theatrical works—except for *Ariosto governatore* (Ariosto the governor)—were primarily concerned with financial and marital problems: classic adulterous triangles, bizarre reversals of situations, money difficulties, and intrigues. His preoccupations with "reality" led to an excess of clutter on the stage, to countless characters superficially delineated, to a minimum of development, to a lack of suspense and excitement, and finally to a negation of theatricality. By imposing restrictions of content and structure upon his dramatic works, Svevo limited himself to a meticulous observation of detail without going deeper into the psychology of the characters, leaving unsaid the most important things. In the pursuit of a veristic credo he applied his theories with more courage than ability. He lost sight of the fact that there is a difference between art and life, between a sense of heightened reality and reality itself, that "the whole art of the theater is precisely the art of illusion."[5]

In addition to following the dictums of verismo, Svevo employed the most accepted and conventional dramatic techniques of the period. In style, structure, language, and theme he imitated the most prominent French, Spanish, and Italian dramatists of the bourgeois theater: Émile Augier (1820–1889), Eugène Scribe (1791–1861), Henry Becque (1837–1899), Sem Benelli (1877–1909), Giuseppe Giacosa (1847–1906), Marco Praga (1862–1929), Sabatino Lopez (1867–1951), and the Quintero Brothers, Álvarez (1871–1938) and Joaquín (1873–1944). However, his early plays were inferior to his models, owing to his youth and artistic naïveté, and he was at first unable to be innovative in the theater or to alter the purpose of playwriting so that it would reveal character and inner thought. Whereas in the novel Svevo prepared the advent of a new prose, a new style, and a new approach, in the theater he kept up with the popular trends of the time; he did not have the vision or the courage to oppose them. However, the merit of his early plays is that they suggest, at least, the makings of an original writer: they contain the seeds of the more mature Svevo and presage nearly all the elements of his future work.[6] It is only in his later plays that we find what Giacomo Debenedetti considered Svevo's strength: the analytical corrosiveness of his narrative texture.[7]

Ariosto governatore (Aristo as governor), an unfinished historical play written when Svevo was only eighteen, betrays the influence of German romantic tragedy, of Shakespeare's *Hamlet,* as well as of the historical plays of Paolo Ferrari (1822–1889) and Paolo Giacometti (1816–1882), rather than the literary creed of realism he later adopted. Also apparent is the stylistic influence of Giacosa, who with his drama *Una partita a scacchi (A Game of Chess),* had tried to revive the use of the *versi martelliani* (Alexandrine heroic verses used in Old French romances). Svevo began his brief seventy-two-line fragment in February 1880. It consists of a long dialogue between Lodovico Ariosto, the Renaissance author of the *Orlando Furioso,* and Mario Equicola, a pupil of Marsilio Ficino's Neoplatonic school of philosophy. In the dialogue Ariosto complains about the loss of his youth, whereas he finds his friend Equicola still looking young and fit. Ariosto complains not only about a real and physical old age but more important, about spiritual and mental aging. No matter how hard the poet tries to convey his pain and suffering, Equicola, lacking the sensitivity to grasp meaningful ideas, cannot understand Ariosto's anguish. At last, Ariosto can no longer control his contempt for Equicola and accuses him of being a calculating spirit who measures everything in life in numerical terms.

Although this embryonic play is lacking in theatricality—there are hardly any stage directions, the characters are barely delineated, and the lines are mediocre, as Svevo himself pointed out—we can, nevertheless, identify many of the themes that Svevo was going to develop in his future writings: the hardships of life, the hypocrisy of society, man's inability to communicate, a concern for justice and equality. Above all, we see a tendency for introspective analysis on the part of man in crisis and in search of identity, as well as an acute concern for aging in both physical and existential terms, what Luti calls "the incurable contrast between youth and old age."[8]

Although Svevo ended, rather abruptly, the fragment of *Ariosto governatore* and never completed it,[9] he did not destroy it, as he had all his previous works, despite his dissatisfaction with it.[10] After this poetic experiment, Svevo never again wrote in verse. Indeed, he even showed some dislike for poetry.[11] Apparently, he felt that it was not possible for him to convey a true picture of life in verse since the genre did not lend itself readily to the characteristics of his art—intuition, psychology, and analysis.

Le ire di Giuliano (Giuliano's anger), written in 1881, a short one-act play set in a typical petit-bourgeois environment, follows the course of a family quarrel that results in an apparent happy ending. Although it has the light weight of a *pochade* (sketch) it nevertheless deals with social and moral questions that offer critical and polemic interest.

Lucia, the young and attractive wife of a rich butcher named Giuliano, leaves her husband after a violent quarrel and goes home to her mother's, planning to go back to her teaching position. But Lucia soon learns that she is not a free agent: her decision means certain ruin for her family since they are all financially dependent upon her husband. Giuliano makes his entrance and tells *his* version of the incident in human and realistic terms that reveal him as a pathetic figure, the victim of enormous pressures from the business world.

The central theme of this play is the inexorable power of money, which controls life to such an extent that it is much stronger than personal sentiments and family ties. The play is therefore an indictment of middle-class society, as seen by young Svevo who grew up in an environment where business transactions left little room for human feelings. Lucia typifies the social injustices that women suffer due to arranged marriages based on materialistic considerations. She is the victim of her husband's injustices and difficulties as well as of the needs of her family, dependent for its sustenance on her behavior as a model wife. She finally succumbs to the realization that she, like Nora Helmer in Ibsen's play, must live in a "doll's house."

Le ire dei Giuliano has all the potential for being a good play, but it fails because the author's propensity for excessive verbosity interferes with the action. The effect on the reader or spectator is that the story is narrated rather than acted out on stage. Despite its conventionality and the relatively brief span of action, the play, at times, is fast-moving, humorous, and ironic, and the degree of character development shows that Svevo regarded character as more important than action. One notes the psychological ability with which Svevo analyzes and probes Giuliano's frustrations and anger, Lucia's dilemma, and her family's indifference to it. Despite its technical and artistic imperfections, it is a young playwright's attempt to find his way and his own mode of expression.

The one-act *Una commedia inedita* (An unpublished comedy) is a lightweight comedy, as its subtitle *Scherzo drammatico in un atto* (Dramatic Scherzo in One Act) indicates. We do not know the exact date of composition, although Umbro Apollonio places it between 1880 and 1890. Most likely it was written shortly after *Le ire de Giuliano* (ca. 1881), when Svevo was still limiting himself to one-act plays. With its central themes of adultery and the unhappiness of women, it follows the conventional form of the bourgeois theater of Giacosa, Becque, and Praga.

Elena Penini refuses to follow her husband, who, for reasons of work, has to move to Venice. Unable to accept his wife's flimsy excuses, he suspects that she is having an affair with Adolfo, a young, aspiring naturalistic playwright. In spite of his jealousy, Penini is forced to admit that he has failed to fulfill his duties as a husband, and that Elena now feels unneeded and bored with marital life. When Penini realizes that Elena has not been unfaithful, he begs forgiveness, promising to seek her advice and treat her as an equal.

Una commedia inedita reveals Svevo's concern with the problems of women in nineteenth-century society. He shows us the inner world of a woman who has been taken for granted both by her husband and her intended lover. Both consider her an object and ignore her spiritual worth and needs. In Elena's case we see how she desperately attempts to find a meaning for her life, to compensate for being childless and for her husband's neglect by toying with the idea of giving herself to another man. Her intended lover, however, turns out to be even more mediocre than her husband. The play ends where it began—on a note of emotional bankruptcy. One hopes that Penini will learn from the episode and will truly mend his ways, but, in view of his insensitivity, one remains skeptical.

This *scherzo*, presented in a humorous but pitiless way, might have developed into a successful and subtle drama of feminine psychology. Like Ibsen, Svevo is not so much a suffragist as an advocate for a maximum of personal realization in a given social milieu. In spite of the limited characterization and the conventionality and naïveté of the ideas and action (the husband hides in an adjoining room hoping to entrap his wife), one cannot dismiss Svevo's psychological acumen, the vivacity of some of the dialogue, and the unusual sarcastic humor that pervades the play. *Una commedia inedita* proves again that Svevo's early theatrical works were the matrix for his later novels and that these characters presaged those of Alfonso Nitti, Emilio Brentani, and even Angiolina. We find in them the same sense of failure and despair so typical of his antiheroic protagonists.

Le teorie del Conte Alberto (Count Albert's theories) is a two-act thesis play written around 1884, most likely as a result of Svevo having reviewed two books dealing with naturalism.[12] Although an avowed naturalist, Svevo did not accept all of the ideas associated with the more deterministic brand of French naturalism. In this play, bearing the subtitle *Scherzo drammatico in due atti* (Dramatic Scherzo in Two Acts), Svevo rejected the atavistic theories popular at that time, and tried to show the danger involved when these doctrines are pushed to an extreme.

In act 1 Count Alberto, a naive pseudoscientist, falls in love with Anna Termigli and asks Lorenzo, his old friend and the girl's legal guardian, for permission to marry her. When the count learns of Anna's questionable family past—her father killed himself in jail and her mother had been unfaithful—he has second thoughts. In act 2 Lorenzo reveals to his friend that he is Anna's natural father but that she does not know this. He convinces him of the absurdity of his scientific theories: there are hereditary traits that can be overcome by education and good example. As Alberto comes to understand that his speculations on heredity work better in theory than in practice, he must choose between his own happiness and the repudiation of his scientific ideas. His heart gains the upper hand and his ideas are not entirely destroyed because after all Anna *is* the daughter of Lorenzo, a distinguished gentleman, whose noble traits she inevitably has inherited.

In writing this play Svevo had not intended to criticize naturalism per se, but only some of its theories. During this period he was completely convinced by the artistic tenets of this school and impressed by the works of Emile Zola, whose use of deterministic postulates provided his work with a coherent structure. In fact, in an 1884 book review he defended Zola against the attacks of Edoardo Scarfoglio (1860–1917) who in his *Il libro di Don Chisciotte* had criticized Zola's naturalistic creed. "Zola is not a scientist," wrote Svevo, "but an artist who describes life by making use of a scientific theory that explains it to him." In the same article Svevo also dealt with theories of heredity, pointing out that they had taken the place that Fate had held in Greek tragedy.[13]

Like *Le ire di Giuliano, Le teorie del Conte Alberto* is ineffective dramatically primarily because of a lack of action. It consists of little more than exits and entrances; of polemical discussions revolving around deterministic theories; of characters, although realistically drawn, not fully developed, distant, and unconvincing. Although Svevo shows a firm grasp of the positivistic ideas he discusses, he does so with a rather clumsy and awkward style that, at times, makes it difficult to understand what is being said. The real import of this play lies in Svevo's insistence that human vitality must not be suppressed by the opinions of conventional society or by pseudoscience. Ironically, these men of science—who "study the actions of man, but not man"—are the ones who theorize the most, but act contrary to their convictions at the first contact with reality.

Prima del ballo (Before the ball), probably written shortly before its publication in 1891, is the only play published during Svevo's lifetime.[14] It is a monodrama, following the classical tradition in vogue at the end of the nineteenth century. This sort of theatrical expression in monologue form was popular for recitals given on special occasions, highlighting as it did the actor's interpretative talents. These monodramas were also performed during the intermission of regular full-length plays or, at times, as a prologue.

Carla is the only character in the play. While waiting for her aunt to take her to a ball, she confides to the audience her private thoughts about society, her family, and other participants at the ball. She reminisces about her first ball and her disappointments; how bored she was because she had followed her mother's advice to be modest and circumspect. Determined not to repeat her mistakes, she resolves to succeed in a world of fools and imbeciles, plan her own techniques of seduction, and avoid all the men who are useless to her purpose.

Prima del ballo is a successful dramatic piece in which, from the very beginning, Svevo offers various dimensions to the situation and to the absent characters, showing in a sarcastic but amusing tone a world torn by contrasts, where people appear divided by indifference, self-indulgence, and lack of feelings. Svevo, the humorist, weaves his truth in this insinuating monodrama. Short as it is, the play documents Svevo's power of psychological observation. This monologue affords us an insight into the nature of the imagination Svevo lends his characters, who are typically immobilized by their introspective musings. In contrast, Carla succeeds in becoming stronger, more determined, and courageous than before. Reminiscent of Strindberg's *The Stronger* (1889), another psychological case history in which the conflict revolves around the question of who is stronger, who is superior, *Prima del ballo* is a tour de force and potentially a superb acting vehicle in which the secondary action takes place in the present, but serves as a background for the analysis of the primary action occurring in the past.

Il ladro in casa: Scene della vita borghese (There's a thief among us: Scenes from bourgeois life), a short four-act play, was probably written around 1892. Apparently Svevo gave the manuscript as a gift to his friend Giulio Piazza (1863–1934), a Triestine vernacular poet, who in 1932 published it in *La Porta Orientale,* a Triestine magazine. Apollonio places it between 1880 and 1890, whereas both Mrs. Svevo and Piazza thought that it was written in 1895. The fact that Svevo signed it E. Samigli, a pseudonym used until the publication of *Una vita* in 1892, would indicate that it must have been written between 1890 and 1892.

The plot was taken from a real event that occurred in the Schmitz family. Some time before 1870 Svevo's aunt Giuseppina (or Peppina) Schmitz fell in love with Ignazio Tedeschi, whom Elio Schmitz describes as small and unattractive, a degenerate loafer who spent all his time reading novels. Svevo's father opposed the marriage, but finally consented, giving Tedeschi a dowry of ten thousand florins with which he opened an oil store. The loss of this capital created great financial difficulties for Francesco Schmitz's business. The morning following the wedding celebration, Aunt Peppina woke up to find that her husband had pawned everything they owned. Nine months later Tedeschi disappeared with all their money, abandoning his pregnant wife penniless.[15]

Similarly, in the play Ignazio wishes to marry Carla because of her considerable dowry. Her brother Carlo, suspicious of Ignazio because he insists on receiving the woman's dowry on the day of the wedding, tries to convince his sister not to marry the rogue, but she is blinded by her desires and insists on the marriage. Carlo is forced to yield and puts his business in jeopardy in order to provide the dowry. After the wedding Ignazio deceives everyone: he defrauds his Uncle Marco and Carlo; he has an affair with Elena, his wife's best friend; and finally, he swindles Elena's husband, a frustrated man of letters. Carla becomes her husband's silent accomplice, helping him make plans to flee the country, not knowing that he is planning to take Elena with him as well as a large sum of illegally obtained money. The police foil Ignazio's escape, and the fugitive hides in Carlo's home, only to be discovered by Carla, who promises not to give him away provided he give back the money. But just when Ignazio thinks he is free, the police arrive and in the ensuing chase he falls from a roof and dies.

Il ladro in casa is a very important play for the study of Svevo's theater because it foreshadows most of the ingredients that are characteristic of his novels. Svevo's psychological probing and analysis, albeit without the same depth and sensitivity as in his novels, bring the characters close to Zeno's world. The perceptive study of human weakness reappears more ruthlessly in *Una vita,* where the psychology of the defeated—the *inetti*—prevails. This drama is an open, critical, social analysis of the Triestine middle class; the subtitle, *Scene di vita borghese,* reveals at the onset the author's intention to examine its moral corruption and avidity.

According to Michele Amato, all the characters "are nailed to the calvary of their inaction, confined to the narrow limits of a desperate loneliness; they only know the joy of things that could have been and that, because of their own lack of faith in themselves, will never materialize."[16] Even Ignazio, who appears to be indifferent and stronger than the others, brings on his own end by leading a life he knows to be self-destructive. A scoundrel who remains consistent and true to his nature throughout the play, Ignazio easily overcomes all that stands in his way because he is completely amoral, without principles or regard for others. He is somewhat like Guido Speier in Svevo's novel *La coscienza di Zeno*: both are typical of those who always have a great need for money and who succeed in obtaining it with remarkable ease, either by lawful or unlawful means. He is a thief of goods and money and also a plunderer of feelings and sentiments. Carlo, on the other hand, has the temperament of a dreamer. He is extremely good, but this goodness has an ambiguous quality which makes us wonder if it may not be caused by incompetence or greed.

In contrast to the men, the women in *Il ladro in casa* show remarkable strength and determination. They are not torn by the doubts and uncertainties that weaken and immobilize their men, but succeed in making bold, if foolish, decisions, regardless of the consequences. Although Carla's passion enslaves her to Ignazio, it also gives her strength and makes her come to life both as a woman and as a character. Ignazio represents for her sensual pleasure as well as freedom from the tedious life she has led in her brother's house. She has no illusions about Ignazio, yet she is determined to hold onto him and even become his accomplice. At the end of the play she garners sufficient courage and nobility of spirit to free herself. Elena, married to a man who writes "big books that nobody reads," is childless and bored by her older husband, who lives in a world withdrawn from the realities of life. Dissatisfied with her own life, Elena works her way into other people's homes to observe, to scheme, and to live their lives vicariously in the hope of escaping her own miserable existence. This propensity makes her an easy mark for the predatory Ignazio, who seduces her. Like

Emma Bovary, Elena is determined to rebel against the constraining social conventions of her class, though she lacks the courage and romantic spirit of Flaubert's heroine. In fact, when Ignazio's plans are thwarted, she does not hesitate to return to her husband, resigned to suffer honorably rather than be exposed to public scorn.

Like many of Svevo's plays, *Il ladro in casa* is pervaded by the theme of money, by characters in constant search of wealth and social position. In this play Svevo manages to contrast the usual triangle plot with that of economic interests, which turn out to be much more dynamic and dramatic. Indeed, the money motif becomes an inseparable part of family relationships: Carla's marriage is dealt with as if it were a commercial transaction; Carlo lends money to Ignazio only because he hopes to make a profit; even Emilio, who seems so remote from the world of business, is induced to give Ignazio some money with the expectation of a quick gain; and finally, both Carla and Elena are pursued by Ignazio primarily on account of their money.

Unlike the previous plays, *Il ladro in casa* is not bogged down by excessive dialogue and inaction. On the contrary, it is full of action both on and off stage. Its swift pace arouses and sustains the interest of the viewer and reader. The total effect is serious, but also comic due to Svevo's biting irony. From the initial scenes the style is terse, vivid, and entertaining. The characters are lifelike and so ably manipulated that the plot progresses with dramatic effectiveness.

When Svevo wrote *Atto unico* (A one-act play), there existed in Italy, alongside the naturalist bourgeois drama, a dialect theater primarily written in the Venetian dialect, whose main exponent was Giacinto Gallina. *Atto unico,* written in 1913, is a lively farce in Triestine dialect; it follows the tradition of the eighteenth-century comic playwright Carlo Goldoni (1707–93) and conveys a true and vivid picture of Svevo's Trieste.[17] Perhaps Svevo's artistic need led him to write in Triestine. In view of his difficulties with standard Italian, it was only natural that he would find it easier and much more rewarding to express himself in his native melodic dialect. Svevo presents with good-natured irony the customs, affectations, language, vices, and virtues of the varied and spirited people of his city. The main attributes of *Atto unico* are the witty female characters, the perceptive social satire, and the spontaneous, free and easy dialogue.

This short play concerns the difficulties of finding good help and how a housewife is even willing to accept crooks as servants. Svevo ridicules Amalia's hypocrisy because she is more interested in having servants for social standing rather than for their practical use. For her, being a lady simply means having at her command a string of servants, ready and eager to obey. This explains why she is determined to do anything in order to keep them, including the dirty work of the house. In her pretentiousness, she loses sight of the fact that she is merely the wife of a modest storekeeper.

Svevo's theatrical genius comes into its own with this hilarious ridicule of affectation and false elegance. The plot is constructed with admirable fluency, and the dramatic turn of events takes place with an air of naturalness and logic. Nothing is strained or improbable. Svevo finds humor in the prankish intrigue and buffoonery, as well as in the characters' behavior, their pretense, and self-importance. As in Goldoni's comedies, Svevo's brilliantly handled satire is directed with equal derision and amiable irony at both master and servant. Still, he shows a preference for the common people and an admiration for the manner in which the servants (thieves) try to resolve their problems. Above all, he admires their humanity, their simplicity, practicality, and discerning cleverness.

Un marito (A Husband), a lengthy three-act drama completed in 1903, is perhaps Svevo's most important and successful play. It is also his most engaging theatrical work because of its complexity and analytical inquiries. *Un marito* was written during an important and fruitful year for Italian theater, which was still completely devoted to the school of verismo: Gabriele D'Annunzio (1863–1938) was staging his *Francesca da Rimini* and *La figlia di Iorio (The Daughter of Iorio)*; Camillo Traversi (1857–1934) was writing his social plays; Gerolamo Rovetta (1852–1910) was making use of verismo in his historical plays; Sabatino Lopez was in full swing with his light, ironic, and moralistic plays; and Marco Praga, the dramatist par excellence of adultery, was writing *La crisi (The Crisis)*. The theme of adultery, against the background of the rising industrial bourgeoisie, was dominant. Although *Un marito* revolves around an adulterous situation, it soon becomes clear that Svevo's verismo is quite different and detached—if not opposite—from that of other plays of the period. *Un marito* is a complicated psychological play. The plot, although interesting and original, is only a pretext for Svevo's analysis of the protagonists and their milieu.

Federico, the husband of the title, killed his first wife, Clara, for infidelity. He lives with the obsessive presence of Clara, whom he still loves although she has been dead for over ten years; everything that has to do with Clara becomes for him a source of pain, anxiety, and, above all, morbid fascination. It is not her death that causes him torment, but rather her betrayal of his love. His second wife, Bice, tries to make him forget the past, but he is obsessively tied to Clara's mother, Arianna, by a pathological dependence and affection. In his infantile and imaginary desires he would like to find in Arianna the embodiment of her dead daughter: "She is not just an old woman! She is the most important person in the world for me . . . Everyone thought that I was anxiously expecting the judges' verdict. Instead, only one important person existed for me: Clara's mother . . . She was there as a witness; but for me as my judge" (255).

When he is presented with letters indicating that Bice too has betrayed him, no longer sure of himself as a dispenser of justice, he faces an unresolvable dilemma: Was he justified in killing Clara, and if so, would it be justice to kill Bice as well? Since he has not been absolved by Arianna, how can he spare Bice and still try to justify himself in the old woman's eyes? His only concern is to be able to face Arianna, who has told him: "You have killed my daughter because she was betraying you. Now you must kill this one too because she has betrayed you as well" (255). He resolves his predicament without having to take any drastic measures: he convinces himself that Bice is innocent. He asks her for forgiveness as a defeated man, destroyed by his passion and violence.

Federico is the victim of a turbulent destiny that persecutes him mercilessly. Like a Greek tragic figure he is in the power of a "capricious and unpredictable fate," which has caused his past to repeat itself. As in Shakespeare's *Othello,* we find an intense study of jealousy where the passions of love, lust, and hate are pushed to an extreme, driving the characters to their doom. In both cases false accusations cause the protagonists to have doubts about their masculinity and their good name. Federico kills and is ready to kill again in the belief that he is performing an act of justice. His tragic flaw may be described best in Othello's lamentation to be "one that loved not wisely but too well."

Arianna is portrayed as a despairing and tragic Hecabe, lamenting the untimely death of her daughter. She is also presented as a modern Fury, eager to avenge and torment Federico for his crime against her own flesh and blood. She is kept alive solely by the hate she feels toward Federico, who has failed to show her any remorse. She loathes his self-righteous conviction that he has killed justly, and that he is ready to do it again. She accuses him of two crimes: "You killed Clara and you tried to convince me, her mother, that she deserved being killed" (229). She appears as a minister of divine justice, as she dramatically apostrophizes Federico: "This is the hand of God in whom you don't believe and who is striking you and freeing me" (230).

The last scene of act 1, the most dramatic and powerful of the play, is filled with deep humanity and pathos. We find this contradictory and strong mother crying and despairing for her daughter's sin and tragic end. She too feels betrayed by Carla's actions, but as a mother she cannot withhold her forgiveness. In addition to her thirst for revenge, she is torn by an uncontrollable love for Federico: "But instead you killed her and I knew no longer whether I loved you or hated you; and today I still don't know" (232).

Bice is a sad and pathetic figure compelled to accept a secondary role to her dead rival. The fall of this strong and impulsive character into a most absurd, unnatural, and cruel position—she must play the role of Clara—gives the play a sinister and powerful dramatic impact. Bice is an Ibsenesque figure struggling toward the affirmation of her own right to be loved. Like Rebecca West of *Rosmersholm,* who has set out to become the second wife and inspiration to an unhappy and tormented man, Bice too is gradually broken down by a force greater than she. She is compelled to assume various masks—wife/sister, wife/mother, wife/nurse, and even wife/daughter—in order to remain at the side of her husband whom she loves in spite of everything. However, this love proves incapable of saving her or Federico as they both yield to Arianna, the contradictory and ambiguous symbol of love and hate. Finally, Bice submits to the shock of being embraced as a daughter by a woman who hates her. At the end of the play, her strength gone, Bice is reduced to a marionette in Federico's hands.

Through a blending of dramaturgical elements, concentration of plot, penetrating diagnosis, and, above all, intense character portrayal, *Un marito* stands as one of Svevo's finest plays. The originality of Svevo's art, which gives the play an explosive quality, lies in the dramatist's search for a moral standpoint. And yet something is missing: one senses that the conflicts have been resolved facilely, and that the resolutions are more apparent than real. Svevo himself was not satisfied with act 3 and turned for help and advice to his friend Silvio Benco.[18] He revised the ending, but was unable to achieve the desired effect. The problem stems from the inexplicable and unexpected catharsis that occurs in this act. Perhaps Svevo wanted to show his perception of life's continuity, his bright view of the future.

Another flaw is the length of the play. Moreover, the copious dialogue at times fails to express fully the drama and vitality of the protagonists' emotions. Svevo's propensity to compose contorted phrases, his wordiness, and lack of emotional speech rhythms mar the drama's performability. Although Svevo was a regular habitué of the theater and a dramatic critic, he failed to learn how to write for actors and to create a sharp and daring dialogue that would be actable and at the same time reveal a wider range of feelings and motivations among the characters.

L'avventura di Maria (Maria's adventure), a three-act play with a simple plot, focuses on the conflict between two different conceptions of love and marriage: that of the traditional and faithful wife, and that of a modern, artistic, and free woman. It also concerns the contrasts between two different societies: that of the artist and that of the commercial middle class. *L'avventura di Maria* progresses on two planes: on one we have a penetrating psychological study of the characters and of the relationships within the Galli home; on the other, a satire and indictment of the provinciality of Triestine middle-class society. Maria, a modern woman who has thrown off the yoke of submission imposed on women by society, no longer has to assert herself because she has become a successful and acclaimed concert violinist. Nevertheless, when she returns home to her native city of Trieste, she becomes aware for the first time of her unfulfilled womanhood and begins to doubt herself and her art. She is torn between the tranquillity that seems to reign in her friend Giulia's home—symbolized by her friend's loom—and her own adventurous life as a gypsy in the pursuit of liberty and art—symbolized by her violin. Maria is fully aware that Giulia's happiness in her marriage to Alberto, a self-styled Don Giovanni, is based upon a series of compromises and false appearances. She reveals Alberto's infidelity to Giulia because she despises the hypocrisy of their marriage, and because her friend has tried to show her that she is the happier of the two. Maria then succumbs to the attention of Alberto because she sees him as a means of fulfilling her frustrated and repressed needs, for which she is ready to do almost anything, including becoming a part of an "honestly and solidly middle-class family." Actually, Maria is a misfit, unable to find real meaning in life whatever her role might be. In her frustrating quest for happiness she has become reluctant to believe that people can really be happy. For her, happiness is but a fleeting thing. At the end of the play, after the inevitable reconciliation between husband and wife, Maria, the victim of this "adventure," resumes her nomadic life—like Svevo, the frustrated artist—in search of an elusive dream of art and freedom.

Giulia is the complete opposite of Maria. She is the exemplary personification—if only in appearance—of placid domestic happiness and fulfillment. Having no outside interests, and as a "perfect housewife . . . born to be the mother of a family" (313), Giulia is a precursor of Augusta, Zeno's wife. In her blindness, resignation, and mediocrity, Giulia differs from Maria's restlessness, inquisitiveness, and vibrant dynamism. She willingly conforms to a conventional pattern of marriage. In fact, she is more offended by Alberto's indiscretions than by his adulterous behavior: as long as appearances are saved, adultery is not considered a serious breach of marriage. As the crisis explodes, she feels no responsibility because she has not deviated from the "regular life" imposed by society. At the end of the play she is no longer able to delude herself about her husband's fidelity, but at least she is certain that his future adventures will be more discreet, and that he will always return to his "domestic sanctuary."

Alberto is a hypocritical weakling who lacks the necessary courage to change his dreary life. He betrays his wife so long as there are no complications, no risks involved. He honestly thinks of himself as a model husband because, as in the case of Zeno, his infidelities make him more affectionate toward his wife. He is unable to go through with his plans with Maria because he is "preoccupied with the idea of a future that inevitably always kills the present" (304); and it is doubtful whether he really intended to leave his home since he was forced into this situation by Maria's impetuousness.

Through Signor Tarelli, Maria's uncle—a typical theatrical *raisonneur* and somewhat unconvincing factotum—Svevo expresses his point of view vis-à-vis the Triestine provincial middle class and reveals his bitter criticism. Unlike Giacosa, the defender of the middle class, Svevo shows its falseness: that it lives by a set of traditional lies and carefully covers up everything that might reveal its falsity. Still, Signor Tarelli, the strong antibourgeois and supporter of freedom, ironically becomes the protector of tradition and, with great satisfaction, achieves the reconciliation of Alberto and Giulia. Svevo's ironic humor stems from the way in which he creates a contradiction of expectations: usually it is the artist leading an adventurous life who appeals to the middle class; here instead, with a twist, the Bohemian is attracted to the regularity of bourgeois life.

Although Svevo has been adroit in giving the play dramatic power, it nevertheless contains a number of weaknesses. All the characters suffer from an inertia that prevents them from taking decisive action. Additionally, the characters are not fully developed and only partially persuasive. We know very little about them: their background remains a mystery, and we see only the results and not the causes that make them what they are. On the whole, the characters are not properly orchestrated and are ill matched. Maria, the obvious protagonist, does not confront a clear antagonist; the conflict, therefore, is between conflicting emotions and life-styles, not between two individuals. Most important, Svevo failed to see that he was guilty of editorialism—bending his characters and actions to the point he wants to make—rather than allowing the point to emerge organically from them. The language, more narrative than dramatic, is at times turgid. Although *L'avventura di Maria* has the potential of being a great drama of ideas, the lack of theatrical technique diminishes its pathos and dramatic movement.

Svevo was fully aware of his limitations as a playwright and his plays never fulfilled his high expectations. He found it difficult to end his plays (there are several endings to some of his dramatic works), and he felt that his composition was not clear enough. In a letter to an unknown dramatist (written ca. 1896–1898), from whom he was seeking help, he wrote: "Everything turns sour in my hands as I add, cut, patch and mangle everything without being able to let any light into the writing that would split in the prism and permit its reconstruction. Is it my ear or hand that should be blamed for this?"[19]

For a better understanding of *L'avventura di Maria,* it would be helpful to know the year in which it was written. Svevo constantly tinkered with his works, never leaving them alone. There are, in fact, three drafts of this play differing only slightly from each other.[20] This constant reelaboration is symptomatic of that strange and often bitter dissatisfaction that characterizes Svevo's personality and that of his protagonists. Apollonio places the play circa 1920. A careful reading of *L'avventura di Maria,* however, offers some internal evidence that places its composition at the turn of the century. In the second draft, for example, the stage directions indicate that the action is taking place in the present and refer to Verdi and Wagner as if they were still alive: Wagner died in 1883 and Verdi in 1901. Furthermore, the well-known

Italian actress Adelaide Ristori, who died in 1906, is also mentioned as if she were still living, another indication that the play, most likely, was written between 1883 and 1906. If so, it was conceived during a most trying time in Svevo's life, when he thought of himself as a defeated man, torn between being Svevo the writer and Schmitz the businessman, between Maria's life-style and that of the Galli household.

Although *La verità* (The truth) is only a one-act play[21] and may at first glance give the appearance and consistency of a *scherzo* aimed at amusing the audience, it is a serious play in which there are no false laughs. The light humor—the lines are funnier than the total effect—was only part of Svevo's intention. *La verità,* completed between 1900 and 1914, is the final result of an earlier preliminary work entitled *La parola* (The word).[22] With *La verità* Svevo broke away from the conventions of the bourgeois drama, followed so closely in his previous plays. We find instead Ibsen's vital motif of falsehood, Pirandellian ideas on the multiplicity of reality, as well as Shavian ideas of freedom combined with irony.

The main theme of the play is the manner in which Silvio Arcetri, a well-to-do gentleman farmer and inconsidered Don Juan, succeeds in creating for himself an imaginary reality that dissolves his wife's discovery of his adulterous episode with the dressmaker. He creates this new reality, full of fantastic alibis and strange circumstances, not because he is truly interested in being forgiven, but because for him life is just a game where one has to play a role, as in Pirandello's *Il giuoco delle parti (The Rules of the Game).* Silvio tries to convince his wife to return so that he may resume his games. His sophistic ploy rests on rejecting with his arguments the idea of absolute truth, while in Pirandellian fashion he proposes the doctrine of the relativity of truth, interpreting reality as a process of constant changes. Since absolute truth is unavailable and because he is more interested in winning the argument than making truth prevail, Silvio turns his concern to the art of debate. Thus with contrived documentation and falsehoods, his frivolous and eristic argumentation degenerates into hair-splitting of words, designed to confuse the issue along with his poor gullible wife: Was his hat crushed when he fled the woman's bed? Was she a blonde or brunette? Was it the dressmaker or another woman? The message of Silvio's sophistry is that truth is unattainable, that there are no genuine moral laws or norms for evaluating his behavior.

After seeing or reading this play, we too are confused about what really takes place. We could come to a Pirandellian conclusion that nothing is absolute, and that human knowledge is only relatively true or certain. Svevo seems to be expressing here a belief that life is a *buffonata* (a joke), a make-believe world similar to that taking place on stage. As in Pirandello's *Così è (se vi pare) (Right You Are If You Think You Are)* we are left with the question, what is truth? what really happened? The answer is that truth is an elusive idea, having many faces. It is not something constant nor easily recognizable, but rather it is a creation, always in flux and at times incoherent and contradictory. Man, endowed with many personalities, is not satisfied to be today what he was yesterday, and consequently desires to be not just one, but many. In his paradoxical search for an alibi or a certain reality Silvio Arcetri exacerbates the conflicts between appearance and reality, normalcy and abnormalcy, the individual's inner world and the external world. Both husband and wife wish to play out their drama from their own perspective, much like Pirandello's *Sei personaggi in cerca d'autore (Six Characters in Search of an Author)*—although in Svevo's case, the protagonists come to some sort of resolution concerning their conflict.

In *La verità* Svevo anticipated the psychological themes of his novels—particularly *La coscienza di Zeno*. Silvio, possessing a keen intellect, impertinence, and rhetorical gusto, wanders from female to female, never satisfied with his conquests, always seeking new thrills and adventures. For him marriage is only a game that society compels him to indulge in. He does not love his wife, or anyone else, because he is incapable of love and tenderness. On the other hand, Fanny's agonizing need for love and self-respect in society compels her to believe and be carried away by Silvio's fanciful alibi. She is determined to save her marriage from a battle she knows she has lost. Thus, in this play marriage, family relations, and adultery are no longer treated within the conventional norms of the bourgeois theater: the individual is scrutinized in a cynical and ironic vein and the psychological element prevails over any given situation.

According to Ruggero Rimini, the play lacks "that force, vitality, that turns a well-written dialogue into real drama . . . [It] strives to rend, but fails to do so."[23] This scant dramatic incisiveness stems from the fact that once the curtain has risen, though there is definite conflict, it exists without crisis. Indeed, it is always clear throughout the play that Fanny eventually will relent and return to her husband. The cards are stacked against her by a mightier antagonist and the issue is settled a priori.

However, Svevo is completely successful in manipulating the incidents, the plot, the characters, and their emotions, maintaining throughout the entire eight scenes a mounting dramatic suspense, even though hardly any action is occurring on the stage. *La verità* has a certain restlessness that makes it a masterpiece of irony. The light and false tone of Silvio's lines and the cleverness of his remarks become more and more refined and subtle as he dazzles Fanny with his relentless logic and his persuasive tongue. The servant Luigi, with his procuring and his funny gags, behaves like the typical gracioso of Spanish classical drama.[24] He provides the comic relief and serves also as a kind of parody of his master, supplying a cynical counterpoint that enhances the theme of the major character. *La verità* is a fairly successful play not only for its style, balanced construction, form and content, but also for the language—Svevo's constant Waterloo—over which he gains absolute control, flexing it and molding it to the dramatic needs of the play.

Terzetto spezzato (Broken Triangle), a one-act fantasy written circa 1920, was presented by the renowned Anton Giulio Bragaglia on the Roman stage in April 1927.[25] Although it was the only play performed during his lifetime,[26] Svevo, who was already sick and old, never saw it because he was unable to undertake the long journey from Trieste to the capital. The play concerns a recently widowed businessman who, having read a book on spiritism, invites his best friend (actually his wife's lover) to take part in raising her ghost in order to obtain favors from her. The séance begins, but when the lover invokes Clelia with too much ardor, the husband becomes jealous. The play reaches its climax when the husband, a coffee importer, asks Clelia to tell him if the price of coffee will rise or fall so that he can make a quick profit. Clelia, realizing why her husband has evoked her spirit, refuses and dematerializes—her derisive laughter echoing in the distance.

Despite the obvious humor, *Terzetto* is also a serious play. The comic scenes are amusing, but most of the humor is deadly; we see the complexity of the characters and the paradoxes that are hidden beneath the surface of each. With sardonic humor, Svevo makes *Terzetto spezzato* a serious satire of the institution of marriage and society as a whole.

In Svevo's plays, as already noted, the male characters are frequently weak and mediocre. Clelia's husband is fearful of her ghost because he realizes that, as a less than ideal spouse, he is vulnerable. Although he suspects his wife's infidelity, he does not seem to be very disturbed by it. His only goal is to gain financially from this spiritistic experiment. Svevo reveals the mediocrity, narrow-mindedness, and greed of this man. We sympathize with Clelia and understand why she sought happiness in the arms of another man.

The lover, on the other hand, is not superior to the husband. In addition to using Clelia as an inspiration for his literary career, he has enjoyed the conveniences of another man's home and wife and taken advantage of the woman's unhappiness. When Clelia materializes, he is not satisfied with just her spiritual presence but, inflamed by his passions, appears to want to make love to her in the presence of the husband who, fortunately, has fainted. The lover, who never showed any jealousy when Clelia was alive, suddenly becomes resentful of her husband and experiences an obsessive urge to reveal his adultery to him. Apparently, he wishes to satisfy his offended ego and obtain a vicarious and perverted pleasure by hurting his friend and rival, whom he also holds responsible for Clelia's death. In addition, he is angry at her for not taking better care of her health and for dying! For the woman, the encounter with her lover is just as disappointing as the one with her husband because both react selfishly to her death.

Clelia is not the only ghost in the play. The husband and lover are shadows of real men whose distinguishing characteristics are lack of style and shallowness of soul. Like the characters of Rosso di San Secondo's *Marionette che passione! (What Passion, Marionettes)* they are both nameless and anonymous. As we get to know them, we find them to be more and more hollow apparitions. Their masculinity is never considered by Svevo; it is thoroughly extinct. The traditional male virtues are prominent only in their absence. Their love is in direct proportion to Clelia's usefulness: the husband is motivated by greed and the lover by preposterous vanity.

Svevo may be considered a pro-feminist in his plays—although not in his novels—because he deals extensively with the position of women in society, considering them victims of a system ruled by a double standard. He intimates that the inequalities between the sexes relegate woman unjustly to a state of complete submission and dependency. Clelia, typical of the Triestine commercial middle class, never really rouses herself enough to wake up from the nightmare of her life, which is marked by sterility, a stagnant existence, emotional torpor, and boredom. She is a product of an environment that taught since childhood that the most important way for a woman to gain love is to accommodate her life to other people's needs and desires. Clelia falls into the role of a dependent wife through conditioning and inertia, and finds that "what she thought was life, turned out to be a kind of death." Clelia appears as a ghost because during her life she was a ghost of a person, directed like a marionette by others. A maimed figure always on the losing side, an incomplete woman with incomplete male relationships, Clelia is somewhat akin to the protagonist of Pirandello's *Il fu Mattia Pascal (The Late Mattia Pascal)* who, according to Debenedetti, is "a character within parentheses, suspended, available."[27] Ironically, her only act of rebellion is to oppose the strict marital customs of her society by betraying her commonplace husband, not with a sympathetic lover, but with a shallow and egotistical man. Clelia realizes—perhaps too late—the hopelessness of maintaining a relationship with the two men. At the play's end her sarcastic laughter echoes at length, mocking them both—a ruthless condemnation of all the compromises, hypocrisy, and wretchedness she was compelled to suffer in this world.

There is much about the play—adultery, the ménage à trois—that conveys a feeling of déjà vu. However, Svevo takes a new approach to the stock variation of this theme which recalls, in this case, the bizarre deformations, contradictions, and paradoxes of the Theater of the Grotesque, as well as German expressionistic theater. For example, the retrospective presentation of adultery does not compel the husband to face his rival and avenge his honor, but rather serves to convince him that it could not have taken place because Clelia has "an unsurmountable aversion to him (the lover) on account of his base desires." Paradoxically, the ménage had worked well as long as Clelia was alive. Now that she is dead, it breaks up because, for the first time, both men are jealous of each other.

It is a measure of Svevo's richness and complexity that *Terzetto* can be read on several levels. The trigger of the play's action is obvious enough—spiritism—but the resonances go much deeper than spiritism itself. It was quite fashionable, during this period, to dabble in the occult. In *La coscienza di Zeno* we find a séance in which Zeno jokingly raises the table, causing the participants—Guido in particular—to believe that they have made contact with a spirit. In this play, too, Svevo creates an amusing and imaginative parody of the occult. He juxtaposes the most important requirement for a medium, an uncommon sensitiveness to disembodied spirits, with the motivation of Clelia's husband, who clearly lacks this qualification because there is nothing sensitive about his greed. More important, by using this spiritistic device, Svevo is able to achieve an unconventional staging of conventional material—to deform and synthesize the subject matter and thus reveal with biting irony the hypocrisy of his environment.

Svevo's intention is not merely to mimic and ridicule the practitioners of this pseudoscience, but rather to make spiritism akin to opening doors onto the mysterious world of the subconscious—as indicated by Zeno who states that "psychoanalysis resembles spiritism."[28] In other words, through the mechanism of the séance, Svevo projects onto the stage the subconscious of the characters—their fears, anxieties, repressions. In Freudian terms, by analyzing the logic of dreams (séance), he wants to show them to be the basis of man's irrational behavior. The subtitle "A One-Act Fantasy" gives rise to several questions: Does Clelia really appear to her two men, or is she the manifestation of the collective subconscious? Or rather, is she the critical spirit of the author who is constantly participating in the unfolding of the drama? By imitating the illogic of dreams, Svevo is free to mix fantasy and reality, in which the only integrating factor occurs in the reader's mind. Like the surrealists, through a distorting mirror, unusual juxtapositions, and shifting planes of reality, Svevo aims at entering into life's essence.

When the play was first performed in 1927, the Roman press dismissed it as being "unusual, original, interesting," while the public did not appreciate it due to a lack of understanding.[29] Nevertheless, it is revealing that Bragaglia selected *Terzetto* for the repertoire of his "Teatro Sperimentale." Since Bragaglia was presenting widely known Italian and European playwrights—such as Pirandello, Rosso di San Secondo, Marinetti, Strindberg, Turgenev, Unamuno, Wedekind, etc., his selection of Svevo's work in such company confirms its theatricality.[30]

Although Svevo's standard of measure remained naturalistic, with *Terzetto spezzato* and *Inferiorità (Inferiority)* he transcended the limitations of naturalistic verisimilitude and penetrated into a more fundamental sphere of reality. His new literary creed became "Felix qui potuit rerum cognoscere causas" (Happy was the man who knew the root causes of things). When Svevo wrote *Inferiorità,* it was clear that Freud, Strindberg, Chekhov, and particularly Ibsen were his new models.[31]

Inferiorità, a short one-act play written in 1921, is the story of a practical joke with tragic consequences perpetrated by two fun-loving noblemen at the expense of a friend, and with the complicity of his servant. Count Alberighi and Baron Squatti have made a bet with Alfredo—a timid man who has been scoffing at the idea that anyone might rob him—that they will be able to prove his cowardice by frightening him into handing over his wallet. The two noblemen convince Alfredo's manservant, Giovanni, to feign an armed robbery by promising him enough money to get married and open an *osteria* (inn). The hoax unexpectedly has a tragic result: Alfredo returns home, and Giovanni (while the two friends are hiding in a closet) timidly goes through with the scheme; however, he loses his nerve when his master faints from fright. Alfredo regains his senses, and Giovanni explains the hoax. At this point the master turns on Giovanni, takes back his wallet, dismisses him on the spot, and refuses to hand over the savings that he has kept for him. Angered, Giovanni shoots Alfredo to death. While the baron and the count are battering on the closet door to be let out, Giovanni quietly puts on his master's hat and coat and flees; as he leaves, he kisses Alfredo's hand, murmuring: "I wanted to be free of you, but now I shall always be with you."

The title of the play refers to the moral inferiority of all the characters and, in particular, to Giovanni's social and psychological inferiority. Giovanni is a fearful peasant, dissatisfied with himself and with the degrading work he does. His inferior position, the strange environment of the city, and his master's bullying tactics cause him grave anxieties and frustrations. Although respectful and servile, he willingly takes advantage of the master who suffers from nerves and is afraid to sleep alone. Giovanni is strongly attached to money which will permit him to get married, buy his inn, and leave the city whose nature he has been unable to comprehend. He frees himself from his state of inferiority when he discovers his master's weaknesses and fears; thus for a few moments he is his master's equal. After he has killed Alfredo, he falls back into his own inherent inadequacy.

In writing this play Svevo uses psychoanalysis for the first time as a logical explanation of man's hidden and irrational motivations and attempts to make psychological states visible in concrete terms. He tries to project Giovanni's inner realities and to objectify his thought and feeling. In Freudian terms Giovanni does not completely understand himself because his conflict is at an unconscious level. He does not know how he views himself, his world, and the people in it. The frustration caused by his personal inadequacies finally results in aggression toward the source of his anguish. After the emotional crisis is over, Giovanni regresses to his earlier behavior, unable to resolve his conflict.

He is caught by his own psychological conditioning of inferiority and tied forever to his master.

The play shows, to a certain degree, Svevo's familiarity with German expressionistic drama: the language, the subjectivity, the grotesqueness of the dramatic action, and the externalization of the writer's inner feelings. In this gloomy portrayal of human frustration Giovanni, who suffers from loneliness and isolation, is unable to free himself or determine his own destiny. He seeks salvation but is caught in a nightmarish tangle. Svevo's characters are all timid people because they are fully aware of their limitations.[32] This, no doubt, is the implication of the title of this hoax in which all the characters exude the painful knowledge of their inevitable defeat.

No doubt, *Inferiorità* is Svevo's best one-act play. Unlike his earlier dramatic works, it is not burdened by the conventions of the naturalistic theater nor by heavy and long dialogues. In *Inferiorità* we see how Svevo masters the form completely by concentrating on the thematic focal point and by compressing long dialogues into dynamic ones. The characters are subtly drawn, while the action, with its well-constructed reversals, resembles a suspense thriller.[33] It is a most remarkable work, haunting in its implications, and a spellbinding study of the realities behind practical joking. It is also a psychological analysis of the odd relationships of a man of low station with his domineering master.

Con la penna d'oro (With a golden pen) is an unfinished four-act play, written in 1926 when Svevo, only two years before his death, was finally being recognized by the world as a new and outstanding European writer. The play shows that Svevo continued to devote himself to the theater, even though he had finally reached fame as a novelist. Unfortunately, a complete and definitive edition of the play does not exist; at present it is available in a version reconstructed by Apollonio, who took various drafts, notes, and fragments and arranged them into an organic and uniform work. This incompleteness and the uncertainty of the sequence of scenes demonstrate in part the difficulties Svevo encountered in composing this theatrical work, but do not detract from its interest, novelty, and beauty.

Con la penna d'oro deals with the themes of charity and dependence. It revolves around the contrast between two female cousins, bound to each other by blood and by emotional interdependence: Alberta, happily married to a wealthy businessman and art collector, requires a constant balancing between gratitude and generosity; her magnanimity—exemplified by the "golden pen"—is proportional to the young widow Alice's degree of submission, dependence, and gratitude.[34] Quite naturally, the high price of Alberta's patronage brings about an intense resentment in Alice, who no longer feels free to lead her own life. She rebels against her cousin's enslaving magnanimity, which offends her pride and dignity.

When their old and ailing Aunt Teresina comes to Trieste, Alberta arbitrarily decides to place her in Alice's house. This arrangement is quite logical and practical for Alberta, since both the aunt and her nurse will be able to keep an eye on Alice and bring some order into her house. The dramatic conflict explodes when Alice discovers her cousin's ploy. She turns on Alberta in a rage at seeing herself treated like a slave.

Eventually, Alice refuses to accept any help from her cousin. Once she is free, her life-style changes drastically: she has a love affair with a painter named Sereni, she neglects her children, and borrows heavily from moneylenders in order to make ends meet. Alice insists on making public the affair and on flaunting it before Alberta, who now feels responsible for her cousin's moral degradation. In the end, Alice forces Alberta into seeing the truth about their relationship and leads her to discover its underlying hatred.

Although the two cousins are the principal characters of the play, Aunt Teresina is one of the most vivid and interesting characters ever created by Svevo.[35] She is old, paralyzed, tragically tied to her wheelchair, and at the mercy of whoever pushes it around. Like Alice, she also is compelled to rely for her subsistence on Alberta's generosity. This economic dependence determines Teresina's behavior and increases the degradation already caused by age and disease. On the surface she appears as an insufferable old spinster constantly remembering her more glorious past, when she was the mistress of her father's household and everyone did her bidding. Now, however, she realizes that she had been the master of her household only in appearance because she was nothing but a slave of duty. As she is shuttled from one home to another, she does not lose her desire to run things, although she is constantly checked by the realization that her former power is gone. In spite of the attention Svevo pays to his character, Teresina remains somewhat of a puzzle for us because the playwright fails to make clear her dramatic role. Does she merely serve to underscore another dimension of Alberta's self-serving generosity with its resulting moral repayment? Or did Svevo plan to use her for a different role in the finished version, which, by the way, could easily have turned her into the principal protagonist?

The multiform incompleteness of *Con la penna d'oro* gives it a poetic quality and a richness representative of the vagaries of life. In writing the play Svevo approaches and imitates the dramatical techniques of Anton Chekhov (1860–1904), the great Russian author and playwright. The play is deliberately static with emphasis on small detail, and the action, which is inconsequential, leads from nowhere to nowhere. However, as in Chekhov's plays, this inactivity is only external because the inner part of the individuals is full of action, indecisions, and inner developments. The play at first seems to lack theatricality because the plot is purposely oversimplified in order to shift the stress upon characterization, environment, and psychological motivation.[36] Svevo is not so much interested in single characters and their fate; he is more concerned with groups of people and their relationships. The female characters—especially Aunt Teresina who has shouted her way through life—all talk, but without any evident exchange of ideas, as if they were too busy with their own preoccupations to bother about other people's problems. Thus Svevo depicts the void that stands between one human being and another, no matter how intimately related.

La rigenerazione (Regeneration), Svevo's last dramatic work, is an extremely lengthy three-act play written in 1927–28, but left unfinished due to the author's death. Apollonio gave it its title, taking it from one of Svevo's youthful literary projects.[37] The play is all about old age and deals with an old man who undergoes a rejuvenation operation.[38] The questions Svevo poses are: What kind of moral, social and ethical problems will result if youth can be regained? Is it legitimate for man to start life all over again? How can an old man get back into everyday life if he is weighed down by haunting memories, past experiences, and regrets?

When the play opens we find Giovanni Chierici, a seventy-four-year-old man, enduring the difficulties caused by his advanced age. His family and friends are constantly reproaching him for being absent-minded and for showing signs of senility. The cast of characters includes his wife Anna, a sweet old lady, entirely devoted to her pet birds and cat; his daughter Emma, whose constant talk about her dead husband creates a funereal atmosphere in the household; his nephew Guido, a greedy and mischievous student of medicine who tries to convince his uncle to submit to a rejuvenation operation; and Rita, the simple and seductive servant who will be the test of the success of the operation.

In act 2 Giovanni is more smartly dressed than before, and walks more energetically, but still with some difficulty. However, he is only rejuvenated in spirit because the physical benefits of the operation require a considerable period of time. Eventually, he arranges to test his virility with Rita, but the test fails. After getting her drunk, he manages only to kiss her before they both fall asleep. When they are found snoring together, no one wants to believe that anything immoral could have taken place.

In act 3 Giovanni suffers numerous humiliations because no one believes in his newly found youth and virility. He has several dreams in which he relives his past and former youth. In the end, realizing that the operation has been a failure, he gives up the struggle to be young and reverts back to his harmless *senilità*.

La rigenerazione is much more freely constructed than Svevo's previous plays; it contains three dream sequences which alternate as intermezzi for the three acts of the play. These dreams serve to project on the stage Giovanni's unconscious, his fears, anxieties, and repressed wishes for his lost youth and virility. In the first oneiric sequence we are shown Giovanni's anxieties about the operation. We see him at the mercy of several doctors who are recommending the surgical procedure. Giovanni hedges about the price and also because he is afraid that he might not be able to assert his manhood with modern women. He is finally convinced when told that a law will be passed compelling all the old men of Trieste to have the operation. As a result, the prices will go up and he might be left as the only old man in the city. The question is settled when he is told that he can have Rita—she lies on a table in the same room—for free since her services are included in the price of the operation.

The intermezzo dream of act 2 represents Giovanni's rebellion against old age and his wife Anna. Here he is young again and in the company of Rita. The past blends with the present as he confuses Rita's face with that of Pauletta, a girl he loved as a young man but did not marry because people thought her extravagant and loose. Pauletta tells him that she had not come before because she was waiting for him to have the operation. He tells her that he had the operation specifically for her and yearns for her lips. She replies that she will be his provided he kills his wife. Giovanni promises and Pauletta becomes his.

The last dream, which concludes the play, expresses Giovanni's repentance and resignation. We see him hoeing a field where he has been led by Rita.[39] He wants to wait for the rains to soften the ground, but the woman tells him that he was selected for this work because he is so young and strong. Anna appears and he rebukes her bitterly for their miserable marital life. Why did they get married? Why did they eat and drink so much at their wedding? Did they stay together because of it? Why did they fall apart after only a few years? When Anna asks him if he ever truly loved her, Giovanni relives in his mind his whole life, but particularly his operation which has made him see that the world is in complete chaos.[40] At the end he understands that he has been only dreaming about his rejuvenation, that the operation was really a failure: that he has been altering the events of his life to satisfy his hidden and unfulfilled desires. The dream ends in the same way as in "La novella del buon vecchio e della bella fanciulla" ("The Story of the Nice Old Man and the Pretty Girl") where the old man understands that his life has been the best possible. He knows that dreams have only symbolized his protest and shortened the road to resignation.

In *La rigenerazione* Svevo found a new style, a new theatrical dimension. He rejected traditional ways of regarding and portraying reality, and attempted to see it in new ways by creating an experimental drama. The psychological awareness, acquired under the inspiration of Freud, the post-World War I experimentations of the European stage, and the recent discovery of Kafka's works—all were nourishing Svevo's creativity. His most significant innovation was the manner in which he deformed the objective reality of the outside world into the subjective reality of the inner states of consciousness. By following the expressionistic dream technique, particularly Strindberg's example, Svevo abandoned the logic of reality for the logic of dreams. Having a deep concern with man's irrational element, he tried to bring what was invisible, unreal, and unconscious into *La rigenerazione*. Svevo also continued to treat the problems of disease, both physical and emotional, as well as the relationships between the ill and the healthy—fundamental problems in modern literature.

La rigenerazione undoubtedly is the most important and most imaginative of all Svevo's plays. It is his literary and artistic testament[41] since it was written after his novels and his long-awaited success. According to Elio Vittorini, this play, together with Svevo's last unfinished works, would have been a masterpiece had it been completed.[42] Its flaws—Rebora calls the text "difficult to deal with, contradictory and elusive"[43]—are minimal, compared to its theatrical and scenic merits. Realizing finally that he was dealing with a form less elastic than the novel, he overcame the stage's rigidities with this newly acquired intuitive scenic talent, finally creating the visual concreteness demanded by the stage, and using all of the technical resources available in the theater. He was able to find for the theater the very same devices and modes he used so successfully in his fiction: mixed time, multiplicity of character, and fluctuation between consciousness and the unconscious, reality and dream. Leon Edel has observed that nothing is more difficult to represent on the stage than the dream state and that "the stage will have to recognize that the novel's modes of subjectivity are proper to the novel. They do not easily serve the other forms."[44] Still, this remarkable and most original play, solidly rooted in Svevo's narrative technique, and sparkling with humor and wisdom, proves the critic to have been wrong.[45]

In Svevo criticism it has been customary until recently to gloss over his theatrical works by assigning him almost exclusively to the history of the novel. Critics have, in fact, considered his drama incidental to his narrative. Undoubtedly, his plays are not flawless and do not reach the perfection of his now-famous novels, However, they have suffered the same kind of misreading and distortions as those of Pirandello, Ionesco, Cocteau, and other avant-garde dramatists because the critics' judgments were based primarily on formal grounds and predicated on a traditional conception of the theater. Svevo's dramatic weaknesses are technical—staging, pacing, dialogue, etc.—rather than substantive. His greatest merit is that his work consists of content and significance rather than mere style. Furthermore, his theatrical production is of extreme importance because it is not only a vital document in the reconstruction of Svevo's history,[46] but also indispensable for a complete and detailed interpretation of Svevo the man, the writer, the novelist. The plays are the genesis of Svevo's fiction and shed new light on his personality and artistic creative process. By removing the mask of the individual and revealing the face for what it really is, Svevo shows us how man's life is a grotesque farce full of absurdities and paradoxes. Nevertheless, his pessimism always reveals a ray of light, humor, and hope, expressed by the characters' strong desire to keep on living. Finally, as in all literary creations, there is in his theater an indefinable poetry born of the melancholy of Svevo, which inspires it.

Chapter Six
Short Stories

We have already seen that Svevo's earliest attempts at writing were for the theater. Elio's diary informs us that in 1881 his brother was also dabbling in short stories, which were never completed. It was not until 1888, however, that the fledgling author made his first appearance as a writer of fiction on the pages of *L'Indipendente,* which serialized his short story "Una lotta" (A contest).[1] His "minor" narrative writings are a potpourri of mainly undated short stories and tales of different lengths, some fragmentary and others sketches of future works never brought to completion. Only seven were ever finished: "Una lotta," "L'assassinio di Via Belpoggio," "La tribù," "La madre," "Una burla riuscita," "La novella del buon vecchio e della bella fanciulla," and "Vino generoso." An eighth, "Lo specifico del dottor Menghi," appears to be complete, except for a fragment missing on the first page. This narrative production—in addition to his plays—belies Svevo's claim of having given up literature after the critical failure of *Senilità* and until the beginning of World War I. What is clear is that, though he may not have submitted many of his creative writings for publication, he continued to practice his craft and to experiment with new narrative forms and techniques.

Published Writings and Finished Works

"Una lotta" seems to be a parody of chivalric romance. The hero, Arturo Marchetti, is a frail, neurotic, but witty poet and theorizer, who at the age of thirty-five feels his youth is slipping away; he regards Rosina as his Dulcinea, and tries like Don Quixote to affirm his heroic spirit. His bravura in threatening his physically more powerful rival, Ariodante Chigi—a handsome, vigorous but inarticulate athlete—and the inevitable deflating result, reveal him to be a true prototype of Svevo's antiheroic characters. The story, written contemporaneously with *Una vita,* anticipates certain basic motifs and characters that Svevo will develop more fully in his novels: the dreamer, the theorizer, the individual whose propensity to think and reflect renders him unprepared for life. Indeed, Arturo resembles Emilio Brentani—both suffer from precocious "senility," both are full of unfulfilled desires. Finally, the contest between Arturo and Ariodante presages those between Alfonso and Macario, Emilio and Stefano, Zeno and Guido. The structure, the language, the intermingling of direct and indirect discourse, but above all the ironic contrast between the rivals whose characterizations are deftly achieved, all reveal Svevo's growing mastery.

Svevo's second short story is far more serious and complicated. Written in 1890 and serialized once again in *L'Indipendente*,[2] "L'assassinio di Via Belpoggio" (Murder on Belpoggio Street) is clearly reminiscent of Dostoyevski's *Crime and Punishment*: an impoverished street-porter, Giorgio, kills Antonio, a casual drinking companion, and robs him of a substantial sum of money in a dark street of Trieste. Like Raskolnikov, Giorgio feels superior to his fellows and has absolutely no remorse for what he has done. Indeed, he sees himself as the wronged party: it was all the fault of Antonio who ought not have shown him the money. The murderer quickly becomes entangled in an intricate snare of motives, conscience, and fears. His true punishment is psychological; the torment of isolation from others makes him abominable to himself until he is arrested and confesses to the murder.

Giorgio is an *inetto*, at odds with both social classes, the middle class that has rejected him as an outcast, and the subproletariat that refuses to accept him. In the brutal attack on Antonio, Giorgio's monotonous and squalid life suddenly becomes dramatic. Like the servant in *Inferiorità* who kills his master, Giorgio frees himself momentarily from his sense of inferiority. The euphoria, however, is fleeting and he falls back immediately into his inherent inadequacy.

In "L'assassinio di Via Belpoggio" Svevo produced something more than a successful thriller. The style is simple, direct, fresh, and vigorous; the somber tone is very persuasive; and the picture of Trieste's low life is vivid and convincing. The story already reveals the mastery of psychological observation and analysis for which Svevo will eventually be esteemed.

In 1897 Svevo wrote "La tribù" ("The Tribe"), his only political narrative. It appeared in *Critica sociale*, the prominent socialist magazine published by Filippo Turati (1857–1932), one of the founders of the Italian Socialist Party in 1892.

The narrative, signed Italo Svevo, deals with a nomadic tribe that settles in a fertile region of the desert. The tribal tents and neat little houses soon disappear, giving way to rich mansions on the one hand and squalid hovels on the other. The tribal leader, Hussein, asks young Ahmed to help the tribe out of its predicament, but Ahmed, who has studied European economic systems, can only suggest the ways of capitalism: first factories, then exploitation, and finally equality. Hussein finds this process too long and tells the tribe that they should skip the first two phases and start with the last. Ahmed, who insists on building a factory, is expelled from the tribe, and the tribesmen thus reach a state of happiness.

Although Svevo's solution to the capitalistic system seems vague, a fabulous and ephemeral resolution to the problem, and although one may view the tale as a parody of Marxist dialectical materialism, or, as Mario Fusco suggests, "an unexpected and humorous hypothesis of Marxist doctrine,"[3] "La tribù" does reflect Svevo's commonsense view of morality and utopian socialism, and clearly points out the incompatibility between progress and happiness. Hussein and his people succeed in a classless society by avoiding the internecine evolutionary class struggle between capitalists and oppressed proletariat. Svevo propounds a philosophy of sense and moderation, and his veiled message is that the functioning of any society, even a primitive and classless one, requires ideals and moral standards.

"La tribù," more charming that persuasive, is memorable for Svevo's laconic wit and the irony of the political allegory.

Composing fables was one of Svevo's lifelong habits. They are central to many of his stories and particularly to his third novel, and Svevo frequently experimented with the form.[4]

"La madre" ("The Mother") concerns several chicks hatched in an incubator who suffer because they do not have a real and nurturing mother,[5] unlike a nearby brood with a mother hen that watches over them with great care.

First written in 1910 and revised for publication in 1927,[6] "La madre" deals in allegorical form with Svevo's exclusion from the Italian literary establishment. The garden with the hen and its homogeneous population of animals represents Italy; while the one with the incubator, populated by chicks of various colors and shapes, is an obvious reference to the city of Trieste at the crossroads of *Mitteleuropa,* the melting pot of various religions and nationalities. The mother, "who was said to be able to give every delight and therefore satisfy ambition and vanity" (131), stands for the Italian establishment, which, until the very last phase of Svevo's career, refused to acknowledge his artistic merits. Indeed, even after the so-called discovery of Svevo by the French literati and Montale, he ran into all sorts of difficulties in trying to have the second edition of *Senilità* published. Furthermore, his writings were attacked by critics like Guido Piovene, who, in a vitriolic review of *Senilità,* wrote: "What is Svevo's merit? Of having come close, more than any other Italian, to that passively analytic literature, which found its apogee in Proust; but it is inferior art, if art is meant to be a product of living and active men. . . ."[7] And finally, the ostracism of the chick Curra reflects not only Svevo's exclusion from the strongholds of Italian culture and learning, but also his position as a Jew without a "true" sense of belonging and acceptance, particularly during the rise of fascism.

"Una burla riuscita" ("The Hoax"), completed in 1926, is a long narrative divided into eight segments; it takes place in Trieste during the last days of World War I.[8] Mario Samigli is an unassuming but devoted office clerk who in his youth published an unappreciated novel entitled *Giovinezza* (Youth).[9] Forty-three years later he has still not gotten over his neglect by the critics. Though he no longer writes for publication, he secretly composes fables whose protagonists are sparrows. Gaia, a former poet who has become a successful traveling salesman, is envious of Mario's faithful commitment to literature. He decides to play a hoax on his friend, leading him to believe that an important Viennese publishing house is interested in buying the rights to his novel. Mario naively falls for the ploy and signs an attractive contract with one of Gaia's accomplices. When eventually he finds out the truth, he confronts Gaia and gives him a sound thrashing. Though the author's ego is deeply wounded, financially the hoax turns out to be rather profitable for him. A speculation performed with nonexistent funds, together with the confusion resulting from the entrance of the Italian Army into Trieste and the collapse of the Austrian currency, give the author a handsome profit of seventy thousand lire.

Aside from the obvious similarities with Svevo's own literary experiences—Lavagetto calls it "a parable of his own existence"[10]—"Una burla riuscita" is extremely important in that it offers an insight into Svevo's self-image as an author right after the initially unsuccessful publication of *La coscienza di Zeno*. Like his namesake and creator, the character Samigli derives relief from the psychic pain of his existence by writing fables. Thus, literature takes on a double valence: protection and shield against the world, and escape and potential cure for his frustrations. In essence, fables are symbolic expressions of wish fulfillment akin to dreams, in which the author finds cathartic release from the tensions and anxieties produced by repressed emotions. Indeed, as the narrator says, Gaia's practical joke remains "powerless against his dreams" (64). The story also offers a psychological study of the motives behind practical joking. Svevo echoes Freud when he explains that Gaia's love for practical joking "was a relic of his suppressed artistic tendencies"; and that he resented Mario because he had remained faithful to his art and become a "silent witness against him" for having given up and repressed his own poetry (92).

"La novella del buon vecchio e della bella fanciulla" ("The Story of the Nice Old Man and the Pretty Girl"), written in 1926, deals with the last love affair of an old man who is clearly the aged successor of Zeno.
During the war in Trieste, while the guns are rumbling in the distance, a rich elderly gentleman meets a young and beautiful girl who quickly becomes his paid mistress. The affair does not last very long because he suddenly falls ill, stricken with angina—no doubt precipitated by the romance—that limits all his activities. One day, as he looks out of his window, he sees her in the company of an attractive young man. Both jealous and guilty for having taken advantage of his wealth to seduce her, he sets out to reform her and write a thesis on the relations between the aged and the young, between health and disease. The girl's reeducation becomes a mere pretext for a profound and desperate examination of his own existence. The narrative ends with the old man's realization that his physical strength is insufficient to bring his thesis to completion. He wraps the pages of his manuscript in a sheet of paper on which, as a final reply to his quest, he writes several times: *Nothing*. The next day he is found dead amidst his writings, with a pen in his mouth.
The story, written in the third person with nameless protagonists, reminds us of Zeno's affair with Carla, and his attempts to appease his guilt feelings. Though similar, the two adventures differ considerably—in this narrative Svevo is merciless toward both the cynical "good" old man and the compliant, mischievous young girl. Both are willing and ready to corrupt and be corrupted by money. Love, as in

La rigenerazione, is seen as a cure for old age and as an escape from degrading physical and emotional conditions. Ironically, however, the cure proves to be fatal for "our old man."

Like most of the short stories written during Svevo's Zeno period, "Vino generoso" ("Generous Wine"), begun in 1914 and revised in 1926, is full of psychological insights and probings on the themes of disease and old age. A sickly old man narrates the story of his niece's wedding. The doctor has given him permission to break his diet and take part in the festivities like everyone less. Taking advantage of this precious and singular opportunity, the old man eats and drinks to excess not because of thirst and hunger, but "from a craving for liberty" from the pills, drops, and powders that have become part of his life. That night he has a nightmare in which all the members of the wedding party call for his death; he, however, offers his daughter's life in exchange for his own. Once awake, he blames the wine, and in order to avoid the recurrence of such a dream, decides to follow the doctor's orders and go back to his diet.

The "generous wine" of the title suggests the opening of doors leading to the subconscious. As the old man becomes more absorbed in analyzing his inner self, guilt and remorse come to the surface. He regrets, in particular, having married the wrong woman and having given up his socialist ideals. The dream clearly shows the late Svevo's familiarity with Franz Kafka's (1883–1924) work. The narrator is caught in a nightmarish tangle of guilt feelings and remorse. His lucid mind, notwithstanding the effects of the wine, finds itself confronting an incomprehensible state of existence. The simplest human conviction—that one deserves respect, affection, and good health, that one has a place in the world—has no basis in his world of altered reality.

"Lo specifico del dottor Menghi" (The specific of Dr. Menghi), one of Svevo's few contributions to science fiction,[11] also concerns itself with the influence of Darwinism. The narrative, written in pseudoscientific and philosophical language, deals with the experiments of Dr. Menghi who, on his deathbed, asks his colleague Dr. Galli to read to the Medical Society a paper dealing with a special serum he has discovered. What follows is the reading in the first person of Dr. Menghi's paper.

The story, written most likely in 1904,[12] contains in a nutshell many of Svevo's favorite themes: the elusiveness of health and the ever-lurking presence of disease, the *senectus* theme and its corresponding debilitating and degenerative effects, the death of a loved one and the ambiguous relationship between son and parent, a skeptical and ironic treatment of doctors and their magical cures. The precarious energy that fascinates Dr. Menghi and constitutes life, and the delicate physiological balance in terms of chemical, physical, and functional processes, maintained by a complex of mechanisms, is what Svevo seems to be searching for both literally and figuratively. Dr. Menghi's specifics, with their potential effect on this vital balance, are very much like the two opposite poles of the Basedowian lifeline that mesmerizes Zeno, namely, the symptomatic characteristics of Graves' disease: hypoactivity and hyperactivity. The story is also significant because it reveals Svevo's attitude toward science, and especially toward those scientists who undertake experimentation without regard for its potentially evil results. "You thought you were helping people," says the doctor's mother, "but instead your invention is nothing but a new scourge" (381). This ominous accusation will be realized, of course, in the momentous ending of *La coscienza di Zeno*. The scientist or individual, although essentially good and well meaning, is tempted by his desire for knowledge to experiment selfishly with life and to end up in a hell of his own making—a very timely theme indeed. Svevo remains faithful to Darwin's law of evolution and "rejects any initiative that might risk modifying the natural equilibrium of the existing forces in nature, however imperfect or unjust the equilibrium might be."[13]

Fragments and Sketches

The sheer volume of unfinished works in Svevo's canon indicates the great difficulty he experienced in bringing his ideas to fruition. Many of these fragments abound in autobiographical data relevant to Svevo's hesitancy and ambivalence about writing, as well as to his ongoing concern with the shifting functions of reality, memory, and death. The fragment "Incontro di vecchi amici" (Old friends meet; ca. 1912) deals with an unsuccessful writer of unfinished stories. Roberto, like Svevo, compensates for his lack of success by becoming a businessman.[14] The character Roberto reappears as an old man in two other unfinished stories, "L'avvenire dei ricordi" (Along memory lane; 1923) and "La morte" ("Death"; 1925), in which the narrator's reminiscences act as a repetition and re-creation of the past, thus slowing the approach of death. Svevo's constant focus on memory and death is also apparent in "Proditoriamente" ("Traitorously"; 1923), a drab meandering narrative that proffers the philosophical message that death is always looming, insidiously awaiting its next victim.

Svevo also explored various theories about the nature of humankind, ranging from the tenets of natural science to the influence of superstition and psychoanalysis. "La buonissima madre" (The Very Good Mother; circa 1919) offers an imaginative reworking of Darwin's theory of natural selection, and echoes Svevo's suspicion—openly stated in his 1907 article "L'uomo e la teoria darwiniana" (Man and the Darwinian Theory)—that man has not, in fact, evolved. In "Il malocchio" (The Evil Eye; circa 1917), Svevo utilizes both superstition and psychoanalytic theory to depict the irrationality and absurdity of human existence, and also to express his well-founded suspicions of modern technology and scientific achievement.

Like his other works, Svevo's fragments reveal his willingness to experiment with more open narrative structures. "Orazio Cima" (ca. 1917) and "Corto viaggio sentimentale" ("Short Sentimental Journey"; 1925–26) are both shaped and given meaning by the consciousness and psychological attitudes of the narrators. The narrator of "Orazio" presents us with a tableau of conflicting values and ideologies, while in the second story the mendacious narrator offers an equally distorted picture of reality. By far the more experimental of the two stories, "Corto viaggio sentimentale" has no principal character other than the narrator's consciousness, no plot, and no structure. Written under the influence of James Joyce, it became Svevo's longest, albeit unfinished, short story; he referred to it as "a long, long serpent curled up in [his] desk drawer."[15]

Svevo's Last Works

In preparation for his projected fourth novel Svevo wrote four alternative segments, in addition to the unfinished "Il vecchione," that seem to be related components for a work intended to crown his literary career.[16] According to Gabriella Contini, although these contain similarities with *La coscienza di Zeno,* and although Zeno reappears as the author/protagonist, Svevo meant to write a novel quite distinct and separate from his previous masterpiece. In her controversial book *Il quarto romanzo di Svevo* Contini argues that the projected novel consists of diverse fragmentary segments, some of which are constituent parts ("Le confessioni del vegliardo," "Umbertino," "Il mio ozio," "Un contratto"), while others are preparatory (*Rigenerazione,* "L'avvenire dei ricordi"), lateral ("Orazio Cima"), or subsidiary ("Vino generoso," "La novella del buon vecchio," "Viaggio sentimentale," "Incontri di vecchi amici," "Proditoriamente," "La morte").[17] Such a novel, according to Contini, is a work in progress, made up of interlocking segments that are readable and comprehensible only if considered in an intertextual relationship.

Regardless of whether Svevo intended these later works to form a fourth novel, it is clear that an idée fixe marks all of Svevo's works written after *La coscienza di Zeno* and serves to bind the disparate parts together. Svevo's overruling concern with old age and declining health is particularly evident in the "constituent parts" of the narrative, in which he picks up where he left off with his third novel, and in which the already-aged Zeno ages still more.

A man of leisure, cut off from all activity, Zeno turns to the past. Rereading his ten-year-old writings, Zeno realizes that what he had already narrated in *La coscienza* was not the most important part of his life. Surprisingly, he seems to have forgotten his past, except for the part recorded in the novel. Faced, however, with his previous confessions, he can suddenly recall other elements of his past. Thus, he begins to inquire philosophically about the meaning of life and to study his past objectively, as if it belonged to someone else. He asks "And now what am I? Not the one who lived, but the one I described."[18] Zeno is surprised to see how the written word can transform life. He envisions a time when, for therapeutic reasons, everyone will be compelled to write, "life will be literalized. . . . And contemplation will be the main business of the day, shielding us from the horridness of actual living. . . ."[19] This realization prompts Zeno to resume writing his diary, which raises the question of whether at the conclusion of *La coscienza di Zeno,* the protagonist was really cured. In any case, as he resumes writing, we may assume that Zeno's former and present writings must have some beneficial effect for him.

In "Un contratto" ("A Contract"), with the advent of peace and a bad business deal that wipes out practically all the money made during the war, Zeno realizes that he no longer has the enterprise required for the more competitive peacetime economy. Aware of his incompetence, Zeno knowingly allows himself to be maneuvered into signing a contract making young Olivi a partner of the business, and relinquishing to him virtually all control. Although Zeno regards it finally as a defeat of old age and a victory of youth, he can't help but smile at the socialist administrator who behaves like a typical capitalist, exploiting his employees and cutting their wages.

In "Le confessioni del vegliardo" ("An Old Man's Confessions")[20] and "Umbertino," Zeno deals with family relations and attempts to fix on paper the present (with all its gradations) and the recent and distant past. Zeno, who still has virtually all of his classic foibles, tries to come to terms with his children, committing the same disastrous mistakes that marred the relationship with his own father. His docile wife Augusta, completely taken with her menagerie, fails to notice the continuous crises he endures on account of his age. Zeno's only consolations are his young grandson, Umbertino, who distracts him with his innocence and curiosity from the dreary routine of his life, and his nephew, Carlo, the son of Ada and Guido Speier.

In "Il mio ozio" ("This Indolence of Mine") Zeno closely analyzes his inertia and discovers that even the present—himself "and the things and people round him"—is made up of various tenses. His "major and interminable present" is his retirement from business and the inertia of his daily life. In this forced indolence he becomes even more preoccupied with the degeneration of his aged body. The companionship of Carlo—very much his father's son—who has his medical degree, stimulates Zeno's curiosity, particularly with the notion that it is the sexual organs and not the heart that sustain our whole organism. According to Zeno, "Mother Nature is a maniac," who maintains life within an organism as long as it is able to reproduce itself. In view of this Zeno sets out to hoodwink Mother Nature by taking a mistress, which for him is equivalent to "going to the chemist's" (146). The cure, however, has a sobering effect when his mistress Felicita, a tobacconist,[21] educates him in his present role as an old man. Zeno, with his unmistakable sense of humor and lack of resolve, decides that it will be his last "fling," and then he adds slyly that he occasionally still keeps "cheating" nature.

With "Il vecchione" ("The Old, Old Man"),[22] written in 1928 and consisting of only a few pages, we have the beginning of the proposed sequel to *La coscienza di Zeno*. A seventy-year-old Zeno, narrating in the first person, relates how on his way home from an outing he felt compelled to greet a pretty young girl as she passed near his car. When Augusta inquires who she is, Zeno explains that she is the daughter of their friend Dondi. Augusta points out that he is mistaken because

Dondi's daughter is older than she, and, therefore, like herself, she too must be an old woman. This encounter triggers in Zeno a myriad of involuntary memories in which time becomes confused as he ponders his life's experiences.

Zeno finds himself constantly frustrated in an absurd and hostile world, in which he is unable to find his proper place. The trivial incident with the pretty girl, like the Proustian madeleine, evokes a rush of memories and the past floods back in its entirety, enabling him to re-create his earlier experiences, but at the same time exposing the illusory nature of his early ideals.[23] He discovers that the past can be recovered by memory, preserved, and even improved in his writings. As he had done once before for his failed psychoanalysis, he records his observations in great detail and analyzes his responses to them, finally rediscovering his vocation as an author. He resolves to write the book that will permit him to "pull himself together" and "rehabilitate" himself (136). Writing assumes a hygienic purpose, because in his memoirs time is crystallized and can always be located if one "knows how to open to the right page" (137). By reading his former and present memoirs, he will find the past always at hand and protected from all confusion.

Zeno's constant concern with the processes of remembering and forgetting reveals his psychological sophistication. The past is forever vanishing, not only materially, but in our minds as well. Time that destroys everything is Zeno's real villain. Still, the past remains enclosed in his unconscious, waiting for the trigger that will release it. But even this recovered past is only a fragment of its totality, since each man's truth is relative to his own needs and psychological constitution.

During the last years of Svevo's life old age became the only subject of his writings. Having written so much about it as a metaphysical condition, as a psychological attitude, and mental frame of mind, Svevo now faced it also in a social and literal sense. Now that he was old and experiencing true old age, he described it as being languid, weakening, and dirty; he saw it as an abject state of enfeeblement.[24] He acquired a new concept: no longer spiritual and emotional, but "physical and chronological" senility.[25] The task was no longer establishing a relationship between the past, the present, and the future, but rather functioning solely in the present. "My situation has simplified itself," says the Old, Old Man, "I continue to struggle between the present and the past, but at least hope—anxious hope for the future—does not intrude. So I go on living in a mixed tense. This is man's destiny. . . ."[26] Old age becomes a privileged point of observation from which life is examined and seen with death on one side and youth on the other. Man's condition is seen as a grammatical problem and lived in a "mixed tense," between past and present; for Svevo there is no future, no ultimate grammatical tense: the present serves only to create future memories. The aged Zeno, in all his manifestations, is a misfit because he vacillates between tenses, between youth and old age. He has always lived in the wrong tense and time.

It is difficult to arrive at an organic assessment of Svevo's numerous and fragmentary narrative writings, often marred by sketchiness, incompleteness, and incongruities. Nonetheless, both his early stories and his post-Zeno production, clearly illustrate the development of Svevo's literary experimentalism. After discovering a fully stratified dimension of memory and time in *La coscienza di Zeno,* in his later stories Svevo created a form based entirely on the present. This "presence," together with the elimination of the future, becomes the conditioning factor of Svevo the man and writer. It explains why he describes, dwells, and lingers on details, often deviating carelessly from the theme at hand. The author arrives also at a juncture where he creates not only an open-ended narrative form—innovative for his time—but also a new relationship between himself and his narrator/protagonist. Indeed, in these "further confessions" Svevo and Zeno become an organic whole no longer separate and distinct. Zeno's presence is that of Svevo, who is also beginning to be cut off from his commercial activity because of age and ill health. He too has lost the future and savors, after many years of struggle and defeat, the present fruits of his literary labors. As he tries to come to terms with his long-awaited success, he ponders his personal obsessions and philosophical anguish over the fate of man, an isolated flimsy spirit condemned to wither and die, while the world that encircles him and assails him remains in a time reduced to the present and a reality made up of a series of discontinuous moments. All this is presented by Svevo in a bristling style, in a work whose inexorable introspective analysis, tempered with irony and sagacity, presages a work to be set beside the great *La coscienza di Zeno.*

Chapter Seven
Conclusion

Almost sixty years after his death Svevo's renown, particularly in the United States, continues to depend in large measure on *La coscienza di Zeno,* a novel of astonishing scope and enormous power. It is quite likely, however, that, even if he had not written this novel, his standing in Italian letters would still be considerable. *Una vita, Senilità,* and several of his plays and short stories would have won him a privileged place among contemporary writers. The novelist Alberto Moravia sees him as "just barely inferior to Manzoni."[1] Because of his extraordinary sensitivity to the times in which he lived, Svevo was able to pick out of the air incipient ideas and movements, and represent the doubts, attitudes, feelings, and aspirations of an entire generation. At the same time, with amused ironical detachment and artistic imagination, he created a revolutionary form of novelistic expression that permitted him to illuminate the destiny of modern man.

Svevo's antiheroic hero has always fascinated readers. Unlike Robert Musil's *The Man Without Qualities,* Svevo's characters are vibrant individuals with many traits. Chief among these are their uncanny ineptitude and apparent uneasiness, their conflicting sense of identity, and bungling attempts to conform to society's expectations—all resulting, however, in discomfort and confusion. Svevo himself recognized that the personality disorders, attitudes, and feelings expressed by Zeno (the older brother of Alfonso and Emilio) could not come from consciousness and therefore had to originate in the levels below consciousness. For Zeno, psychoanalysis was clearly insufficient to clarify the causes of his problems. In *Gli anni della psicanalisi* (The Years of Psychoanalysis) Giorgio Voghera writes that, according to Umberto Saba, the dilemma of the Triestine Jews was that they had been brought up between two truths, that of their family and that of the surrounding Christian world. Voghera adds that almost all the Triestini who took an active interest in Freud's ideas were either Jews or half-Jews, thus suggesting that this propensity was perhaps related to their characteristic identity crisis.[2]

Svevo the agnostic, the nonpracticing Jew who had submitted to the

Church only to please his wife—Saba called him "psychologically Jewish down to the very marrow of his bones"[3]—could not ignore the problems facing the European Jews of his day (the Dreyfus Case, Zionism, Theodor Herzl, Palestine, pogroms, the vitriolic anti-Semitic articles in the world press), nor could he repress his own indistinct yet ever-present Jewish consciousness, the uneasiness of the Jew in Western society. In spite of the favorable conditions enjoyed for many years under the Austrian crown, the Jews of Trieste—like those in other parts of nineteenth- and twentieth-century Europe, who felt comfortable and even integrated in all aspects of life—continued to feel and be treated as aliens, as the Other, as sojourners rather than permanent and indigenous inhabitants of the land. Despite their success and contributions, they realized deep down that they had not helped to forge the conscience of the land that was and continued to be Christian. Svevo and his peers certainly gave Trieste—the famous clearing house of European ideas—a particular flavor and contributed immensely to the arts, commerce, letters, science, etc. In the Italian or Triestine imagination, however, they could never exist as equals, only as Jews whose presence was peripheral, irrelevant to Christian/Italian self-consciousness. Like many of his correligionists, Svevo was fated to be a prisoner of his race and culture, no matter how hard he tried to prevent this. In Jungian terms, behind Svevo's "unconscious"—the obstructed residue of the past—lay the "collective unconscious" of the Jew, the memory of his racial past. It is precisely this "primordial" image, shaped by the experiences of his family and ancestors, that becomes recognizable as an element, perhaps the most important element, of his literary experience as a whole. The plight of the Jew, his dark experiences of exile and persecution, his unending drama, molds and colors the nature of Svevo's antiheroic characters. In the case of Zeno Cosini his condition, his illness, has been caused not only by undisclosed traumas and neuroses, but primarily by the author's Jewishness, which, whether we like it or not, cannot be dismissed in any critical assessment of Svevo's life and work.

The persuasive power of his writings stems from his humanity, from the outcry of a disheartened and wounded mankind. Nevertheless, Zeno and his fellow characters—genuinely and profoundly symbolic of modern man—are all infused with an almost miraculous force that allows them to survive. Svevo's outlook is not totally despairing, for he still sees life as fascinating in its richness of experience. When Guido complains that life is hard and unjust, Zeno replies philosophically that "life is neither good nor bad; it is original" (299).

Notes and References

Chapter One

1. *Lettere a Italo Svevo. Diario di Elio Schmitz*, ed. Bruno Maier (Milan: dall'Oglio, 1973), 246. This volume contains some of Livia Veneziani's letters to her husband, as well as Elio Schmitz's "Diary." The present and all subsequent translations are mine.
2. Giacinto Spagnoletti, "La giovinezza e la formazione letteraria di Italo Svevo," *Studi Urbinati di Storia, Filosofia e Letteratura* 27 (1953):191.
3. Elio Schmitz, *Diario*, 246. The text reads: "after keeping him waiting for ages, nothing came of it because the applicant was an Israelite."
4. Livia Veneziani Svevo, *Vita di mio marito con altri inediti di Italo Svevo* (Trieste: Zibaldone, 1958), 21–22.
5. Elio Schmitz, *Diario*, 254.
6. For a description of literary salons in Trieste see Charles C. Russell, *Italo Svevo. The Writer from Trieste* (Ravenna: Longo Editore, 1978), 50–51.
7. Italo Svevo, *Opera Omnia: Racconti, Saggi, Pagine sparse*, ed. Bruno Maier (Milan: dall'Oglio, 1968), 799; hereafter cited as *Racconti, Saggi, Pagine*.
8. Elio Schmitz, *Diario*, 244–45. According to Bruno Maier, the editor of this volume, the entry is undated. We have used the date provided by Veneziani, *Vita*, 25–26. *Hoci-lai-ki* is one of the best-known Chinese plays of the Yuan dynasty (1259–1368), attributed to either Li Hsing-tao or to Li ch'ien-fu. The English title of the play is *The Circle of Chalk*. Brecht's *Caucasian Chalk Circle* (1945) is based on this play.
9. Spagnoletti, *Studi Urbinati*, 197.
10. *Racconti, Saggi, Pagine*, 813–14.
11. Guido Tamaro, "Ricordi da una dedica sveviana," *Adige Panorama* (December 1979), n.p. (clipping available in Svevo Miscellanea, at the Biblioteca Civica of Trieste).
12. Veneziani, *Vita*, 32–33.
13. *Racconti, Saggi, Pagine*, 803.
14. The expression "caso Svevo" refers to the author's inability to gain recognition from Italian critics. This was, in part, due to his being a Jew from Trieste, not being completely Italian, as well as to his particular style and language, and the choice of subject matter and type of characters.
15. *Racconti, Saggi, Pagine*, 557. The article bearing the title "Shylock" appeared in *L'Indipendente* on 2 December 1880.
16. Veneziani, *Vita*, 231. Livia writes about herself in the third person.
17. Marie-Anne Comnène, "Italo Svevo," in *Europe*, Paris, September

1960, 111–16. Quoted from Enrico Ghidetti, *Italo Svevo. La coscienza di un borghese triestino* (Roma: Editori Riuniti, 1980), 136. Marie-Anne Comnène was the wife of the well-known critic and editor Benjamin Crémieux. See also P. N. Furbank, *Italo Svevo. The Man and the Writer* (London: Secker and Warburg, 1966), 50.

18. According to Furbank (50), Svevo was baptized after Letizia's birth. However, more recently Giuseppe Antonio Camerino, who was able to consult all pertinent documents at the Archivi della Curia Arcivescovile of Trieste, points out that the civil ceremony took place on 30 July 1896, the religious rite on 25 August 1897, and that Letizia was born on 20 September 1897. The requests for the baptism, for the special dispensation (given the fact that they were cousins), and for the wedding were filed on 7 July 1897. See Giuseppe Antonio Camerino, *Italo Svevo* (Turin: UTET, 1981), 165–67. See also Enrico Ghidetti, *Italo Svevo*, 136 for additional information regarding the baptism.

19. Svevo, *Opera Omnia: Commedie*, ed. Umbro Apollonio (Milan: dall'Oglio Editore, 1969), 393.

20. Svevo, *Opera Omnia: Epistolario*, ed. Bruno Maier (Milan: dall'Oglio, 1966), 229.

21. Ibid., 562–63.

22. Ibid., 348.

23. Veneziani, *Vita*, 48.

24. Ibid.

25. *Racconti, Saggi, Pagine*, 816.

26. Ibid., 818.

27. Ibid., 685–705.

28. Svevo participated actively in the resistance against the Austrians. He refused to give them the secret formula for the submarine paints produced in his factory. He gave the Austrian military forces a falsified formula and consequently, in reprisal, they dismantled the entire factory and confiscated everything. See Veneziani, *Vita*, 88–89.

29. Ibid., 97.

30. See B. Weiss, *"Terzetto spezzato:* Svevo's Spiritistic Fantasy," *Italica* 55 (1978):221–22.

31. Veneziani, *Vita*, 144–45.

32. Information gathered from interviews with Letizia Fonda Savio Svevo.

33. Eugenio Montale, *Eugenio Montale Lettere Italo Svevo con gli scritti di Montale su Svevo* (Bari: De Donato, 1966), 143.

34. ". . . we have the sensation that we are faced with a convenient, probably unconscious, no doubt very profitable rationalization." Mario Lavagetto, *L'impiegato Schmitz e altri saggi su Svevo* (Turin: Einaudi, 1975), 11–12.

35. ". . . every commerce with literature . . . ends up being equivalent to an extramarital adventure." Ibid., 10.

36. The pseudonyms are not chosen completely at random: Erode is close to Ettore, the initial *E* is constant in E. Muranese and in E. Samigli, while this last pen name has both Ettore Schmitz's own initials. It is worth mentioning that at home his family used to call him "Tajè" and that at Segnitz his friends called him "Halomes" or "Halomespeter" which in Hebrew means a dreamer, someone in the clouds.

37. Brian Moloney, "Svevo as a Jewish Writer," *Italian Studies* 28 (1973):52.

38. Lavagetto, *L'impiegato Schmitz,* unnumbered last page.

Chapter Two

1. On 19 December 1889 Svevo wrote: "Exactly two years ago I began that novel which was supposed to be God knows what. Instead it's mere rubbish that will nauseate me sooner or later." *Racconti, Saggi, Pagine,* 813–14.

2. Emile Zola, preface to *Thérèse Raquin.*

3. Veneziani, *Vita,* 211.

4. All quotations from the novel come from Italo Svevo, *A Life,* trans. Archibald Colquhoun, (New York: Alfred A. Knopf, 1963). Page numbers are shown in the text in parentheses.

5. Veneziani, *Vita,* 213. "Certainly, for the author, the relationship between Alfonso and Annetta, the rich daughter of the banker Maller, is the important part of the novel."

6. Giacinto Spagnoletti, "Pirandello e Svevo," in *Romanzieri italiani del nostro secolo* (Turin: ERI, 1967), 19.

7. Octavio Paz, *A Draft of Shadows and Other Poems* (New York: New Directions, 1979), 155.

8. Edouard Roditi, "A Note on Svevo," in Italo Svevo, *As a Man Grows Older,* trans. Beryl De Zoete (New York: Bantam Books, 1968), xiii.

9. Notice the homophony between "Nitti" and "inetti."

10. Michele Amato, *La genesi narrativa in Italo Svevo* (Cosenza: Pellegrini, 1966), 44.

11. Giacomo Debenedetti, "Svevo e Schmitz" in *Saggi Critici* (Milan: Mondadori, 1955), 63, 67.

12. Otto Weininger, *Geschlecht und Charakter (Sex and Character)* (Vienna, 1903). In this anti-Semitic work Weininger attempted to establish a philosophy of the sexes which he conceived of as representatives respectively of good and evil: the male representing the positive, the female the negative. He identified Judaism with the negative principle and Christianity with the positive. His wild accusations against the Jews were used later by Hitler and the Nazis. Weininger, who had converted from Judaism, killed himself shortly after the publication of this book.

13. Quoted from Roditi "A Note," xiv.

14. Gabriella Galmonte, "Italo Svevo" (Thesis, Università di Roma,

1966), 141. Albert Goldman writes perceptively on this topic: "As James Joyce divined, when he made the hero of *Ulysses* Leopold Bloom, *the Jew with his 'hangups,' his self-doubt, his self-hate, and his awkward, alienated stance is a twentieth-century symbol for Everyman.*" In Albert Goldman, "Boy-man, schlemiel: the Jewish element in American humor," *Explorations,* ed. Murray Mindlin (Chicago: Quadrangle Books, 1968), 6.

15. In April 1927 Svevo wrote to an anonymous critic: "You probably have noticed that in my whole life I have written only one novel." Cf. Veneziani, *Vita,* 149. The idea of thematic immutability in Svevo's works has been studied by Giorgio Luti (*Italo Svevo e altri studi sulla letteratura italiana del primo Novecento* [Milan, 1961], 253) and by Elio Vittorini (*Diario in pubblico* [Milan, 1957], 18).

16. Renato Poggioli, Introduction to *Confessions of Zeno,* trans. Beryl De Zoete (New York: Putnam, 1948).

17. Michel Eyquem de Montaigne, *Essais,* Book 3 "Essay 1," quoted from W. A. Nitze and E. P. Dargan, *A History of French Literature* (New York, 1922), 201.

18. Montale, *Lettere Italo Svevo,* 121.

19. Roditi, "A Note," xv.

20. In his play *Un marito (A Husband)* Svevo refers to it as "capricious and irrational fate." *Commedie,* 217.

21. Maria Punter, *I caratteri e l'ambiente dell'arte sveviana* (Parenzo: Coana, 1934), 104.

22. In his "Autobiographical Sketch" Svevo tells us that B. Crémieux compared Zeno to Chaplin's screen character because both characters constantly stumble through life (Cf. Veneziani, *Vita,* 223). Alberto Rossi draws a parallel between Chaplin's *Modern Times* and Svevo's characters. Both Chaplin's and Svevo's characters are always surprised by the unexpected realities they come up against when they pursue their own impossible fancies. Cf. "Svevo e Charlot," *La Gazzetta del Popolo* (Torino), 5 July 1928.

23. Brian Moloney, *Italo Svevo A Critical Introduction* (Edinburgh: Edinburgh University Press, 1974), 36.

24. Cf. Matteo Palumbo, *La coscienza di Svevo* (Naples: Liguori, 1976), 26. Eduardo Saccone, *Il poeta travestito. Otto scritti su Svevo* (Pisa: Pacini, 1977), 119.

25. Veneziani, *Vita,* 217.

26. Roditi, "A Note," xvii.

27. Iris Origo, *Leopardi.A Study in Solitude* (London: Hamish Hamilton, 1953), 53.

28. Cf. Saccone, *Il poeta,* 148, and Gian-Paolo Biasin, *Literary Diseases* (Austin: University of Texas Press, 1975), 66.

29. Renato Poggioli, "A Note on Italo Svevo" in *The Spirit of the Letter. Essays in European Literature* (Cambridge: Harvard University Press, 1965), 176.

30. Furbank, *Italo Svevo*, 159.
31. Veneziani, *Vita*, 211.
32. J. B. Priestley, *Literature and Western Man* (New York: Harper & Row, 1960), 197.
33. Quoted from Will Durant, *The Story of Philosophy* (New York: Pocket Books, 1954), 329.
34. Veneziani, *Vita*, 213. Svevo writes in his autobiographical sketch: "The author, certainly, though already in this thirties, still showed in it a certain immaturity."
35. Svevo, *Epistolario*, 759–60.
36. Luigi Barzini, "Italian Writers," *New York Review of Books* 13 (9 October 1969):36.
37. Veneziani, *Vita*, 214.
38. In Trieste, unlike other parts of Italy, everyone speaks the local dialect no matter what the social or cultural position of the individual. It is not unusual to hear highly educated and sophisticated people converse in Triestine without the slightest inhibition.
39. Giacomo Devoto, *Studi di stilistica* (Florence: Le Monnier, 1950), 173–93.
40. Carlo Bo, "Per un ritratto di Svevo," in *Riflessioni Critiche* (Firenze: Sansoni, 1953), 447.
41. J. O'Brien, "Italo Svevo," *Bookman* (February 1931), 566–71.
42. The book, published in 1863, details the construction of a play: Rising action (exposition and complication), climax, and falling action (reversal and catastrophe). See C. Hugh Holman, *A Handbook to Literature* (Indianapolis: Bobbs-Merrill, 1981), 196.
43. Domenico Oliva, *Il Corriere della Sera*, 11 December 1892.
44. Furbank, *Svevo*, 162.
45. Eugenio Montale, *Carteggio con gli scritti di Montale su Svevo* (Milan: Mondadori, 1976), 129.
46. Geno Pampaloni, "Italo Svevo narratore: da *Una vita a Senilità*," in *Italo Svevo Oggi. Atti del Convegno, Firenze 3–4 Febbraio 1979*, ed. Marco Marchi (Florence: Vallecchi, 1980), 116.

Chapter Three

1. Numbers in parenthesis in the text and notes refer to Italo Svevo, *As a Man Grows Older*, trans. Beryl De Zoete (New York: Bantam Books, 1968).
2. Silvio Benco, "Italo Svevo," *Il Resto del Carlino*, 18 September 1931. According to Livia Veneziani's somewhat contemptuous description of her, she was a beautiful florid young working-class woman who, after the affair, ran away from Trieste—presumably with another man—and ended up in a circus as an equestrienne (Veneziani, *Vita*, 47). Veruda drew a picture of her that

accentuates her femininity and grace. Veruda's drawing is now the property of Bruno Pincherle of Trieste. It has been published in Tullio Kezich, *Svevo e Zeno: Vite Parallele* (Milan: All'insegna del pesce d'oro, 1970), plate 11.

3. "Profilo autobiografico" in *Racconti, Saggi, Pagine,* 804. The same substitution of the fictional for the real name occurs in a letter to Valerio Jahier, where the author repeats: ". . . in part it was written to be read by Angiolina and to educate her." Svevo, *Epistolario,* 863–64.

4. "Profilo autobiografico," in *Racconti, Saggi, Pagine,* 805.

5. Svevo, *Epistolario,* 39–40.

6. On 24 February 1896 Svevo writes: "The first period of my life ends here and the new one begins." On 2 March another entry reads: "In any case the most important thing is that henceforth a new life begins for me." Italo Svevo, *Diario per la fidanzata* (1896), ed. Bruno Maier and Anita Pittoni (Trieste: Edizioni dello Zibaldone, 1962), 105,114.

7. It is not clear how long the affair lasted; nor do we know precisely when Giuseppina left Trieste.

8. Svevo, *Epistolario,* 64.

9. It appeared in serialized form from 15 June to 16 September 1898. That same year it was also published by Vram at Svevo's expense.

10. I should point out that De Zoete's translation of the end of the last sentence of this passage does not fully convey the meaning of the original text, which reads "gli altri non avrebbero trovato mai piú la quaresima." (The others would never find their way back to Lent.) By implication this means that there would be no more Carnivals for them.

11. This is the only instance in which the author uses the word *senile.*

12. Giorgio Luti, *Svevo* (Florence: La Nuova Italia, Il Castoro, 1967), 50.

13. Svevo, *Diario per la fidanzata,* 102.

14. Svevo, *Senilità* (Milan: dall'Oglio, 1971), 7–8. According to Stanislaus Joyce, even his brother James did not like the title and suggested in 1932 *As a Man Grows Older* for the English version of the novel. Cf. Stanislaus Joyce, "Introduction" in *As a Man Grows Older,* ix.

15. Quoted from Furbank, 32.

16. Veneziani, *Vita,* 33.

17. Ibid.

18. "Profilo" in Veneziani, *Vita,* 212. The portrait is at the Galleria d'Arte Moderna, Palazzo Pesaro, Venice. Benco's review of the novel's second edition appeared in the *Piccolo della Sera* (Trieste), 8 September 1927. For a fuller description of Veruda, see Charles C. Russell, *Italo Svevo. The Writer from Trieste. Reflections on his Background and his Work* (Ravenna: Longo Editore, 1978), 111–14.

19. Svevo, *Epistolario,* 879–80.

20. Giacinto Spagnoletti, *Svevo: la vita, il pensiero i testi esemplari* (Milan: Edizioni Accademia, 1972), 53.

21. Emilio even fabricates a dream in which he catches Balli with Angiolina and berates him with words "full of burning hatred and contempt to punish him with" (109). In another dream Balli takes advantage of "Amalia's abject submission" and refuses to "make any honourable amends" (110).
22. Eduardo Saccone, "Un'educazione sentimentale?" in *Il poeta travestito*, 167.
23. Ibid., 172.
24. Bruno Maier, *Italo Svevo*, 4th ed. (Milan: Mursia, 1975), 82.
25. Benco writes that Veruda "with the broad and secure vision of a talented artist" refined Svevo's "sensitivity of the eye" and taught him how to look at things with the eye of an artist. "The grey of the first novel is often opaque; the grey of the second . . . is all transparencies of color. All this due to his intimacy with Veruda." Benco, "Italo Svevo" in *La coscienza di Zeno*. (Milan: dall'Oglio, 1957), 13.
26. Benedetto Croce, *Estetica come scienza dell'espressione e linguistica generale* (Bari: Laterza, 1950). In English, cf. G. N. G. Orsini, *Benedetto Croce Philosopher of Art and Literary Critic* (Carbondale: Southern Illinois Press, 1961).
27. Russell, *Svevo*, 153, 154.
28. Geno Pampaloni, "Italo Svevo" in *Storia della Letteratura Italiana*, ed. Emilio Cecchi and Natalino Sapegno (Milan: Garzanti, 1969), vol. 9, 510.
29. Russell, *Svevo*, 156.
30. "Profilo" in Veneziani, *Vita*, 216.
31. Quoted from Geno Pampaloni, "Italo Svevo," *Terzo Programma* (Turin), no. 2 (1964), 102.
32. This identification was first made by Letizia Fonda Savio-Svevo, the author's daughter, in an interview on Radio Trieste (20 February 1961). Subsequently she expanded on this information in another interview with Charles C. Russell. Cf. Russell, *Svevo*, 135–36. The information concerning Maria Rossi's addiction comes from Camerino, *Svevo*, 184.
33. "Profilo" in Veneziani, *Vita*, 215.
34. Furbank, *Svevo*, 170.
35. "For some years he remembered with regret a girl called Maria, with pale hair of purest gold and a straight figure which seemed not to notice all the weight of gold she bore on her head." *A Life*, 77.
36. Giorgio Luti, *Italo Svevo e altri studi sulla letteratura italiana del primo Novecento* (Milan: Lerici, 1961), 271.
37. See G. Pontiggia, "La tecnica narrativa di Italo Svevo," in *Il Verri* 4, no. 5 (October 1960), 165.
38. *Racconti, Saggi, Pagine*, 832. The diary entry is dated 6 June 1917.
39. "Preface" to 2d ed. *Senilità*, 5.
40. Actually, Svevo's claim that except for *L'Indipendente* (12 October 1898), there had been total silence is not accurate. In fact, reviews of the

novel appeared in several Italian papers: *L'idea italiana* (Rovigno, 15 October 1898), *Il corriere di Gorizia* (Gorizia, 18 October 1898), *Il sole* (Milan, 12 November 1898), *Supplemento al Caffaro* (Genoa, 11 February 1899), and *Il Marzocco* (Florence, 12 March 1899). Ironically, *Il Piccolo,* Trieste's leading Italian daily for which Svevo was still working, refused to acknowledge the publication of *Senilità* because it had first appeared on the pages of the rival paper.

41. Heyse's letter to Svevo is dated 26 November 1898. Cf. Veneziani, *Vita,* 47–48.

42. "Preface" to 2d ed., *Senilità,* 5.

43. A calming drug. See Roland A. Champagne, "A Displacement of Plato's *Pharmakon*: A study of Italo Svevo's Short Fiction," *Modern Fiction Studies* 21:564–72.

Chapter Four

1. See Giuditta Rosowsky, "Théorie et pratique psychoanalytiques dans La coscienza di Zeno," *Revue des Études Italiennes* 16 (1970): 49–70.

2. According to Kumar, "Another possible link with Bergson's philosophy is Italo Svevo with whom Joyce lived on terms of close intimacy and whose novels represent Bergsonian theories of time, memory and consciousness." Shiv K. Kumar, *Bergson and the Stream of Consciousness Novel* (New York: New York University Press, 1963), 105.

3. James Joyce, *Finnegans Wake* (New York: Penguin Books, 1978), 186.

4. Sandro Maxia, *Svevo e la prosa del Novecento* (Roma-Bari: Laterza, 1977) [Letteratura Italiana Laterza 61], 34.

5. Ibid.

6. Dr. Weiss, who was also a distant relative of Svevo, believed that he had been the first to introduce Svevo to psychoanalysis. Cf. G. Voghera, "Considerazioni 'eretiche' sulla scrittura di Italo Svevo," in *Gli anni della psicanalisi* (Pordenone: Edizioni Studio Tesi, 1980), 41–42.

7. Numbers in parenthesis in the text and notes refer to Italo Svevo, *Confessions of Zeno,* trans. Beryl De Zoete (New York: Vintage Books, 1958).

8. Svevo was possibly inspired by the concluding moment of World War I, which ended on the *11th hour* of the *11th day* of the *11th month* of 1918.

9. Sigmund Freud, in *The Question of Analysis* (chap. 5), observes that illness may be used as a protection, to excuse incapacity at work, or in family life as a means of obtaining sacrifice, affection from others, or even to impose one's will upon others. The patient, however, is unaware of his behavior.

10. "Profilo autobiografico," in *Racconti, Saggi, Pagine,* 809.

11. Richard Gilman, "News from the Past," *New Republic,* (2 November 1963), 19.

12. Russell, *Svevo*, 211.
13. According to Russell, ibid., 217 "This fat man was actually Svevo's old friend, Giulio Ventura, the fellow who dabbled in dialect poetry and who once tried his hand at a novel."
14. "Profilo autobiografico," in *Racconti, Saggi, Pagine*, 807.
15. Ibid.
16. In *Problems of Anxiety* Freud states that the physical act of writing, which consists in allowing a fluid to flow from a tube upon paper, has acquired the symbolic meaning of coitus.
17. Zeno, of course, admits openly to his numerous lies: "I remembered that among the many lies I had imposed on that profound observer, Dr. S., one was that I had never betrayed my wife after Ada went away" (382).
18. Anthony Wilden, "Death, Desire, and Repetition in Svevo's 'Zeno,'" in *Modern Language Notes* 84 (1969):102.
19. "Profilo autobiografico," in *Racconti, Saggi, Pagine*, 809.
20. Ibid.
21. Quoted from Albert Goldman, "Boy-man, schlemiel: the Jewish element in American humor," 7.
22. Ruth R. Wisse, *The Schlemiel as Modern Hero* (Chicago: University of Chicago Press, 1971), 23. Theodore Reik in his *Jewish Wit* (New York: Gamut Press, 1962), 41, characterizes the schlemiel as "a masochistic character who has strong unconscious will to fail and spoil his chances."
23. Goldman, "Boy-man, schlemiel," 13.
24. Marina Beer argues unconvincingly that Svevo, being familiar with Adalbert von Chamisso's novel *Peter Schlemihl* (1814), may have been influenced by it to choose E. Samigli as one of his pseudonyms, due to its homophonic closeness to both Schmitz and Samigli. See Marina Beer, "Alcune note su Ettore Schmitz e i suoi nomi: per una ricerca sulle fonti di Italo Svevo," in *Contributi Sveviani*, ed. Riccardo Scrivano (Trieste: Edizioni LINT, 1979), 11–30.
25. The original text is far more poignant: "*15.4. 1890 ore 4 1/2. Muore mio padre. U. S. Per chi non lo sapesse quelle due ultime lettere non significano United States, ma ultima sigaretta.*" (For those who may not know, the last two letters do not mean United States, but stand for last cigarette.)
26. Furbank, *Svevo*, 174–203.
27. André Bouissy, "Les fondaments idéologiques de l'oeuvre d'Italo Svevo," *Revue des Études Italiennes* 12 (1966):26.
28. Paula Robinson, "Svevo: Secrets of the Confessional" *Literature and Psychology* 20 (1970):107.
29. Edoardo Saccone, *Commento a "Zeno"* (Bologna: il Mulino, 1973), 111–20.
30. Carlo Fonda, *Svevo e Freud. Proposta di interpretazione della "Coscienza di Zeno"* (Ravenna: Longo Editore, 1978), 99–106.
31. Ibid., 105.

32. Russell, *Svevo*, 221.
33. Montale, "Leggenda e verità di Svevo," in *Eugenio Montale Lettere Italo Svevo con gli scritti di Montale su Svevo*, 125–26.
34. Tullio Kezich, *Svevo e Zeno. Vite parallele* (Milan: All'Insegna del Pesce d'Oro, 1970), 10–11.
35. Veneziani, *Vita*, 52.
36. Deuteronomy 6, 11. Cf. J. H. Hertz, ed., *The Pentateuch and Haftorahs* (London: Soncino Press, 1973), 769–71.
37. Veneziani, *Vita*, 147.
38. Benjamin Crémieux called Zeno "the Triestine bourgeois Charlot." Cf. Crémieux's review of *Zeno* in *Les Annales*, Paris, 1 March 1928, 214.
39. Fausta Cialente, in her autobiographical novel *Le quattro ragazze Wiselberger* (Milano: Oscar Mondadori, 1980), 18, writes that in her mother's family three sisters had names beginning with *A*: Alice, Alba, Adele; the fourth one, named Elsa, had danced on several occasions with Ettore Schmitz to whom she did not pay much attention because he was not young and beautiful as she. "He was, however, very charming and such a considerate and honorable man."
40. In *The Limping Hero. Grotesques in Literature* (New York: New York University Press, 1971), Peter L. Hays states that maimed figures represent their author's view of life as sterile and severely limited.
41. While they are in the coffee shop, Guido suddenly begins to berate women, spouting forth the misogynous ideas of Weininger. Zeno is so fascinated by this that he will read the racist book entitled *Sex and Character*.
42. Fonda, *Svevo e Freud*, 109.
43. Beno Weiss, review of Carlo Fonda, *Svevo e Freud. Proposta di interpretazione della "Coscienza di Zeno," Italica* 58 (1981):329.
44. "The Dream-Work," in *The Basic Writings of Sigmund Freud*, trans. and ed. A. A. Brill (New York: Random House, 1938), 371–72.
45. When Ada and Guido are married and he betrays her with his secretary, she comes to loathe his violin playing. Ada will hate him for the very same qualities for which she once loved him.
46. The French edition of the novel, done under Svevo's supervision, corroborates my interpretation: "Je saisis maintenant pourquoi Adeline aimait tant votre Bach déformé. Vous jouiez très bien, mais il y a des choses sacrées que de justes lois devraient mettre à l'abri de toute souillure." [Now I grasp why Ada loved so much your distorted Bach. You played very well, but there are certain sacred things which good laws should protect from any kind of soiling (or profanation)]. *La Conscience de Zeno*, trans. Paul-Henri Michel (Paris: Gallimard, 1954), 140.
47. The text reads: "Questa era la vera chiarezza." This was true clarity, a true epiphany.
48. Mario Fusco, *Italo Svevo: Coscienza e realtà*, trans. Paola Bimbi (Palermo: Sellerio editore, 1984), 171.

49. Teresa de Lauretis, "Dreams as Metalanguage in Svevo's *Confessions of Zeno*," *Language and Style* 4 (1971):218.

50. Svevo's wife had beautiful long hair. When Joyce asked for permission to use her name and hair as models for Anna Livia Plurabelle, Svevo and Livia sent him as a gift a beautiful painting by Veruda, in which Livia's hair shone in splendid beauty. The painting (now part of the James Joyce Collection at the University of Buffalo) was meant to show Svevo's gratitude to Joyce. Joyce once remarked to an Italian journalist: "They say I have immortalized Svevo, but I've also immortalized the tresses of Signora Svevo. These were long and reddish-blond. My sister who used to see them let down told me about them. The river at Dublin passes dye-houses and so has reddish water. So I have playfully compared these two things in the book I'm writing. A lady in it will have the tresses which are really Signora Svevo's." Quoted from Richard Ellman, *James Joyce* (New York: Oxford University Press, 1965), 572.

51. At the end of the affair with Carla, Zeno muses: ". . . it was inexcusable that I should suffer so much when I had such a unique opportunity for freeing myself" (243). The original reads "una opportunità unica di svezzamento," meaning a unique opportunity for being *weaned*.

52. Zeno actually makes an unsuccessful pass at Carmen, thinking that he might be doing a good turn to Ada, but without causing Augusta any harm. Women respectable enough to be married by Zeno and his equals have names beginning with *A*; Carla and Carmen, the two mistresses, have names that begin with *C*. Zeno, whose name is so distant from the first letter of the alphabet, can easily shift from one to the other. His children's names are Antonia and Alfio.

53. Fonda, *Svevo e Freud*, 143.

54. In a short story entitled "Lo specifico del dottor Menghi" (The specific of Dr. Menghi) the doctor discovers a drug that either increases or decreases the body's activity. When the metabolism slows down, one's mental and perceptive abilities become intensified. The *pharmakon* is called Annina.

55. Furbank, *Svevo*, 190.

56. A. Robbe-Grillet, *Pour un nouveau roman* (Paris: Gallimard, 1963), 81.

57. Illness, as Biasin points out, is a reflection of certain sociological and historical phenomena. Cf. Gian-Paolo Biasin, *Literary Diseases. Theme and Metaphor in the Italian Novel* (Austin: University of Texas Press, 1975).

58. Giacinto Spagnoletti, *La Coscienza di Zeno di Italo Svevo* (Milan: Biblioteca Universale Rizzoli, 1978), 115.

59. The word *untore* (anointer has a specific meaning in Italian lore because it immediately brings to mind Manzoni's romantic novel *I promessi sposi (The Betrothed)* and its "appendix," *Storia della Colonna Infame*. As reported there, during the 1629–30 plague that ravaged Lombardy, it was believed that anointers were spreading the dreaded disease by painting "doors and walls

with a yellowish or whitish filth." Renzo, one of the principal characters, is mistakenly taken for an anointer and barely escapes with his life, as a menacing Milanese crowd chases him down a street shouting, "Get him! Get the dirty anointer!" Cf. Alessandro Manzoni, *The Betrothed*, trans. Bruce Pennman (Harmondsworth: Penguin Books, 1983), 644.

60. Sigmund Freud, *The Interpretation of Dreams*, ed. and trans. James Strachey (New York: Basic Books, 1955), 269–71. Otto's dream 269–71; Staircase Dreams, 247, 355, 364–66, 369–72, 384.

61. Fonda, *Svevo e Freud*, 139–43.

62. Freud, *The Interpretation of Dreams*, 397.

63. Ibid., 398.

64. Wilhelm Stekel, *The Interpretation of Dreams*, trans. Eden and Cedar Paul (New York: Washington Square Press, 1967), 14. Svevo met Stekel in 1911.

65. Saccone, *Commento a "Zeno,"* 200.

66. Ibid., 199.

67. In this particular vision, Zeno is under the table playing with marbles. He moves closer to his mother because he wants her to play with him. Suddenly, he pulls on the tablecloth and a bottle of ink falls on him staining both of his parents' clothing. The father is about to give him a kick, but his mother intervenes. The playing under the table is reminiscent of James Joyce's *A Portrait of the Artist as a Young Man*. Stephen Dedalus, as a young boy, also used to play under that table. Svevo was familiar with this work because Joyce once asked him to read it as a class assignment and to comment upon it.

68. In Stoic philosophy this is an attitude of indifference: all the things that do not depend directly on ourselves (life, death, pleasure, and suffering) are neither virtue nor vice, neither good nor evil.

69. Svevo, *Epistolario*, (letter dated 10 December 1927) 857–58; (letter dated 27 December 1927), 859–60.

70. Fonda, *Svevo e Freud*, 147.

71. Sigmund Freud, *New Introductory Lectures on Psychoanalysis*, chap. 3, quoted from *Freud: Dictionary of Psychoanalysis*, ed. N. Fodor and F. Gaynor (Greenwich: Fawcett, 1963), 123 [A Premier Book].

Chapter Five

1. Svevo's plays have been collected in Italo Svevo, *Opera Omnia: Commedie*, ed. Umbro Apollonio (Milan: dall'Oglio, 1969). Numbers in parentheseses in the text refer to this edition.

2. The protagonist of "Il vecchione" ("The Old, Old Man") states that he has to write in order to feel alive: "Writing, therefore, which I shall do every evening just before taking my physic, will serve a hygienic purpose." Svevo, "Il vecchione," *Racconti, Saggi, Pagine*, 137.

3. Veneziani, *Vita*, 151.

Notes and References

4. See Roberto Rebora, "Il teatro per Italo Svevo non è una distrazione domenicale," *Sipario* (May 1961), 2. See also Ruggero Rimini, *La morte nel salotto: Guida al teatro d'Italo Svevo* (Florence: Vallecchi, 1974).

5. Richard N. Coe, *Eugene Ionesco* (New York: Grove Press, 1961), 1.

6. Professor Michele Amato in *La genesi narrativa in Italo Svevo* (Cosenza: Pellegrini, 1966) points out that Svevo's early plays were the genesis of his novels.

7. Giacomo Debenedetti, *Il romanzo del Novecento* (Milan: Garzanti, 1971), 527.

8. Giorgio Luti, *Svevo* (Firenze: La Nuova Italia, 1967), 50.

9. When Ettore showed the play to his brother-in-law, Samuele Salmona, he counseled him to give up poetry and write in prose. *Lettere a Svevo. Diario di Elio Schmitz,* ed. Bruno Maier (Milan: Dall'Oglio, 1973), 221. The text of *Ariosto governatore* is on 222–24.

10. During 1880–1881 Svevo either planned or wrote other plays of which only the titles remain: *Il primo amore* (First love), *Le roi est mort, vive le roi* (The king is dead, Long live the king), *I due poeti* (Two poets), *I fiori del perdono* (Flowers of forgiveness), *Fra il corpo insegnante* (Within the teaching body), *La rigenerazione* (Regeneration), *La gente superiore* (Superior people), *Difetto moderno* (Modern defect), and *Tre caratteri* (Three characters). Cf. *Diario di Elio*, 230–37, 244–45.

11. Veneziani, *Vita,* 24.

12. The first review "*La joie de vivre di Emilio Zola*" appeared in *L'Indipendente* on 8 March 1884 and the other "*Il libro di Don Chisciotte di Edoardo Scarfoglio*" appeared in the same publication on 18 September 1884. Cf. Svevo, *Racconti, Saggi, Pagine,* 575–77, 588–91. The play is undated. Umbro Apollonio, the editor of *Commedie,* believes that it was written circa 1880. Svevo's wife, on the other hand, places it around 1884 and Bruno Maier between 1885 and 1892. I tend to agree with Ruggero Rimini who is convinced that *Le teorie del Conte Alberto* was written after *Le ire di Giuliano* and *Una commedia inedita,* both one-act plays. With this play, however, which has two acts, Svevo showed a certain mastering of the art—albeit imperfect—in being able to expand both time and action. Cf. Rimini, *La morte nel salotto,* 36–38.

13. Svevo, *Racconti, Saggi, Pagine,* 590.

14. It was published in *Befana,* a literary supplement of *L'Indipendente,* (55–60, 1891 issue).

15. Tedeschi was eventually arrested upon landing in Alexandria, Egypt. Peppina moved back into the Francesco Schmitz residence where she gave birth to a child and was rejoined by her husband, who had served six months in jail. The child, Mario, died at two, ostensibly as a result of a venereal disease contracted by his father. Elio fails to tell us what eventually happened to Tedeschi. Apparently he and his wife continued to live in the Schmitz household. We know that Peppina had three other children, Silvio, Steno, and Rita. Steno Tedeschi (1881–1911), who became a philosophy pro-

fessor in Trieste, took his own life, driven by his mother's illness. His *Studi filosofici ed altri scritti* (Genova: Formiggini, 1913) was published posthumously. Cf. Elio Schmitz, *Lettere a Svevo. Diario di Elio Schmitz*, 198, 235, 260.

16. Amato, *La genesi narrativa*, 44.

17. It was written most likely in 1913 or 1914. In scene 2 Amalia notices that Giuseppe held his last job in 1909 and asks him to account for the four years during which he has not worked, unaware that he spent the time in jail.

18. Veneziani, *Vita*, 152–53.

19. Svevo, *Epistolario*, 56.

20. One version is of act 1 of the play, with minor insignificant variations. The third version has three acts, but bears the title *Casa Galli* (The Galli Home), again with minor variations (581–633).

21. At first the play was bylined Italo Svevo; the name was subsequently crossed out and replaced by E.[ttore] Muranese, a pseudonym used only on this occasion. Possibly, the name derives from Murano, an island in the Venetian lagoon where the Veneziani firm had a paint factory. Between 1900 and 1914 Svevo spent frequent periods in Murano, and the play was most likely written during one of these stays. Svevo wrote several short stories ("Marianno," "Cimutti," "Senerella"), whose protagonists are from Murano. The Murano branch of the factory remained open until 1918.

22. Dramatically, *La parola* is not as effective as *La verità* owing to the lengthy secondary plot, which, though an absorbing story, halts what little action there is. Both plays are similar in many respects, except for minor variations of plot, but the polemical question concerning reality and its dissolution is not treated as extensively as in *La verità*. Svevo's hypothesis is that the individual who tells only the truth is not believed, and therefore he is at times forced to withhold it. As Alemanno appropriately has pointed out, the subtitle of the play should have been "or better still, the triumph of falsehood." Cf. Anna Maria Alemanno, "Cronache di teatro: Tre atti unici di Italo Svevo," *Il Pensiero Nazionale*, 16 September 1967.

La verità touches *La coscienza di Zeno* at several points. Both Silvio and Zeno suffer from a nervous disease and are treated with shock therapy; both like intriguing numerical combinations; and most interesting, Zeno's father also betrayed his wife with her dressmaker, but she never succeeded in making him confess this infidelity and died in the belief that she had been mistaken (*Confessions of Zeno*, 29). In view of these similarities, we can now come back to the problem of dating the two plays. Apollonio, who used a handwriting expert to approximate the dates of composition, places both plays in 1880; whereas Maier proposes that *La parola* was written in 1901 and *La verità* between 1921 and 1925 or 1926. Cf. Bruno Maier, *Italo Svevo*, 137, 151. Most likely, *La parola* was written circa 1900 and *La verità*, on account of its relationship to the novel, just before Svevo began to write *La coscienza di Zeno*.

Furthermore, the play had to be written prior to 1918, when Trieste became part of Italy and Italian currency was first used. In the play Austrian currency is used instead.

23. Rimini, *La morte nel salotto*, 73.

24. Usually a servant, a comic character who has the confidence of his master.

25. It premiered on 1 April 1927 at Bragaglia's Teatro Sperimentale Degli Indipendenti and was first published in *Il Convegno* (Milan), 23 April 1931. This segment dealing with *Terzetto* is a partial rendering of my essay "*Terzetto spezzato*: Svevo's Spiritistic Fantasy," *Italica* 55 (1978):211–24.

26. Apollonio places it around 1890. However, certain 1910 Svevo writings show a remarkable similarity with parts of this play, causing serious doubts as to the exact date of composition. See Svevo, *Saggi e pagine sparse*, ed. Umbro Apollonio (Milano: Mondadori, 1954) 296–97. Bruno Maier argues that *Terzetto* was written during the so-called "Zeno period," or immediately after (between 1919 and 1927). Cf. Bruno Maier, "Proposta cronologica per *Terzetto spezzato di Italo Svevo*," in *Studi in memoria di Luigi Russo* (Pisa: Nistri Lischi, 1974), 319–27. The following two pieces of evidence will strengthen his chronology: In scene 3 the husband boasts: "I am the biggest coffee importer in the Kingdom" (187). Trieste, where the action of the play takes place, only became part of the Kingdom of Italy in 1919. Therefore, the play must have been written either in 1919 or after. This polemic has been partially laid to rest by a newly discovered letter (12 April 1927) which Svevo wrote to Montale while *Terzetto* was being performed in Rome: "I wrote that stuff about fifteen years ago, and a friend took it away from me. I feel as if I were concluding my multicolored life with a play." *Carteggio Svevo Montale*, ed. Giorgio Zampa (Milan:Mondadori, 1976), 54,55.

27. Debenedetti, *Il romanzo del Novecento*, 338–48.

28. *Confessions of Zeno*, 379.

29. Cf. Veneziani, *Vita*, 151, 250. Although there is disagreement concerning the merits of Svevo's plays, the critics agree on the dramatic effectiveness of *Terzetto*. Leone De Castris (*Italo Svevo* [Pisa: Nistri-Lischi, 1959], 50) sees it as a "smiling criticism of a life filled with hypocrisies and social conventions, articulated in a moving and very stirring dialogue." Maurizio Mazzotta ("La passione sbagliata di Svevo: il teatro," *La Voce del Sud* (Lecce), 6 January 1962) feels that Svevo is at his best in this play. Even Furbank, who usually has a negative opinion of Svevo's theater, admits that *Terzetto* is "altogether wittier and more original." Furbank, *Svevo, The Man and the Writer* (London: Secker & Warburg, 1966), p. 210.

30. Nino Meloni, who convinced Bragaglia to stage the play, wrote to Svevo: "Bragaglia only knew you by name; once he read the script, he was very impressed and although he is not too keen on psychological drama . . . he favored *Terzetto* over the extremely modern works normally preferred by him." Quoted from *Lettere a Svevo. Diario di Elio Schmitz*, 132–33.

31. This segment dealing with *Inferiorità* is a partial rendering of my article "Svevo's *Inferiorità*," *Modern Fiction Studies* 28 (Spring 1972): 45–51, copyright © 1972 by Purdue Research Foundation. Reprinted with permission.

32. Apollonio sums it up quite well: "*Inferiorità*, to an extent, is the story of a timid man, and Svevo's entire literary production frequently develops the theme of timidity, that is to say, a psychic situation against which no one's help is of any use." See "Introduzione" in *Commedie*, 7.

33. According to Furbank, "The play is a study in contagion, worked out with all Svevo's acute perception of consequences, and for once, as a dramatist, Svevo is economical—his quick reversals really surprise and his ironies are truly dramatic." The contagion mentioned by Furbank refers to the reciprocal bullying that takes place among all the characters of the play. Cf. Furbank, *Svevo*, 211.

34. It is quite possible that the title has no relationship to the action of the play. When Svevo began writing *Con la penna d'oro*, his wife gave him as a gift a golden pen with which to write the play. He consequently chose the title in homage to his benefactor. In a very successful 1977 production of the play the director Massimo De Francovich staged it under the more appropriate title of *Le due cugine* (The two cousins).

35. There are striking similarities between Teresina and Aunt Rosina of *La coscienza di Zeno*, the irascible sister of Giovanni Malfenti. Both women resemble Fanny Wolf Moravia (1822–1895), Livia Veneziani's dictatorial grandmother, Svevo's aunt and wife of Giuseppe Moravia, the founder of what eventually became the Veneziani Paint Company. It was she, however, who was the real spirit and control behind this successful business venture.

36. Eugenio Montale considers the play "a dramatized novel," unsuited for the stage. Cf. Eugenio Montale, *Lettere Italo Svevo con gli altri scritti di Montale su Svevo* (Bari: De Donato Editore, 1966), 173.

37. On 24 February 1881 Svevo wrote in Elio's diary: "*Regeneration*. Unfortunately I completed two acts and I wish I hadn't. Something that could have been included in one act, I tried to expand into four." See Elio Schmitz, *Diario*, 245.

38. It is most likely the Voronoff cure that attracted great publicity in the Triestine press of the period. Serge Voronoff (1866–1951) was a Russian physician and biologist known for his experiments on rejuvenation by means of transplanting genital glands from monkeys.

39. A scene reminiscent of *Candide*, Voltaire's parody of optimism, summed up by "'Tis well said, but we must cultivate our garden."

40. In "Il vecchione," which deals with the same topic, we read: "The disorder of the present gave way to the disorder of the past." *Raccconti, Saggi, Pagine*, 139.

41. Antonio Valenti, "*La rigenerazione* al Teatro della Loggetta. Uno

Notes and References

Svevo comico che sa di Brecht e di Beckett," *Il Giornale di Brescia*, 22 November 1967.

42. Elio Vittorini, *Diario in pubblico* (Milano: Bompiani, 1957), 16–21.
43. Roberto Rebora, "Italo Svevo e l'opera di ricerca. *La rigenerazione* di Italo Svevo," *Sipario*, 1 February 1968, 40.
44. Leon Edel, *The Modern Psychological Novel* (New York: Grosset & Dunlap, 1964), 197. [Universal Library]
45. The play was staged by Tino Buazzelli's "La compagnia di Prosa" under the direction of Edmo Fenoglio. It achieved a phenomenal critical and box-office success (more than 200 performances) in Italy and Europe, winning the Idi-Saint Vincent Prize for best Italian dramatic work for the 1973–74 theatrical season.
46. Michele Tondo, "Teatro di Svevo," *La gazzetta del mezzogiorno* (Bari), 23 December 1960.

Chapter Six

1. It was serialized on 6, 7, 8 January 1888. Now available in Luciano Nanni, *Leggere Svevo. Antologia della critica sveviana* (Bologna: Zanichelli, 1974), 380–87. Except for "Una lotta," all the short stories and fables are in Svevo, *Racconti, Saggi, Pagine*. Numbers in parenthesis refer to this edition.
2. It appeared in nine installments between 4 and 13 October 1890.
3. Fusco, *Svevo*, 215–16.
4. Svevo wrote many fables, now collected in *Racconti, Saggi, Pagine*, 751-63.
5. It appears that the Venezianis owned an incubator appropriately called "La Foster-Mother" and that while in England, Svevo inquired as to its proper functioning. Cf. Svevo, *Epistolario*, 426.
6. Svevo wrote three versions of the tale: the 1910 version has been lost to us; the second was published on 7 December 1924 in *Sera della Domenica* (Svevo considered it "mutilated"), and the third appeared on 15 March 1927 in *Il Convegno*. See Svevo, *Epistolario*, 830.
7. Guido Piovene in *La parola e il libro*, no. 9-10 (September-October 1927), 253.
8. The story is based on a real-life incident as well as on a dream. Cf. Furbank, *Svevo*, 136–37.
9. Samigli, of course, is the name Svevo used to sign his first writings in *L'Indipendente*.
10. Lavagetto, *L'impiegato Schmitz*, 112.
11. In the original MS one reads under the title: "Short story of a fantastic nature. Warning: you are requested not to laugh . . . right away. No. 298." In Svevo, *Saggi e pagine sparse*, ed. Apollonio, 388.
12. In a letter dated 4 May 1904 Svevo signed off in a postscript: "The

inventor of Annina [the name of the serum] and all its applications, practical and impractical." See *Epistolario,* 400.

13. Fusco, *Svevo,* 221–22.

14. Most likely, it was written when Svevo, like Roberto Erls, had become a successful businessman and no longer suffered the humiliation of failure, so well described in *Una vita.* The treatment of the inferiority complex suggests also that Svevo was by now familiar with Freud's ideas.

15. Svevo, *Epistolario,* 770. See 768, 796, 799, 809 for other references to his difficulties with the story.

16. It is difficult to establish their order of composition, except for "Le confessioni del vegliardo" which bears the date 4 April 1928. The English edition of the sequel to Zeno, which includes the play *La rigenerazione,* is appropriately entitled *Further Confessions of Zeno.*

17. Gabriella Contini, *Il quarto romanzo di Svevo* (Turin: Einaudi, 1980), 28–30.

18. "Le confessioni del vegliardo," *Racconti, Saggi, Pagine,* 372.

19. Ibid.

20. The manuscript bears no title. The present title was chosen by Umbro Apollonio. Cf. Svevo, *Corto viaggio sentimentale e altri racconti inediti,* ed. Umbro Apollonio (Milan: Mondadori, 1966), 411.

21. Svevo ironically links love and tobacco into one organic pleasure.

22. In a letter to B. Crémieux (16 May 1928) Svevo indicates that the story's title will be "Il vecchione." In a subsequent letter to Marie Anne Comnène [Crémieux] (19 August 1928), he uses the title "Il vegliardo." Cf. *Epistolario,* 876–77, 888.

23. By now Svevo was familiar with Proust's writings and most likely was influenced by them when he wrote "Il vecchione."

24. At this point in his life Svevo was weighed down by many ailments: he suffered from chronic asthma and emphysema (as a result of smoking 60 cigarettes a day), arteriosclerosis, intestinal disturbances, arthritis, nervousness (for which he took tranquillizers), and baldness. Cf. Carlo Baiocco, "Intervista alla signora Letizia Svevo Fonda Savio" in *Analisi del personaggio sveviano in relazione alle immagini di lotta e malattia* (Roma: Centro Informazioni Stampa Universitaria, 1984), 126–29.

25. Maier, *Svevo,* 121.

26. "Il vecchione," *Racconti, Saggi, Pagine,* 138.

Chapter Seven

1. *Alberto Moravia, Intervista sullo scrittore scomodo,* ed. Nello Ajello (Rome and Bari: Laterza, 1978), 117–18.

2. Giorgio Voghera, *Gli anni della psicanalisi* (Pordenone: Studio Tesi, 1980), 3–42.

3. Ibid., 16.

Selected Bibliography

PRIMARY SOURCES

See *Notes and References* for further bibliographical orientation. For a complete bibliography (1892–1969), see Bruno Maier's "Bibliografia delle edizioni" and "Bibliografia della critica," in Italo Svevo, *Opera Omnia: Romanzi,* vol. 2, pt. 2, 1105–1228; see also Julia M. and Peter E. Bondanella, "American Criticism of Italo Svevo: A Checklist of Recent Translations and Critical Articles," in *Bulletin of Bibliography* 28 (1971):49–50, 59; Francis C. Bloodgood and John W. Van Voorhis, "Criticism of Italo Svevo: A Selected Checklist," in *Modern Fiction Studies* 18 (1972): 119–29; Ernesto Guidorizzi, "Rassegna sveviana," in *Lettere Italiane* 25, no. 3 (1973):360–85; Beno Weiss, *An Annotated Bibliography on the Theatre of Italo Svevo* (University Park: Pennsylvania State University Libraries), 1974; Bruno Maier, *Italo Svevo* (Milano: Mursia, 1978), 205–20; and "Bibliografia" in Italo Svevo, *Romanzi,* ed. Pietro Sarzana (Milano: Mondadori, 1985), 1209–26.

The standard edition of Svevo's works in Italian is *Opera Omnia,* ed. Bruno Maier (Milano: dall'Oglio Editore): vol. I, *Epistolario,* 1966; vol. 2, pt. 1, *I romanzi (Una vita & Senilità,* 1927 ed.), 1969; vol. 2, pt. 2, *I romanzi (La coscienza di Zeno & Senilità,* 1898 ed.), 1969; vol. 3, *Racconti, saggi, pagine sparse,* 1968; vol. 4, *Commedie,* 1969. Maier has written the introductions to vols. 1, 2, 3, and the "Aggiornamento" for vol. 2, pt. 2; Umbro Apollonio has written the "Introduction" and the "Notes" for vol. 4.

1. Novels
A Life. Translated by Archibald Colquhoun. London: Secker & Warburg, 1963. Vol. 3 in the Uniform Edition of Svevo's Works.
As a Man Grows Older. Translated by Beryl De Zoete. London: Secker & Warburg, 1962. Vol. 2 in the Uniform Edition of Svevo's Works.
Confessions of Zeno. Translated by Beryl De Zoete. London: Secker & Warburg, 1962. Vol. 1 in the Uniform Edition of Svevo's Works.

2. Short Stories
"The Tribe." In P. N. Furbank, *Italo Svevo the Man and the Writer.* London: Secker & Warburg, 1966, 217–23.

Short Sentimental Journey and Other Stories. Translated by Beryl De Zoete, L. Collison-Morley, and Ben Johnson. London: Secker & Warburg, 1967. Vol. 4 in the Uniform Edition of Svevo's Works. The volume includes "The Hoax," "The Story of the Nice Old Man and the Pretty Girl," "Generous Wine," "Traitorously," "Argo and his Master," "The Mother," "Short Sentimental Journey," and "Death."

Further Confessions of Zeno. Translated by Ben Johnson and P. N. Furbank. London: Secker & Warburg, 1969. Vol. 5 in the Uniform Edition of Svevo's Works. The volume includes "The Old, Old Man," "An Old Man's Confessions," "Umbertino," "A Contract," "This Indolence of Mine," and *Regeneration* (a play).

3. Plays

The Broken Triangle. Anonymously translated. In *Atlas* 1 (1967): 42–51.

Inferiority. Translated by P. N. Furbank. In *Essays on Italo Svevo,* University of Tulsa Monograph Series no. 6, 1969.

Regeneration. A Comedy in Three Acts. Translated by P. N. Furbank. In *Further Confessions of Zeno.* London: Secker & Warburg, 1969.

A Husband. Translated by Beno Weiss. In *Modern International Drama* 6 (1972): 43–88.

4. Essays

James Joyce (1927 lecture). Translated by Stanislaus Joyce. New York: New Directions, 1950.

"The Story of Elio." Translated by Beno Weiss. In *Journal of Modern Literature* 9 (1981/82): 148–50.

SECONDARY SOURCES

1. Books

Amato, Michele. *La genesi narrativa in Italo Svevo.* Cosenza: Pellegrini, 1966. Brief, intelligent discussion of how plays were the genesis of Svevo's narrative. Somewhat outdated.

Anzelotti, Fulvio. *Il segreto di Svevo.* Pordenone: Edizioni Studio Tesi, 1985. A personal view of Svevo, particularly of the Moravia, Schmitz, and Veneziani families. The misleading title refers to the family formula for manufacturing underwater paints. It provides new insights in Svevo's personality.

Baiocco, Carlo. *Analisi del personaggio sveviano in relazione alle immagini di lotta e malattia.* Rome: Centro Informazione Stampa Universitaria, 1984. Analyzes illness in its various manifestations by reconstructing Svevo's own medical knowledge.

Barilli, Renato. *La linea Svevo-Pirandello.* Milan: Mursia, 1972. Disparate chapters in which works by both authors are analyzed and related to certain themes and tendencies: naturalism, decadence, and psychoanalysis. Barilli expounds the author's poetics. Like Debenedetti, he points out the conservative nature of Svevo's novelistic structure and technique, in spite of his ethical and epistemological originality.

Bon, Adriano. *Come leggere "La coscienza di Zeno" di Italo Svevo.* Milan: Mursia, 1977. Provides information for a basic understanding of the novel; also biography, social/historical background, and sketchy history of criticism.

Borghello, Giampaolo. *La coscienza borghese. Saggio sulla narrativa di Svevo.* Rome: Savelli, 1977. Marxist analysis of the role and meaning of decadentism; examination of Svevo's political ideology through his works. Presents Svevo as a bourgeois *Mitteleuropean* author who courageously and candidly experienced the torments of his class.

Briosi, Sandro. *La critica e Svevo.* Bologna: Cappelli, 1975. Anthology of excerpted critical essays by 54 authors. Via a synchronic analysis, Briosi tries to show that differing methodological approaches reveal more analogies than differences.

Camerino, Giuseppe Antonio. *Italo Svevo e la crisi della Mitteleuropa.* Florence: Le Monnier, 1974. Links Svevo and the themes of ineptitude, senility, and disease to the Jewish *Mitteleuropean* (Austro-Hungarian) literary tradition. Unlike authors such as Kafka and Joseph Roth, who formulate a sociopolitical polemic, Svevo outlines in his characters the plight of the East European Jew rejected by his tribe, which is composed of assimilated and enriched Jews.

———. *Italo Svevo.* Turin: UTET, 1981. Interesting biography with ample documentation pertaining to cultural, social, and political life of Habsburg Trieste, indicating that Svevo gave Trieste a *Mitteleuropean* imprint, not vice versa.

Cappelli, Elisabetta and Nardi, Isabella. *Italo Svevo.* Florence: La Nuova Italia Editrice, 1976. Reconstruction of alternate phases in the history of Svevo criticism.

Contini, Gabriella. *Le lettere malate di Svevo.* Naples: Guida Editori, 1979. Svevo's epistolary activity during his so-called 25 years of silence is seen as proving ground for his future narrative production.

———. *Il quarto romanzo di Svevo.* Turin: Einaudi, 1980. Although there are similarities between *La coscienza* and the fragmentary writings for his projected fourth novel, Svevo intended to write a distinct and separate novel, viewed by Contini as a work in progress, composed of linking segments that are readable and comprehensible only if considered intertextually.

———. *Il romanzo inevitabile.* Milan: Mondadori, 1983. Themes and narrative techniques in *La coscienza di Zeno.*

De Castris, Arcangelo Leone. *Italo Svevo.* Pisa: Nistri-Lischi, 1959. According to the Marxist critic, Svevo lacked the necessary drive to make it on his own as an artist. His characters reflect the ideological and ethical crisis of bourgeois society. Zeno, the "anti-hero of Decadentism" laughs at society without any judgmental resentment. Humor is corrective.

De Lauretis, Teresa. *La sintassi del desiderio. Struttura e forme del romanzo sveviano.* Ravenna: Longo Editore, 1976. Using structuralist and semiotic methodologies, De Lauretis shows that the novels are variations of the same text, and the characters are successive incarnations expressing a similar psychological constitution.

Del Missier, Silvano. *Italo Svevo. Introduzione e guida allo studio dell'opera sveviana. Storia e Antologia della critica.* Florence: Le Monnier, 1976. Extremely useful introductory work which discusses Svevo's life, thought, and writings.

Fonda, Carlo. *Svevo e Freud. Proposta di interpretazione della "Coscienza di Zeno."* Ravenna: Longo Editore, 1978. Personal and stimulating psychoanalytic study. Fonda rejects the opinion that Svevo universalized himself through Zeno. The key for an understanding of the novel lies in the trauma Zeno suffered at being weaned at the time of his brother's death. A large segment is devoted to the role of Trieste in the aesthetics of the novel and to a refutation of Debenedetti's stand on Svevo's Jewishness.

Forti, Marco. *Svevo romanziere.* Milan: All'insegna del pesce d'oro, 1966. By means of "internal itineraries," Forti traces Svevo's model for *La coscienza* to *Senilità,* stressing the modernity of Emilio. The structure of *La coscienza* is defined as "binocular" due to the sequential overlapping of episodes.

Furbank, P[hilip] N[icholas]. *Italo Svevo, The Man and the Writer.* London: Secker & Warburg, 1966. First full-length biographical study in English. Extremely well written, it furnishes abundant and valuable data, and includes a critical analysis of Svevo's major writings.

Fusco, Mario. *Italo Svevo. Conscience et réalité.* Paris: Éditions Gallimard, 1973. Lacanian psychoanalytic study of Svevo's writings; Fusco shows that there exists a fundamental narcissistic relationship that ties Svevo to his works.

Ghidetti, Enrico. *Italo Svevo. La coscienza di un borghese triestino.* Rome: Editori Riuniti, 1980. By far the best, most informative, and well-documented biography.

Gioanola, Elio. *L'esistenza alienata: Svevo e Pirandello.* Turin: Società Editrice Internazionale, 1976. Useful introduction to Svevo's writings and their convergence with those of Pirandello.

———. *Un killer dolcissimo. Indagine psicanalitica sull'opera di Italo Svevo.* Genoa: Il Melangolo, 1979. Extremely interesting and illuminating clinical reading (via Freud and Melanie Klein): Svevo's work is inseparable from his personality. Zeno suffers from hysteria and not from obsessive neuroses (Rosowsky, Saccone, Fusco), and Svevo's "obsessive metaphors" are tied to his characters' "homicidal phantoms."

Jonard, Norbert. *Italo Svevo et la crise de la bourgeoisie européenne.* Paris: Belles Lettres, 1969. Via a psychoanalytic reading, Svevo's heroes are seen as the author's double. Svevo's aesthetics placed in relation to the crisis of the European bourgeoisie.

Kezich, Tullio. *Svevo e Zeno. Vite parallele.* 2d rev. ed. Milan: Il Formichiere, 1978. Comparative chronology of Svevo's and Zeno's lives.

Lavagetto, Mario. *L'impiegato Schmitz e altri saggi su Svevo.* Turin: Einaudi, 1975. Four essays focusing on the relationship between author and his *écriture*. In this Freudian and Marxist study, the critic maintains that Svevo tried to create a fictitious personality for himself.

Lebowitz, Naomi. *Italo Svevo.* New Brunswick, N. J.: Rutgers University Press, 1978. Analysis of Svevo's major, last period and significant influence on it by Freud and Montaigne.

Lunetta, Mario. *Invito alla lettura di Svevo.* Milan: Mursia, 1972. Useful introduction to Svevo's major writings. A brief portrait of Svevo shows that Trieste's milieu favored his propensity for introspection.

Luti, Giorgio. *Italo Svevo e altri studi sulla letteratura italiana del primo Novecento.* Milan: Lerici, 1961. In Marxist terms, Luti bases his analysis on Svevo's relationship to the crisis suffered by European bourgeois society. His thematics and style evolve in relation to historical-social changes.

Maier, Bruno. *Italo Svevo.* 5th rev. ed. Milan: Mursia, 1978. Historical, eclectic approach; Maier studies disease, senility, death, originality, and life's unpredictability as the fundamental themes of Svevo's work. His introspectiveness, autobiographic nature, and behavioral difficulties are also those of other Triestine writers.

Marchi, Marco, ed. *Italo Svevo Oggi. Atti del Convegno Firenze 3–4 Febbraio 1979.* Florence: Vallecchi, 1980. Essays by C. Bo on Svevo the man; G. Stampa on Svevo and Habsburg culture; C. Magris on Svevo's life and his representation of life; G. Pampaloni on *Una vita* as the prototype for Svevo's subsequent writings; M. Lavagetto, corrections for Zeno whose intent is to evade and deceive; T. Kezich, on the fortunes and misfortunes of Svevo's theater; B. Maier, problems of a critical edition of Svevo's works.

Maxia, Sandro. *Svevo.* Palermo: Palumbo, 1975. Despite the novelty and modernity of his inspiration, Svevo failed to arrive at a corresponding theoretical formulation and failed to break coherently with traditional literary schemes. The reader faces unresolved problems requiring an intense critical collaboration due to Svevo's ambiguousness. Maxia also provides an account of the changing critical evaluation of Svevo's work.

Meynaud, Jeuland M. *Zeno e i suoi fratelli. La creazione del personaggio nei romanzi di Italo Svevo.* Bologna: Pàtron Editore, 1985. The critic refutes the idea of Svevo as *engagé* writer. His intent was not to show that society and the individual are in crisis, but rather to assert the right of the individual to be different (neurotic, antiheroic, etc.).

Moloney, Brian. *Italo Svevo. A Critical Introduction.* Edinburgh: Edinburgh University Press, 1974. A stimulating personal view, useful because it offers an overview of Svevo's works and life. Good for the non-experienced reader coming to Svevo for the first time. Moloney shows why Svevo bears no resemblance to any other Italian novelist.

Nanni, Luciano. *Leggere Svevo. Antologia della critica sveviana.* Bologna: Zanichelli, 1974. Extremely useful anthology of critical writings on Svevo. Volume includes synopses of Svevo's novels, short stories, and plays.

Palumbo, Matteo. *La coscienza di Svevo. Negazione e utopia tra "Una vita" e "Senilità."* Naples: Liguori, 1976. Structuralist Marxist approach which rejects impressionistic and psychological interpretations.

Petroni, Franco. *L'inconscio e le strutture formali. Saggi su Italo Svevo.* Padua: Liviana, 1979. Petroni refutes the notion that Svevo did not know how to write well. Svevo was fully aware of the role played by formal narrative structures in the expression of "repressed" inner reality.

Petronio, Giuseppe, ed. *Il caso Svevo.* Palermo: Palumbo, 1976. Six essays: E. Apih analyzes Triestine society in Svevo's time; C. Magris discusses German culture in Trieste and Svevo's relationship to it; M. Fusco discusses Svevo and psychoanalysis; S. Maxia analyzes Svevo's first two novels; L. Martinelli, Svevo's last writings; F. Petroni provides an ideological and structural analysis of *Senilità*.

Ricciardi, Mario. *L'educazione del personaggio nella narrativa di Italo Svevo.* Palermo: Flaccovio, 1972. Socioeconomic view of Svevo and his characters. In the first two novels Svevo confronts the conflict art/ideal bourgeois life with a progressive and reductive resolution: art for art's sake. After *Senilità*, there occurs a poetic change in the writer who finds an accommodation with life.

Rimini, Ruggero. *La morte nel salotto. Guida al teatro d'Italo Svevo.* Florence: Vallecchi, 1974. Indispensable. Only full-length study of Svevo's plays. Includes Svevo's position vis-à-vis contemporary bourgeois drama.

Russell, Charles C. *Italo Svevo. The Writer from Trieste. Reflections on his Background and his Work.* Ravenna: Longo Editore, 1978. Detailed examination of Triestine life at the turn of the century and the cultural environment in which Svevo wrote. The city is seen as a key to a deeper understanding of the author.

Saccone, Eduardo. *Commento a Zeno.* Bologna: Il Mulino, 1973. A perceptive, extremely valuable Freudian/structuralist (Lacanian) analysis of illness and the novel's semantic system consisting of a combination of various "signifiers": metaphor, metonymy, and catachresis. Zeno does not recount his life, only his illness (obsessive neurosis).

———. *Il poeta travestito. Otto scritti su Svevo.* Pisa: Pacini Editore, 1977.

Eight seminal essays (6 previously published): "Il poeta travestito" (analysis of "Corto viaggio sentimentale"); "I dolori del giovane Schmitz (1880–1889)"; "Delitto e castigo" (analysis of "Assasinio di via Belpoggio"); "Un'educazione sentimentale" (analysis of *Senilità*); "La trasgressione" (analysis of *Inferiorità*); "I vecchi e i giovani, i vecchi giovani, i giovani vecchi" (analysis of *La rigenerazione*); "Svevo, Zeno e la psicanalisi"; and "Ancora su Svevo e la psicanalisi."

Scrivano, Riccardo, ed. *Contributi sveviani*. Trieste: Edizioni LINT, 1979. Eight essays: M. Beer, examines Svevo's pseudonyms; G. Savarese, Svevo's critical writings; S. Maira, metaphor in *Una vita*; M. Serri, the presence of death in Zeno; G. A. Camerino, Svevo's theater; A. Gareffi, Svevo's theater as destiny, analogy, and transgression; R. Scrivano, humor and its function, literature as transgression and falsehood; N. Longo, the interpretation of "La novella del buon vecchio e della bella fanciulla."

Spagnoletti, Giacinto. *Svevo. La vita, il pensiero, i testi esemplari*. Milan: Edizioni Accademia, 1972. Portrays Zeno as an opportunist who manages his neuroses profitably.

———. *La coscienza di Zeno di Italo Svevo*. Milan: Rizzoli, 1978. Examines the internal structure of the novel, its characters and key parts, placing it in relation to nineteenth-century novelistic tradition and contemporary culture, particularly Freud.

Svevo, Letizia Fonda Savio in collaboration with Bruno Maier. *Iconografia sveviana*. Pardenone: Edizioni Studio Tesi, 1984. Svevo's daughter's intimate portrait of her father, based on personal recollections. 96 photos.

Svevo, Livia Veneziani in collaboration with Lina Galli. *Vita di mio marito con altri inediti di Italo Svevo*. Edited by Anita Pittoni. 2d ed. Trieste: Edizioni dello Zibaldone, 1958. First significant biography, by Svevo's wife; this intimate assessment of Svevo is a must for an understanding of the author.

Testa, Antonio. *Italo Svevo*. Ravenna: Longo Editore, 1968. Useful introduction to the roots of Svevo's analytic stance in German romantic aesthetics (Schopenhauer and Jean Paul Richter), and to its evolution into a problematic fusion between truth and poetry, morality and literature.

Tuscano, Pasquale. *L'integrazione impossibile. Letteratura e vita in Italo Svevo*. Milan: Istituto Propaganda Libraria, 1985. Interesting careful study using the latest critical information to determine the values and limits of Svevo as interpreter of decadent society.

2. Special Issues

Essays on Italo Svevo. Edited by Thomas F. Staley. University of Tulsa Monograph Series, no. 6. Tulsa, Okla. 1969. Articles by T. F. Staley, J. Gatt-Rutter, J. P. Malocsay, B. Moloney, B. Maier, R. S. Baker, O. Ragusa, M. Frampton.

Modern Fiction Studies. Svevo Issue. Edited by Thomas F. Staley. Vol. 18, no.

1 (Spring 1972). Includes articles by Letizia Svevo Fonda Savio, T. F. Staley, Gian-Paolo Biasin, P. Robinson, B. Weiss, R M. Treitel, D. Cernecca, T. de Lauretis, N. Rocco-Bergera, L. Galli, F. C. Bloodgood, and J. W. Van Voorkin.

3. Articles and Chapters

Almansi, Guido. "The Italian Proust." *Adam International Review*, nos. 310–12 (1966), 115–18. Any comparison with Proust is more improbable than ever.

———. "Il Tema dell'incesto nelle opere di Svevo." *Paragone*, no. 264 (Feb. 1972), 47–60. Indicates frequency of fetishism, particularly of the "the well shod foot."

Battaglia, Salvatore. "La coscienza della realtà nei romanzi di Svevo." *Filologia e Letteratura* 10 (1964):225–48. Identifies unitary nature of Svevo's work and distances him from Freud's doctrine.

Biasin, Gian-Paolo. "Zeno's Last Bomb." In *Literary Diseases: Theme and Metaphor in the Italian Novel*, 63–99. Austin: University of Texas Press, 1975. A comprehensive analysis of the metaphorical and symbolic force of disease; Zeno's introspection is related to the bourgeois disease of the *fin de siècle* and seen as a symbol of modern man's alienation.

Bo, Carlo. "Per un ritratto di Svevo." In *Riflessioni Critiche*, 443–64. Florence: Sansoni, 1953. Identifies the characteristics that differentiate Svevo from the naturalistic search for truth. Disposes of the linguistic polemic concerning Svevo's language, pointing out that it has the capacity for critical observation, and achieves the "interior documentation" sought by Svevo.

Bonora, Ettore. "Italo Svevo" and "Gli inediti di Italo Svevo." In *Gli ipocriti di Malebolge e altri saggi di letteratura italiana e francese*, 86–105, 106–11. Milan and Naples: Ricciardi, 1953. Seminal work. Reformulation of all the critical problems concerning Svevo's work. Underlines Svevo's tendency to write an antinovel and defines his language problems as syntactical and not lexical.

Bouissy, André. "Les fondements idéologiques de l'oeuvre d'Italo Svevo." *Revue des Études Italiennes* 12 (1966):209–45, 350–73; 13 (1967):23–50. Discusses the ideological formation of Svevo, who shared in Schopenhauer's perspectives, in the ideas of socialism, Freud, and Darwin without relying on their solutions.

Cambon, Glauco. "Zino come anti-Faust." *Il Verri* 8 (Dec. 1963):67–76. Health and disease are identified with innocence and self-awareness; common themes in both characters are identified; Zeno is seen as a parody of Faust.

Champagne, R. A. "A Displacement of Plato's *Pharmakon*: A Study of Italo Svevo's Short Fiction." *Modern Fiction Studies* 21:564–72. Svevo implements a writing that is a *pharmakon*, that is, a remedy and a poison for the human situation.

David, Michel. *La psicoanalisi nella cultura italiana,* 379–404, 436–42. Turin: Boringheri, 1966. Although there are definite psychoanalytic elements in *La coscienza di Zeno,* there are nevertheless substantial lacunae and heterodoxies.

Debenedetti, Giacomo. "Svevo e Schmitz." In *Saggi critici–Nuova Serie,* 25–102. Rome: Edizioni del Secolo, 1945. Ties Svevo's continuous "analytic corrosion of narrative texture" to the uneasiness of the Jew in Western society. Locates correspondences between Weininger's work and Svevo's characters. The novels are "small" because the characters lack a necessary fuller dimension which is denied them by the Svevo who covers up his Jewishness.

———. *Il romanzo del Novecento,* 513–616. Milan: Garzanti, 1971. Svevo, the great subverter of the traditional novel, is placed among the precursors of modern literature. His debt to Joyce and Proust is minimized. In *Zeno* he discovers a "fourth dimension both spatial and temporal."

De Lauretis, Teresa. "Dreams as Metalanguage in Svevo's *Confessions of Zeno,*" *Language and Style* 4 (1971):208–20. The innovative element of Svevo's narrative technique is the use of dreams as a system of signs; the novel is encoded in the symbolic language of the unconscious.

Devoto, Giacomo. "Decenni per Svevo." In *Studi di stilistica,* 175–93. Florence: Le Monnier, 1950. Analysis of linguistic objection: lack of grace, philological overbearance, barbarisms, antiliterary style, a-syntactical and archaic forms, improper use of antecedent tenses.

Freccero, John. "Zeno's Last Cigarette." *Modern Language Notes* 77 (1962):3–23. Compares *La coscienza* to the literature of "confession" or the "conversion" novel involving a process of spiritual death and resurrection. In Zeno's spatial imagination, the moment is present and conditioned by the preceding one, which in turn is conditioned by its predecessors, etc. For Zeno memory has no essence, since he has no moments to look back upon; therefore one cigarette is exactly like another.

Gilman, Richard. "News from the Past." *New Republic,* 2 November 1963, 19–23. Deals with technique in novels. In *La coscienza* he sees a repudiation of narrative, conventional plot, and psychological coherence. We discover that Svevo cures us of our desire to be cured.

Guglielmi, Guido. "Glosse a Svevo." In *Letteratura come sistema e come funzione,* 104–27. Turin: Einaudi, 1967. Structuralist analysis dealing with Svevo's awareness of "reality's irreducibility to its definition." Writing assumes only a practical value; in *La coscienza,* the first-person narrator is nonjudgmental.

Gulgielminetti, Marziano. "Il monologo di Svevo." In *Struttura e sintassi del romanzo italiano del primo Novecento,* 118–52. Milan: Silva, 1964, 1967. Analyzes the modality of tenses in Svevo's works. In *Una vita* Svevo manipulates verbal tenses, while in *Senilità* the imperfect becomes the most constant voice of the narrator. Svevo's monologue has a syntactic structure created not for objective presentation of facts, but rather to create a dialogue between the actor and the author who insinuates himself into the character's consciousness in order to comment and judge.

Jacqmain, M. "Alexander Portnoy, pronipote di Zeno Cosini." *Rivista di Letterature Moderne e Comparate* 32 (1979):138–48. Parallels between Zeno and Portnoy; both are obsessed with illness.

Musatti, Cesare. "Svevo e la psicoanalisi." *Belfagor* 29, no. 2 (1974):129–41. Although Svevo's empirical autoanalysis cannot free Zeno from his problems, it is nevertheless valid because it reveals some external reasons for his behavior.

Nelson, Lowry, Jr. "A Survey of Svevo." *Italian Quarterly* 3 (1959):3–33. Traces a progression in form and technique from the first two novels to the formlessness of the last, which reflects life more accurately.

Pacifici, Sergio. "Italo Svevo's Antiheroes." In *The Modern Italian Novel from Manzoni to Svevo*, 149–83. Carbondale: Southern Illinois University Press, 1967. Svevo's style sets him apart; he professed little interest in the social, political, and cultural issues of the time.

Petroni, Franco. "L'intreccio della *Coscienza di Zeno*." *Belfagor* 32, no. 3 (1977):261–80. Argues that in the novel Svevo represents the impossibility of a rational interpretion of reality.

———. "La coscienza di Zeno." *Nuovi Argomenti*, no. 58 (1978), 217–30. Formalist analysis of cause and effect in the narratology of the novel.

Poggioli, Renato. "A Note on Italo Svevo." In *The Spirit of the Letter*, 171–79, 217–20. Cambridge: Harvard University Press, 1965. Svevo accepts the bourgeois spirit as a frame or state of mind and does not see any conflict between it and the artist. He sees time as a foolish and amusing prankster playing a recurring and successful hoax.

Pontiggia, G. "La tecnica narrativa di Italo Svevo." *Il Verri* 4, no. 5 (1960):150–66. Attempt to evaluate Svevo's narrative technique in the light of Henry James's poetics.

Porcelli, Bruno. "L'evoluzione dell'ideologia e della narrativa sveviane." In *Momenti dell'antinaturalismo. Fogazzaro, Svevo, Corazzini*, 53–100. Ravenna: Longo Editore, 1975. Points out Svevo's bourgeois ideology and his antinaturalism after 1900. Argues that in his novels Svevo moves from a work closed by a narrow circle of well-defined relationships into an open one.

Robbe-Grillet, Alain. Review of *La coscienza*. *La Nouvelle Revue Française*, 1 July 1954, 139-41. Zeno tells us that in modern society nothing is natural anymore and that man no longer laments this fact.

———. "La conscience malade de Zéno." In *Pour un nouveau roman*, 77–81. Paris: Éditions de Miniut, 1963. Analyzes modern man's concept of the "pathological" and "sick conscience" in Svevo's last novel, which is regarded as a precursor for twentieth-century avant-garde novelistic forms.

Robinson, Paula. "Svevo: Secrets of the Confessional." *Literature and Psychology* 20 (1970):101–14. *La coscienza* and subsequent writings display a detailed awareness of Freudian psychodynamics. Svevo's humor stems from the contrast between repressed desire and an innocent exterior; it is a defense mechanism against life's tragedy and man's neuroses.

Roditi, Edouard. "A Note on Svevo." In Italo Svevo, *As a Man Grows Older*. Translated by Beryl De Zoete, xi–xxii. New York: Bantam Books, 1968. Svevo's works are difficult to place in the tradition of the Italian novel. The society described is not typically Italian; his characters illustrate qualities and faults of the Austrian bourgeoisie.

Rosowsky, Giuditta. "Théorie et pratique psychoanalytiques dans *La coscienza di Zeno*." *Revue des Études Italiennes* 16 (1970):49–70. Lacanian interpretation. Both Zeno and Dr. S use the first person as mode of expression. *La coscienza* is an open work that requires the reader's intervention. Svevo's Freudianism is ambiguous.

Wagner, Roland C. "Italo Svevo: The Vocation of Old Age." *Hartford Studies in Literature* 2 (1970):214–28. A close analysis of Zeno shows that he becomes saner as he grows older despite his mad behavior. The theme of old age is carried to new dimensions.

Weiss, Beno. "*Terzetto spezzato*: Svevo's Spiritistic Fantasy." *Italica* 55 (1978):211–24. Discusses the play in a way that throws light on Svevo's other works.

———. "La otra pasión de Svevo." *Sin Nombre* 11, no. 3 (1980):16–21. General introduction to Svevo's theater.

Wilden, Anthony. "Death, Desire and Repetition in Svevo's *Zeno*." *Modern Language Notes* 84, (1969):98–119. The greatest part of Zeno's life is intertwined with death, desire, and repetition; Zeno, therefore, is always postponing his own death by focusing on that of his father or of others.

Wlassics, Tibor. "La poesia delle mende: note sul linguaggio dell'ultimo Svevo." *Lingua Nostra* 32, (1971):45–48. The problem of language has always dominated Svevo criticism. Argues for a linguistic reinstatement of Svevo.

———. "Sulla 'Novella' di Svevo." *Nuova Antologia* 6, no. 2046, (1971):248–55. Close reading of "La novella del buon vecchio e della bella fanciulla." The real story is written between the lines: the reader must create it, by becoming a pliant receptacle of Svevo's occult alchemies.

Zingale, A. "La crisi dell'uomo contemporaneo nella narrativa sveviana." *Nuova Antologia* 527:269–74. Discusses Svevo's view of human destiny and argues that it is still relevant.

Index

adultery, 94, 96–97, 103, 113; *see also* ménage à trois
Allen, Woody, 58, 63
Amato, Michele, 22, 101
antiheroes, 22–24, 80, 83, 97, 122, 134; *see also* disease and health, *inetti,* inferiority
Apollonio, Umbro, 96, 100, 108, 116, 118
Ariosto governatore (Ariosto as Governor), 3, 18, 39, 94–95
As a Man Grows Older. See Senilità
Atto unico (A one-act play), 102–3
autobiography in the fiction, 22–23, 36–37, 39–40, 43–44, 59–60, 66–67, 75, 100, 124–26, 128–29

Balzac, Honoré de, 4
Basedow's (Grave's) disease, 83, 86–88, 121
Becque, Henry, 94, 97
Benco, Silvio, 5, 13, 40, 51, 93, 105
Boccacio, Giovanni, 4, 55
bourgeois, the, 23–24, 84, 103, 106; *see also* business world; capitalism; money; Schmitz, Aron Hector, and the middle class
Bragaglia, Anton Giulio, 13, 111, 114
breast feeding, 61, 79, 80
business world, the, 69–70, 80–88; *see also* bourgeois, the

capitalism, 123; *see also* bourgeois, the
Caprin, Giulio, 13
Carducci, Giosue, 4
Carnival, the, 37–38, 39
Chekov, Anton, 114, 118
cigarettes. *See* smoking
Circolo Artistico, 4
Circolo Musicale, 4
city life and country life, 20–21, 27–28

Confessions of Zeno. See La coscienza di Zeno
Con la penna d'oro (*With a Golden Pen*), 10, 116–18
Contini, Gabriella, 129–30; *Il quarto romanzo di Svevo,* 129
"Corto viaggio sentimentale" (Short Sentimental Journey), 129, 130
coscienzia, 92
Cremieux, Benjamin, 13
Critica sociale, 123
Croce, Benedetto, 33, 44

D'Annunzio, Gabriele, 33, 42; *Francesca da Rimini,* 103; *La figli di Iorio,* 103
Dante, *Divine Comedy,* 38
Darwin, Charles, 85, 127, 128, 129
death, 50, 58, 63–69, 90, 128–29
Debenedetti, Giacomo, 22, 23, 94
dialectical materialism, 123
Diario per la fidanzata (*Diary for My Fiancee*), 37
disaggradevole, 32
disease and health, 58–59, 74–77, 83–92, 120, 126, 127–28
Dostoyevski, Fyodor, 11; *Crime and Punishment,* 123
dreams, 78–80, 86–88, 89, 114, 119–20, 126, 127; *see also* unconscious, the

Einstein, Albert, 85
Eleatic School, 56
Esame, 13
expressionistic drama, German, 113, 116, 120

fables, 123, 125, 126
fascism, 84, 124
father figures, 62, 65, 77, 88; *see also* oedipal triangle

166

Index

Ferrari, Paolo, 6
Fitzi, Dr. Aurelio, 59
Flaubert, Gustave, 4, 27
Fonda, Carlo, 65, 66, 72, 83, 87, 90
free association, 53, 60
Freud, Sigmund, 12, 27, 53, 54, 59, 63, 65, 72, 78–79, 85, 86, 87, 90, 114, 120, 126; *The Interpretation of Dreams*, 12, 59, 86
Freytag, Gustav, *Technique of the Drama*, 32
Furbank, P. N., 27, 33, 50, 65, 84

Gabersi, Giulia, 7
Giacosa, Giuseppe, 6, 94, 95, 97, 107
Goethe, Johann Wolfgang von, 2, 3

Heine, Heinrich, 3, 63
Heyse, Paul von, 51
Hortis, Attilio, 4, 5
hysteria, 66

Ibsen, Henrik, 11, 96, 97, 114
Il Corriere della Sera, 13, 32
Il ladro in casa: Scene della vita borghese (There's a thief among us: Scenes from bourgeois life), 99–102
illness. *See* disease and health
"Il malocchio" (The Evil Eye), 129
"Il mio ozio" (This Indolence of Mine), 129, 131
Il Piccolo, 11
"Il vecchione" (The Old, Old Man), 131–33
impressionism, 44–45, 46, 47
"Incontro di vecchi amici" (Old Friends Meet), 128, 130
inetti (the inept), 22, 50, 101, 123; *see also* antiheroes, disease and health, inferiority
Inferiorità (*Inferiority*), 114–16, 123
inferiority, 62, 71–72, 77, 114–16

Jahier, Valerio, 90
Jewishness, 23, 68–69, 125, 134–35; *see also* Schmitz, Aron Hector: and Jewishness

Joyce, James, 12, 13, 15, 30, 52, 129; *Ulysses*, 15

Kafka, Franz, 14, 120, 127

"La buonissima madre" (The Very Good Mother), 129
La coscienza di Zeno (*Confessions of Zeno*), 12–13, 14, 27, 50, 52–93, 101, 110, 113, 125, 128, 129, 130, 131, 133, 134
"La madre," (The Mother), 122, 124–25
"La morte" (Death), 128, 130
La Nazione, 13, 39
"La novella del buon vecchio e della bella fanciulla" (The Story of the Nice Old Man and the Pretty Girl), 120, 122, 126–27, 130
Larbaud, Valery, 13, 30, 39
La rigenerazione (*Regeneration*), 118–21, 127, 130
"L'assassinio di Via Belpoggio" (Murder on Belpoggio Street), 7, 122, 123
"La tribù" (The Tribe), 122, 123–24
"L'avenire dei ricordi" (Along Memory Lane), 128, 130
La Verità (*The Truth*), 109–11
L'avventura di Maria (*Maria's Adventure*), 106–9
"Le confessioni del vegliardo" (An Old Man's Confessions), 129, 131
Le ire di Giuliano (*Giuliano's Anger*), 6, 95–96, 98
Le Navire d'Argent, 13
Le teorie del conte Alberto (*Count Albert's Theories*), 6, 97–98
Life, A. *See Una vita*
L'Indipendente, 5, 6, 7, 11, 51, 122, 123
literature and writing, 21–22, 60; *see also* Schmitz, Aron Hector, as writer
"Lo specifico del dottor Menghi" (The Specific of Dr. Menghi), 127–28
"L'uomo e la teoria darwiniana" (Man and the Darwinian Theory), 129

Maier, Bruno, 43
Mann, Thomas, *Death in Venice*, 75

Maupassant, Guy de, 33
Maxia, Sandro, 52
memory, 66, 67, 74, 83, 128, 132
ménage à trois, 69–80; see also adultery
middle class, the. See bourgeois, the; business world; money; Schmitz, Aron Hector, and the middle class
Minerva, the, 4
Moloney, Brian, 24
money, 94, 95, 102, 115, 126; see also bourgeois, the; business world; Schmitz, Aron Hector, and the middle class
Montaigne, 23
Montale, Eugenio, 13, 14, 24, 66, 125
mother figures, 67; see also breast feeding, dreams, father figures, oedipal triangle

narrative, 50–51, 52
naturalism, 4, 12, 18–20, 47–48, 93, 97–98

oedipal triangle, 62, 65, 77, 79, 87
old age, 40–41, 118–21, 127, 129, 131–32
Oliva, Domenico, 33
oral fixation, 79
"Orazio Cima," 129, 130

Pampaloni, Gena, 33
paradox, 56–57, 58, 67, 71
Paz, Octavio, 21
Piazza, Giulio, 100
Pirandello, Luigi, 109, 113, 114; Così è (se vi pare), 110; Il fu Mattia Pascal, 113; Il giuoco delle parti, 109; Sei personaggi in cerca d'autore, 110
Poggiolo, Renato, 23, 27
practical joking, 126
Praga, Marco, 6, 94, 97, 103
Primo del ballo (Before the Ball), 99
procrastination, 57–58
"Proditoriamente" (Traitorously), 129, 130

"Profilo autobiografico" (Autobiographical Sketch), 15, 59
Proust, Marcel, 13, 52, 55, 125
psychoanalysis, 52, 53, 57, 59–60, 62, 67, 88–92, 115, 129, 132, 134
psychosomatic disorders, 71

realism, 19; see also naturalism, verism
renunciation, 28–29
Richter, Friedrich, 2
romanticism, 18
Roncoldier, Carlo, 7
Roncoldier, Giuseppe, 7
Russell, Charles C., 46, 59, 66
Russian Revolution, 84

Salvini, Tomaso, 2
Samigli, E. (first pen name), 5, 100
Sanctis, Francesco de, 4
Schiller, Friedrich, 2, 3
schlemiel, the, 63, 69
Schmitz, Abraham Adolfo (grandfather), 1
Schmitz, Adolfo (brother), 1, 2
Schmitz, Allegra Moravia (mother), 1, 8, 36
Schmitz, Aron Hector (or Ettore): as banker, 3–4, 19; as businessman, 11–12; and Catholic conversion, 8–11, 66; death of, 14, 69; and Jewishness, 1–2, 8–11, 14, 15, 23, 63, 66, 68–69, 125, 134–35; life of, 1–16; marriage of, 8; and the middle class, 4; pen names of, 5, 15; pessimism of, 7, 84; and psychological observation, 48; self-criticism of, 5–7; as student, 2; and the theater, 2–3, 12, 13, 93–121; and violin, 13; as writer, 11–12, 18–19, 30–31, 44–45, 93, 94

WORKS: NOVELS
La coscienza di Zeno (*Confessions of Zeno*), 12–13, 14, 27, 50, 52–93, 101, 110, 113, 125, 128, 129, 130, 131, 133, 134
Senilità (*As a Man Grows Older*), 7, 8, 12, 39–51, 122, 134

Index

Una vita (*A Life*), 4, 5, 6–8, *16–33,* 47, 48, 50–51, 100–1, 122, 134

WORKS: PLAYS
Ariosto governatore (*Ariosto as Governor*), 3, 18, 39, 94–95
Atto unico (*A one-act play*), 102–3
Con la penna d'oro (*With a Golden Pen*), 10, 116–18
Il ladro in casa: Scene della vita borghese (*There's a thief among us: Scenes from bourgeois life*), 99–102
Inferiorità (*Inferiority*), 114–16, 123
La rigenerazione (*Regeneration*), 118–21, 127, 130
La Verità (*The Truth*), 109–11
L'avventura di Maria (*The Adventure of Maria*), 106–9
Le ire di Giuliano (*Giuliano's Anger*), 6, 95–96, 98
Le teorie del conte Alberto (*Count Albert's Theories*), 6, 97–98
Primo del ballo (*Before the Ball*), 99
Terzetto spezzato (*The Broken Triangle*), 13, 93, 111–14
Un marito (*A Husband*), 103–6
Una commedia inedita (*An Unpublished Comedy*), 6, 96–97

WORKS: STORIES, FRAGMENTS, AND SKETCHES
"Corto viaggio sentimentale" (Short Sentimental Journey), 129, 130
"Il malocchio" (The Evil Eye), 129
"Il mio ozio" (This Indolence of Mine), 129, 131
"Il vecchione" (The Old, Old Man), 131–33
"Incontro di vecchi amici" (Old Friends Meet), 128, 130
"La buonissima madre" (The Very Good Mother), 129
"La madre," (The Mother), 122, 124–25
"La morte" (Death), 128, 130
"La novella del buon vecchio e della bella fanciulla" (The Story of the Nice Old Man and the Pretty Girl), 120, 122, 126–27, 130
"L'assassinio di Via Belpoggio" (Murder on Belpoggio Street), 7, 122, 123
"La tribù" (The Tribe), 122, 123–24
"L'avenirre dei ricordi" (Along Memory Lane), 128, 130
"Le confessioni del vegliardo" (An Old Man's Confessions), 129, 131
"Lo specifico del dottor Menghi" (The Specific of Dr. Menghi), 127–28
"L'uomo e la teoria darwiniana" (Man and the Darwinian Theory) 129 (essay)
"Orazio Cima," 129, 130
"Proditoriamente" (Traitorously), 129, 130
"Profilo autobiografico" (Autobiographical Sketch), 15, 59 (essay)
"Shylock," 5 (essay)
"Umbertino," 129
"Una burla riuscita" (The Hoax), 122, 125–26
"Una lotta" (A Contest), 122
"Un contratto" (A Contract), 129–30, 130–31
"Vino generoso" (Generous Wine), 122, 127, 130

Schmitz, Elio (brother), 1, 2–3, 6, 13, 15, 67, 75, 100
Schmitz, Francesco (father), 1, 3, 100
Schmitz, Giuseppina (aunt), 100
Schmitz, Letizia (daughter), 8, 15
Schmitz, Livia Veneziani (wife), 4, 7, 8–11, 14, 36, 37, 40, 100; *Vita di mio marito* (*Life of My Husband*), 9, 14
Schmitz, Natalia (sister), 1
Schmitz, Noemi (sister), 1
Schmitz, Ortensia (sister), 1
Schmitz, Ottavio (brother), 1
Schmitz, Paola (sister), 1
Schopenhauer, Arthur, 2, 27–29; *The World as Will and Idea, Senilità* (*As*

a Man Grows Older), 7, 8, 12, 39–51, 122, 134
senility, 39, 118–21, 123
Shakespeare, 2, 12; *Hamlet,* 94; *Othello,* 104
Shema, the, 68; *see also* Jewishness; Schmitz, Aron Hector, and Jewishness
"Shylock," 5
sibling rivalry, 61, 72
smoking, 54–63, 67
Soggiorno londinese (London Sojourn), 12
Spagnoletti, Giacinto, 3, 6, 42, 84
spiritism, 113–14
Stekel, Wilhelm, 88
Strindberg, August, 12, 114, 120; *The Stronger,* 99
suicide, 29
Svevo, Italo. *See* Schmitz, Aron Hector (or Ettore)

Tagliapietra-Cambon, Elisa, 4
Tedeschi, Ignazio, 100
Terzetto spezzato (*Broken Triangle*), 13, 93, 111–14
theater, the, 94–121
Turati, Filippo, 123
Turgeneev, Ivan Sergeyevich, 2, 114
Tuscan Italian, 61

"Umbertino," 129
"Una burla riuscita" (The Hoax), 122, 125–26

Una commedia inedita (*An Unpublished Comedy*), 6, 96–97
"Una lotta" (A Contest), 122
Una vita (*A Life*), 4, 5, 6–8, 16–33, 47, 48, 50–51, 100–1, 122, 134
Unamuno y Jugo, de, 27, 86, 114; *Niebla,* 27
unconscious, the, 52–53, 60, 61, 74, 78, 87, 91, 115, 119, 132; *see also* dreams; Freud, Sigmund
"Un contratto" (A Contract), 129–30, 130–31
Un marito (*A Husband*), 103–6

verism, 93, 103
Veruda, Umberto, 7, 12, 40–41, 43, 65
"Vino generoso" (Generous Wine), 122, 127, 130
violin, the, 13, 72–73

Weiss, Edoardo, 53
Williams, Tennessee, *The Glass Menagerie,* 49
wish fulfillment, 79, 126
women, as characters, 45–47, 77, 96–97, 101–2, 106–8
World War I, 13, 56, 122, 125

Zeno of Citium, 90
Zeno of Eleas, 56
Zergol, Giuseppina, 36, 37, 75
Zola, Émile, 4, 93